VOICES OF THE

FOREIGN LEGION

VOICES OF THE
FOREIGN
LEGION

THE HISTORY OF THE WORLD'S
MOST FAMOUS FIGHTING CORPS

ADRIAN D. GILBERT

A HERMAN GRAF BOOK
SKYHORSE PUBLISHING

Skyhorse Publishing books may be purchased in bulk at special discounts for sales promotion, corporate gifts, fund-raising, or educational purposes. Special editions can also be created to specifications. For details, contact the Special Sales Department, Skyhorse Publishing, 555 Eighth Avenue, Suite 903, New York, NY 10018 or info@skyhorsepublishing.com.

www.skyhorsepublishing.com

10 9 8 7 6 5 4 3 2 1

Library of Congress Cataloging-in-Publication Data

Gilbert, Adrian D.
  Voices of the Foreign Legion : the history of the world's most famous fighting corps / Adrian D. Gilbert.
      p. cm.
  Includes bibliographical references and index.
  ISBN 978-1-61608-032-7
  1. France. Armie. Ligion itranghre. [1. France. Army. Foreign Legion.] I. Title.
  UA703.L5G553 2010
  355.3'590944--dc22
                                    2010001065

Printed in the United States of America

ACKNOWLEDGEMENTS

The Imperial War Museum is always a treasure trove of information on any military subject, and my thanks go to the keepers and staff of the departments of Printed Books and of Documents and to the Sound Archive. The British Library and the London Library were also invaluable as a source of essential books.

I would also like to thank Brigadier Tony Hunter-Choat OBE of the Foreign Legion Association of Great Britain, who kindly pointed the way towards a number of former legionnaires. Among these, I would especially like to thank Dave Cunliffe, Carl 'Jacko' Jackson, Matt Rake and David Taylor. My thanks also extend to Mrs E. P. Deman (widow of Peter [formerly Erwin] Deman) and Kevin Foster for their permission to use material via the IWM's Sound Archive. My gratitude also goes to the help provided by others who wish to remain anonymous.

I am grateful to the authors, agents and publishers who have granted me permission to use material from the following works: Leslie Aparvary, *A Legionnaire's Journey* (Detselig Enterprises); Gareth Carins, *Diary of a Legionnaire: My Life in the French Foreign Legion* (Grosvenor House, © 2007 – author website: www. diaryofalegionnaire.com); Blaise Cendrars, *Lice* (Peter Owen); Anthony Delmayne, *Sahara Desert Escape* (Jarrolds), reprinted by permission of the Random House Group; Christian Jennings, *Mouthful of Rocks: Through Africa and Corsica in the French*

VOICES OF THE FOREIGN LEGION

Foreign Legion (Bloomsbury); Simon Low, *The Boys from Baghdad* (Mainstream); Pádraig O'Keeffe with Ralph Riegel, *Hidden Soldier: An Irish Legionnaire's Wars from Bosnia to Iraq* (The O'Brien Press Ltd, Dublin © Padraig O'Keeffe and Ralph Riegel); Simon Murray, *Legionnaire: An Englishman in the French Foreign Legion* (Sidgwick & Jackson); John Parker, *Inside the Foreign Legion: The Sensational Story of the World's Toughest Army* (Piatkus/Little Brown); Jaime Salazar, *Legion of the Lost: The True Experience of an American in the French Foreign Legion* (Berkley Caliber), represented by Andrew Lownie; Howard Simpson, *Dien Bien Phu: The Epic Battle America Forgot* (Potomac Books); Zosa Szajkowski, *Jews and the French Foreign Legion* (KTAV); Jacques Weygand, *Légionnaire: Life with the Foreign Legion Cavalry* (© Jacques Weygand, 1952), reproduced by permission of Chambers Harrap Publishers Ltd; James Worden, *Wayward Legionnaire* (Robert Hale, © 1988), reproduced by permission of James Worden and Pollinger Ltd.

I would also like to thank publishers and agents for their help in attempting to secure copyright holders of these works: Jo Capka, *Red Sky at Night* and Ernst Löhndorff, *Hell in the Foreign Legion* (HarperCollins); Pierre Leuliette, *St Michael and the Dragon*, John Lodwick, *Bid the Soldiers Shoot*, Susan Travers, *Tomorrow be Brave* (Random House); Adrian Liddell Hart, *Strange Company* and Colin John, *Nothing to Lose* (Orion Publishing Group); G. Ward Price, *In Morocco with the Legion* (Random House and Curtis Brown).

Every effort has been made to clear permissions, and all omissions are unintentional. If permission has not been granted please contact the publisher, who will include a credit in subsequent printings and editions.

Thanks too to my agent Andrew Lownie, and to Graeme Blaikie, Iain MacGregor and Kate McLelland at Mainstream Publishing. And a special thanks to Victoria.

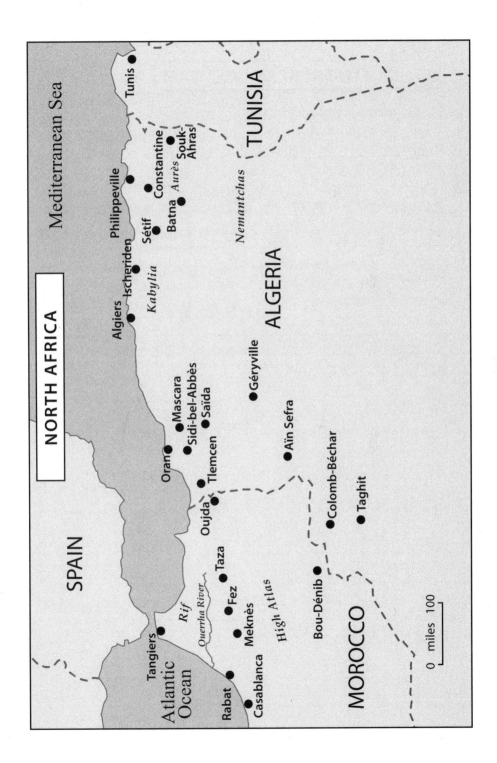

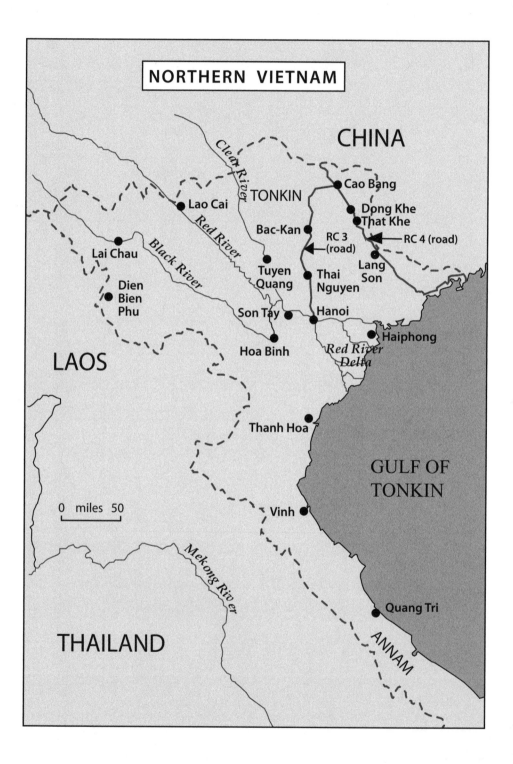

NORTHERN VIETNAM

CHINA

Clear River

TONKIN

Lao Cai

Cao Bang

Dong Khe
That Khe

Bac-Kan

RC 3
(road)

RC 4 (road)

Red River

Lai Chau

Black River

Lang
Son

Tuyen
Quang

Thai
Nguyen

Dien
Bien
Phu

Son Tay

Hanoi

LAOS

Hoa Binh

Haiphong

Red River
Delta

0   miles   50

Thanh Hoa

GULF OF
TONKIN

Vinh

Mekong River

Quang Tri

THAILAND

ANNAM

CONTENTS

PART I

THE MAKING OF A
LEGIONNAIRE

Pain is only weakness leaving the body . . .

(Traditional Legion maxim)

CHAPTER 1

CROSSING THE LINE

Simon Low made his decision to join the French Foreign Legion while sitting in a south London pub in 1988. After seven years' service in the British armed forces he wanted another challenge, and putting down his unfinished pint he returned to his flat, packed his belongings and took the train for Paris. It was a hard-thought choice, however, and Low had misgivings as he took the metro across the city to the Legion's recruiting office at Fort de Nogent:

> Never has a tube ride been so nerve-wracking; counting the stations still to come, I was aching to get there and get it over with. At the same time, I didn't want the journey to end. When it did, I rapidly climbed the stairs two at a time to ground level. I asked an official-looking chap in a 50-pence-shaped, peaked cap directions for the Foreign Legion. '*Où Légion Étrangère?*' Without batting an eyelid, he pointed along a tree-lined road, '*Par là, par là*' [There].
>
> Two minutes' brisk walk found me staring at a sign above two large wooden arched fort gates – *Légion Étrangère*. Taking a deep breath and holding my grip over my right shoulder, I walked towards the small door set into the larger wooden gates, my heart beating ten to the dozen, and rapped loudly with my knuckles. Immediately, a slit in the door snapped open. A pair of eyes peered from within, scrutinising me. I waited for a few seconds while the eyes continued their hard stare, then, pointing to myself, I said, '*Moi, Légion Étrangère.*'

The eyes disappeared, and there was a scraping of bolts before the small wooden door opened inwards. It revealed a legionnaire in combats and kepi, assault rifle slung across his chest. He motioned me to step inside, where I was first searched and then led to a bare stone-arched room. He uttered two words: '*Assis toi*' [Sit down]. I sat on one of the old wooden chairs positioned against the wall. The legionnaire then left, closing the solid wooden door with a resounding bang. Now alone, I looked towards the ceiling, stretched my legs out in front of me and breathed a massive sigh of relief. I had done it. I had crossed the fateful line and into the unknown.

Low's description would find an echo in almost all those who have crossed that line. David Taylor had to overcome second thoughts when he volunteered in 1983:

It was a very daunting walk up the hill from the station to the old fort with its huge wooden gate about 20 feet high. I did what I'm sure many guys did, and that is turn around and walk back to the station to have a beer and think things over. I then went back up, knocked on the door, and went through it right into the Legion.

By its very nature, the Legion has accepted men from all nationalities and walks of life. In the past, if the volunteers were between 17 and 40 years old and were able to meet the Legion's physical requirements they were seldom rejected. The idealistic adventurer – of the type made famous in the *Beau Geste* novels of P. C. Wren – was actively discouraged, however. As far back as 1890, Frederic Martyn was surprised to find his recruiting officer trying to dissuade him from signing the standard five-year contract. The officer – believing the well-bred Martyn would find life unduly hard – remarked: 'There are many, too many, who join the Legion with no sort of qualification for a soldier's life, and these men do no good to themselves or France by enlisting.' Similar reservations were displayed by a Legion non-commissioned officer (NCO), when a be-suited, public school-educated Simon Murray announced his intention of joining the Legion in February 1960:

There was a sergeant sitting behind the table who looked me up and down and said nothing. I broke the ice and said in English that I had come to join the Foreign Legion and he gave me a look that was a mixture of wonder and sympathy. He spoke reasonable English with a German accent and asked me, 'Why?'

I said something conventional about adventure and so on and he said I had come to the wrong place. He said five years in the Legion would be long and hard, that I should forget the romantic idea that the English have of the Legion and that I would do well to go away and reconsider the whole thing. I said I had given it a lot of thought and had come a long way and eventually he said 'OK' with a sigh and led me upstairs and into an assembly hall.

When, in 1999, American would-be legionnaire Jaime Salazar said that he too was looking for adventure, he was openly laughed at by his recruiting NCO, a Japanese *caporal-chef*. But after some preliminary questions, the corporal handed copies of the contract for Salazar to sign:

The pen trembled in my hand. God alone knew what I was agreeing to and what rights I was signing away. But once I had signed, I felt an indescribable release. I'd finally done it!

I was made to change into a green tracksuit smelling of sweat and vomit with a hole in the crotch, and was thrown into a room with the other new arrivals, a collection of humanity's rejects. The Legion has always had a bizarre mix passing through its gates, from the legendary gentlemen who joined in top hats and tails to men who arrived in tatters and signed with an X.

One after another, men in the new intake returned from the bureau waving pieces of paper printed with their *nom de guerre*, the new identity under which they were joining the Foreign Legion. Some were guys with a past that they needed to put behind them; some were even French. According to its founding statutes, the Foreign Legion is an army of non-French mercenaries. On paper, apart from the officers, there are no French nationals serving in the ranks. Any Frenchmen are listed as Belgians, Swiss or French-Canadians. Recruits are [sometimes] given names based on their real initials so that I, as Jaime Salazar, would become Juan Sanchez. Jasper Benson, a black American, was given the name James Bond.

The offer of anonymity has been central to the Legion. It has given men an opportunity to escape their pasts, and, under a different name, forge a new identity. In Western Europe and the United States, a prime motivating factor for signing up has been a love of adventure; in an increasingly safe world the Legion remains one of the ultimate tests of manhood. But economic and social problems have played their part as well. This was certainly the case for former British paratrooper Carl Jackson:

> In some ways I joined the Foreign Legion to forget; as it gave me time *not* to think about the many problems I had left behind me. After 12 years' service in the British Army I was back in my home town of Aberystwyth, back to the reality of electric, gas and water bills – something we never had to deal with in our protected Army environment. However, it was a very disappointing homecoming as I didn't feel the ex-military were being well treated; I couldn't find work and nobody wanted to know.
>
> My first marriage had just broken up, which had not been very amicable, with Brett, my young three-and-a-half-year-old son, being right in the centre of an argument concerning right of access, which made life extremely stressful. I felt that if I didn't sort my life out soon I was probably going to end up being the guest of Her Majesty's Prison Service in Swansea, getting three square meals a day and sewing mail bags for a living. In the end I drew my own conclusion, which was to get away and start afresh.

Regarding the Legion as a whole, poverty and political repression have been the most persuasive recruiting sergeants, and not the betrayals in love that became so popular in Legion novels. During the nineteenth century – and well into the twentieth – pay was so poor that it was only the most desperate who volunteered for economic reasons: in order to put clothes on their backs and food in their mess tins. An old maxim ran: '*La Légion c'est dur – mais gamelle c'est sur!*' [The Legion is hard – but food is for sure!]

Erwin Rosen, a German journalist who had travelled extensively in America, signed up for the Legion in 1905. At a recruiting office in Belfort he was pushed into a room to await his medical examination, and there was shocked at the desperate state of his fellow recruits:

> The atmosphere of the close little room was unspeakable. It was foul with the smell of unwashed humanity, sweat, dirt and unwashed clothes. Long benches stood against the wall and men sat there, candidates for the Foreign Legion, waiting for the medical examination, waiting to know whether their bodies were still worth five centimes daily pay.
>
> One of them sat there naked, shivering in the chill October air. It needed no doctor's eye to see that he was half starved. His emaciated body told the whole story. Another folded his pants with almost touching care, although they had been patched so often that they were now tired of service and in a state of continuous strike. An enormous tear in an important part had ruined them hopelessly. These pants and that tear had probably settled the question of the wearer's enlisting in the Foreign Legion.
>
> A dozen men were there. Some of them were mere boys, with only a shadow of beard on their faces; youths with deep-set hungry eyes and deep lines around their mouths; men with hard, wrinkled features telling the old story of drink very plainly.

Adrian Liddell Hart – son of the military theorist and historian Sir Basil Liddell Hart – volunteered in 1951. He analysed why men joined the Legion. Having accepted that some would have enlisted out of economic necessity, he suggested two other reasons:

> There are a number of men who join for strictly professional reasons. They are men who want to be professional soldiers and cannot soldier in their own countries or have decided that it is anyhow better to soldier in the Legion. For them the Legion has certain concrete advantages. There are plenty of opportunities for active service – and for action. Promotion in the non-commissioned ranks can be rapid, with corresponding benefits, and for some, at least, it is easier to become an officer in the Legion than it might be in their national forces.

In the second place there remain a proportion of men who have sought sanctuary in the most literal sense. A few of them, even today, are escaping from their police for civil offences. Many more are escaping from their governments for political reasons. In the modern world the Legion is not, perhaps, such a sure refuge in this sense as it used to be. But there is no doubt that it still makes the effort to protect this kind of individual, once he is accepted, against the ever-increasing power of the modern state. And whether he likes the Legion or not, it is surely better than sitting in a concentration camp or, in many instances, in an ordinary gaol.

Since the 1960s – and the Legion's move from Algeria to France – improved pay and prospects have made the Legion attractive to a wider range of economic migrants, and following the collapse of the Iron Curtain in 1989 many of these have come from Eastern Europe. Another inducement has been the offer of French citizenship when the legionnaire's contract has been successfully completed. In the twenty-first century, the ranks of the Legion are being joined by increasing numbers from South America, Asia and Africa seeking a better life in the West.

Something of the difference between Westerners and those from more economically deprived countries can be seen in a conversation between the university-educated Jaime Salazar and a former Polish law student called Sadlowski, who rebuked Salazar for his reason for joining:

> I can't understand what you wanted to join up for. You had a good life in America. It was totally different for me; the Legion's my lifeline. Things back in Poland are desperate – there's crime and corruption everywhere. The only people making money are the mafia. I liked my studies but how could I live on three hundred US dollars a month? If I make the cut, I'll join the parachute regiment where I hear you can earn fifteen thousand francs a month and more on mission to Africa!

If economic deprivation provided a steady stream of recruits then war, revolution and other political upheavals produced the great surges of enlistment that became such a part of the Legion's history.

White Russians entered the Legion in large numbers in the early 1920s, following their defeat by the Bolsheviks in the Russian Civil War. After both world wars, displaced Germans continued to volunteer for the Legion, despite their recent enmity with France. The Soviet invasion of Hungary in 1956 saw Hungarians leave their homeland for the Legion. Similarly, there were influxes of Czechs after the repression of the 'Prague Spring' in 1968, and Portuguese recruits after the 1974 overthrow of the Spinoza regime. In 1981 Colonel Robert Devouges, a veteran Legion officer, said of recent upheavals: 'We reflect the troubles of the world. Laos, Cambodia, Bangladesh – you name the event, and we'll have the men.'

These surges of manpower from specific nations inevitably modified the character of the Legion – before being absorbed into it with minimal trouble. A. R. Cooper, a legionnaire in 1914, was bemused by the strange national, social and political mix of the Legion when he rejoined in 1919:

> I found that half my Legion comrades were Germans, the very people I had been trying to kill for four years in the bloodiest war of all time. I had to admit that the Germans were the better elements. The majority had belonged to the Spartacist group of Marxists, and others were monarchists who had enlisted to avoid serving the new [German] republic. The monarchists were mainly former Prussian officers. Most of the Spartacists, on the other hand, were schoolteachers, intellectuals and engineers.
>
> Russians had been virtually unknown in the Legion before the war. They flocked to the service of France after the failure of the White Russian movement, many of them still wearing Cossack uniforms with cartridge belts across their chests. Here was a paradox: Spartacist revolutionaries and White Russians, opponents of Communism, working amicably together in a force that also included Prussian aristocrats.

Apart from its obvious multinational nature, the Legion was marked out by the social range of its recruits, even if the majority came from the lower rungs of society. While officers within the Legion numbered several princes, as well as the future King Peter of Serbia and Pierre Messmer, a French prime minister, the ranks of enlisted men included Giuseppe Bottai, a former education minister in Mussolini's government, Shapour Bakhtiar, the Shah of Iran's last prime minister, and Siegfried Freytag, a Luftwaffe ace (102 official victories) who joined the Legion after the Second World War, served in Indochina and died in the Legion's retirement home in 2003. The Legion traditionally attracted writers and artists, among whom were the German painter Hans Hartung, the American poet Alan Seeger, the German writer Ernst Jünger and the Hungarian intellectual Arthur Koestler.

From Fort de Nogent, and the other recruiting centres dotted across France, the recruit is despatched to the Legion's headquarters and administrative centre at Aubagne, a few miles north of Marseilles. The recruit will spend around three weeks at Aubagne, where his suitability for the Legion is assessed, before going on to commence basic training at Castelnaudary, where he is classified as an *engagé volontaire* (EV). Christian Jennings, a British volunteer in 1984, described his arrival at Aubagne after a coach trip from Paris:

> Driving up to the gates of the camp, I saw my first legionnaire in parade uniform; he was wearing a white kepi, a green tie and blue cummerbund. He saluted the coach and we drove through the gates and up a hill past the enormous parade ground at the far end of which I could see the *Monument aux Morts*, the memorial to every dead legionnaire. It took the form of a huge bronze globe supported by an enormous stone plinth. It had originally occupied a position at Sidi-bel-Abbès, but when the Legion left Algeria it had been dismantled stone by stone and brought to its present resting place at Aubagne. Behind it was a stone wall on which was written in bronze letters the motto of the Legion, '*Legio Patria Nostra*' [the Legion is Our Country].
>
> It was only 7.30 a.m. but already it was getting hot. The camp was full of pine trees and flowerbeds of bougainvillea and hibiscus. Square white buildings, three storeys high, sat at regular intervals on the slope, all looking down towards the parade ground. Uniformed legionnaires marched around, and there was a group of convicts from the regimental prison in filthy fatigues and greasy boots who were emptying the dustbins and sweeping

the roads. A body of soldiers in sports kit marched past in a slow, rhythmic pace, singing loudly. They were all in step and looked very smart. We drove to the top of the road and drew up outside a compound surrounded by a wire fence; inside was a large white building surrounded by an expanse of gravel on which a huge group of people were drawn up in lines. This was the '*Section Engagés Volontaires*', the department that dealt with all prospective recruits.

Pádraig O'Keeffe, previously a hotel chef in Cork, recalled his time at Aubagne in 1991:

I spent three weeks in Aubagne, and it was very much an acclimatisation for Legion life. You learned to march, you learned to keep your gear in order, you learned to salute properly and you began your introduction to what it meant to be a legionnaire. And I had my first introduction to the dreaded *corvée* – the cleaning routine. Being on *corvée* duties meant spending your whole day cleaning – first your barracks, then the floor, then the toilets and finally, perhaps, the entire parade ground. If one thing in Legion life was to be avoided at all costs, it was *corvée* duty, and, needless to say, that was impossible.

The prime reason behind the volunteer's stint at Aubagne has been to weed out the unsuitable, and each recruit is subjected to a series of basic physical, intelligence and psychological tests. In the modern, post-colonial period the number of would-be legionnaires has not diminished and the Legion can afford to be choosy in who it takes on, as Major Karli, a vocations officer during the 1990s, outlined:

There is a certain turnover in the Legion and the gaps have to be filled but at present we have more candidates than we can use. We are now accepting about one in eight, so you can see the selection is fairly rigorous. The person's background is taken into consideration. Previous military experience is helpful but not necessary. Civilian experiences can be just as important. We may even accept someone fresh out of school if we feel he has the right attitude and potential to make it as a legionnaire.

While at Aubagne the recruit also undergoes rigorous security checks by the *2ème Bureau* – the intelligence section nicknamed the 'Gestapo' – as O'Keeffe explained:

> This was a series of interviews, which bordered on interrogation, about your previous life. The first session lasted about three hours and was like an A–Z of your life to date. It was a grilling that went on for several further sessions over an entire week, and if any aspect of your story didn't gel, you were out. The Legion interrogators were incredibly adept at indentifying recruits who were trying to hide something in their past – in most cases a criminal conviction or an ongoing problem with the police. If they were suspicious, they could devote two entire sessions to asking the same question in about two hundred different ways. One of the worst crimes in the Legion is to be caught lying, and it's not something that would be sorted out the easy way – at the receiving end of a fist or boot.
>
> Traditionally, the Legion was willing to turn a blind eye to recruits who had misunderstandings with the law in their own countries – unless, of course, it involved murder (and other serious crimes). But the Legion insisted on knowing *why* recruits wanted to be legionnaires and any criminal past was a crucial factor in that.

Before Aubagne became the Legion's home in the 1960s, its headquarters was at Sidi-bel-Abbès in Algeria. Recruits were assembled at Marseilles before being shipped over to Africa. Adrian Liddell Hart described his experiences in the old and squalid Fort St Nicholas in Marseilles:

> In the dawn, through overcast days, in the chill, damp dusk as we gazed across the harbour at the pin-points of lights, through the bleak barrack-rooms hazy with the smoke of acrid French tobacco, would reverberate an interminable roll-call over the loudspeaker. Here and there figures would detach themselves from the windswept huddles and slip away to the orderly office. We might not see them again. An empty bunk that night, its rugs returned to the store and waiting for the next occupant, would remind us of final rejection.

We were not yet legionnaires. But we had ceased, for practical purposes, to be civilians. We were not citizens or even aliens. We were prisoners, it seemed, without the limited rights and minimum security which are generally enjoyed by prisoners, convicted or remanded. We were informed of no rights and assured of no prospects. We were liable to be kept in suspense and then rejected without ever knowing the reason.

Our daily lives were controlled by the large German corporal who had interviewed me on my arrival. As several hundred eccentrics and an unknown number of desperados from the ends of the earth were turning up each week, the corporal earned his modest chevrons. He relied on whistle and shout freely supplemented by his boot. Occasionally someone tried to resist. He would be hustled off by a group of legionnaires, who materialised at short notice, amidst a hail of blows. Sometimes he was not seen again. Sometimes he returned the worse for wear, from the cells, where it was rumoured others languished indefinitely.

Simon Murray also successfully went through the selection process in Marseilles. He wrote in his diary:

We leave for Algeria tomorrow. Excitement is running high. Imaginations are working overtime. We have been given Legion haircuts – clean sweep, bald as eggs, known as a *boule à zero*. We look more like convicts than ever. I am looking forward to getting out of this rat hole.

Reveille at five o'clock and we piled into trucks that took us down to the harbour. We left Marseilles under a clear blue sky aboard the SS *Sidi-bel-Abbès*, a 5,000-ton troop-carrier-cum-cattle ship. The sleeping quarters are in the bowels of the ship and consist of a thousand deckchairs facing in every direction and packed as tightly as sardines in a tin. I stood on deck until the last pencil-line of land became invisible. I said goodbye to old Europe and turned to face Africa and God knows what.

After a stormy Mediterranean crossing, Murray and his fellow recruits arrived in Oran, before being transferred, first to Sidi-bel-Abbès and then Mascara to undertake '*instruction*'. In today's Legion, those who have passed the selection course at Aubagne are sent to Castelnaudary in south-west France to begin four months of hard basic training.

CHAPTER 2

THE POWER OF TRADITION

Before leaving Aubgane for basic training at Castelnaudary, the *engagé volontaire* (EV) will be taken around the Legion's museum. This is not intended as a pleasant recreational trip, rather it is one of the first steps designed to inculcate the recruit with the mystique of the Legion, above all its separateness from any other military corps. British legionnaire John Yeowell, who signed up in 1938 and was sent to Sidi-bel-Abbès, described how the Legion used its past as a training tool:

> We now began our period of indoctrination. It was to fill our heads with the traditions of the Legion. One of the first things they did was to take you around the museum of the Legion, the *Salle d'Honneur*, where the great battles of the past were described to us, along with exploits of the heroes. We saw the captured battle colours, ancient swords, rifles and other relics. They gave us each a little book with our names inscribed inside, which highlighted the Legion of the past. It really did work. Every day on the parade ground there was some kind of traditional activity going on with the Legion band playing all the trumpet calls which we had to memorise and which always ended with a performance of '*Le Boudin*' [the regimental march]. It was all very moving. And the traditions of the Legion began to sink in.

Nearly half a century later, Christian Jennings was given the tour of the museum at Aubagne, as well as a two-hour lecture celebrating the Legion's history:

> We visited the Legion's museum and wandered round looking at the different flags of the units which had fought all over the world for 150 years. There were displays of medals, weapons, uniforms and pictures. We went down into the crypt where the wooden hand of *Capitaine* Danjou [hero of the fight at Camerone] lay in a glass case. It was the focal point of the room, and whenever visiting dignitaries and military authorities came to visit Aubagne they would be taken down to the crypt where they would stand and salute the hand. There was a poem on the wall written by an American legionnaire called Alan Seeger during World War I:
>
>> But I've a rendezvous with Death
>> At midnight in some flaming town,
>> When Spring trips north again this year,
>> And I to my pledged word am true,
>> I shall not fail that rendezvous.
>
> There were tattered flags from Dien Bien Phu and Algeria, and collections of medals belonging to famous Legion soldiers. I walked over and stood respectfully in front of *Capitaine* Danjou's false limb. It was made of dark wood and looked like a graceful gorilla's paw. I read another poem on the wall written by a God-fearing captain who had been killed in Algeria, in which he implored God to look sparingly on humble soldiers performing their divine task as warriors of Christianity. It effectively conjured up the mixture of religion, fighting prowess and romanticism which the Legion held so dear.

Central to the Legion's idea of itself is the engagement at Camerone, fought in Mexico on 30 April 1863, when the Legion was part of an invading French Army attempting to set the Archduke Maximilian upon the throne of Mexico. Although the campaign ended in failure, the defence of Camerone has become a sacred event in the Legion calendar. A special Camerone Day is set aside on 30 April, and the following official account is read out to all men in the Legion:

The French army was besieging Puebla. The Legion had been ordered to protect traffic and ensure the security of convoys over seventy-five kilometres of road.

On 29 April 1863 the commanding officer, Colonel Jeanningros, was informed that a large convoy, carrying three million francs in specie, siege material and ammunition, was en route for Puebla. Captain Danjou, his second-in-command, persuaded him to send one company ahead of the convoy. No. 3 Company of the Foreign Legion Regiment was detailed but it had no officers available. Captain Danjou took command himself and 2nd-Lieutenants Maudet of the colour party and Vilain, the paymaster, volunteered to join him.

At 1 a.m. on 30 April No. 3 Company set off at a strength of three officers and sixty-two men. By 7 a.m. it had covered some twelve miles when it stopped to brew coffee at Palo Verde. At this moment the enemy appeared and fighting started at once. Captain Danjou formed square and, during his withdrawal, successfully repulsed several cavalry charges, inflicting his first severe losses on the enemy.

On reaching Camerone inn, a vast building including a courtyard surrounded by a 9-ft-high wall, he decided to dig in there in order to pin the enemy down and delay to the maximum the time at which the convoy might be attacked.

While the men were hurriedly organising the defence of this building a Mexican officer summoned Captain Danjou to surrender, pointing out the vast disparity of numbers. Captain Danjou replied: 'We have ammunition and we shall not surrender.' Then, raising his hand, he swore to defend himself to the death and required his men to swear the same oath. It was now 10 a.m. Until 6 p.m. these sixty men, who had neither eaten nor drunk since the previous day and despite extreme heat, hunger and thirst, defended themselves against 2,000 Mexicans – 800 cavalry, 1,200 infantry.

At midday Captain Danjou was killed by a bullet through the heart. At 2 p.m. 2nd-Lieutenant Vilain fell with a bullet in the head. At this point the Mexican colonel succeeded in setting fire to the inn.

Despite their sufferings, increased by heat and smoke, the legionnaires held on but many of them had been hit. By 5 p.m. there remained only twelve men to fight, grouped around 2nd-Lieutenant Maudet.

At this point the Mexican colonel assembled his men and emphasised to them the disgrace which would attach to them if they were unable to overcome this handful of brave men (a legionnaire who understood Spanish translated his speech as it was made). The Mexicans prepared for a general assault through the breaches which they had succeeded in opening but Colonel Milan first sent another surrender call to 2nd-Lieutenant Maudet. It was scornfully rejected.

The final assault took place. Soon there remained only five men around Maudet – Corporal Maine and Legionnaires Catteau, Wenzel, Constantin and Leonhart. Each still had one round in their rifles and their bayonets were fixed; in a corner of the courtyard, their backs to the wall, they faced their enemies; at a given signal they fired point blank at the enemy and then charged with the bayonet. Second-Lieutenant Maudet and two legionnaires fell, mortally wounded. Maine and his two legionaries were about to be massacred when a Mexican officer dashed forward and saved them, shouting 'Surrender'. 'We will surrender if you promise to collect and care for our wounded and if you leave us our weapons,' Maine replied. The three men still had their bayonets lowered. 'We can refuse nothing to men like you,' the officer answered.

Captain Danjou's sixty men had kept their oath to the end; for eleven hours they had held up 2,000 enemy, of whom they had killed 300 and wounded a similar number. By their sacrifice and by saving the convoy, they had carried out their orders.

The Emperor Napoleon III decided that Camerone be inscribed as a battle honour on the colours of the Foreign Legion and the names of Danjou, Vilain and Maudet be engraved in letters of gold on the walls of Les Invalides in Paris.

In 1892 a memorial was built on the scene of the fighting. Ever since then, when Mexican troops pass the memorial, they present arms.

In the early 1960s, foreign correspondent Geoffrey Bocca asked a group of legionnaires why Camerone was so important to them, especially when it was little more than a skirmish and virtually unknown outside the Legion. One of them, a Sicilian *sergent-chef* called LaBella, replied:

> The appeal of Camerone to a legionnaire is as natural as instinct. He reaches out to it in his own heart, because it is part of his own pain. It is the great reminder to the legionnaire that the sand is always blowing in his eyes, the battleground is always ill-chosen, the odds are too great, the cause insufficient to justify his death, and the tools at hand always the wrong ones. And, above all, nobody cares whether he wins or loses, lives or dies. Camerone gives the legionnaire strength to live with his despair. It reminds him that he cannot win, but it makes him feel that there is dignity in being a loser.

As part of its separateness, the Legion likes to see itself as a family – albeit a rough one – in which every legionnaire is an exclusive member. James Worden, a former RAF officer who joined the Legion in the late 1950s, pointed out the legionnaire's true loyalty to this extended family became apparent on completion of his basic training:

> It is at this time that the almost fully trained recruit realises that, although on enlistment he swore an oath of allegiance to the French flag, that flag is wholly represented by the Legion, and only the Legion. He may be termed a soldier but he is not part of the French Army, and for him there will only exist the Legion and its officers. The French regular army is as remote as the man on the moon, and will not even exist in his mental make-up.

At the great military display in Paris on Bastille Day (14 June) the Legion brings up the rear of the march-past because of its unusually slow parade march, set at 88 paces per minute instead of the more usual 120. Along with its white kepi and distinctive parade uniform this is another means of keeping a distance between the Legion and the rest of the French armed forces. Dave Cunliffe, a sergeant in the 1990s, took part in two Bastille Day parades, where the crowd gave the Legion the loudest cheer:

> On Bastille Day the Legion marches last down the Champs Elysées in Paris. There they exaggerate the slow march, instead of the Legion's actual regulation 88 paces a minute they bring it down to 60-odd paces a minute for effect. You're practically falling over, you're going so slow. But it is pretty impressive, and it is good to be in that platoon or squad when you're marching.

Raymond L. Bruckberger – an American traveller in North Africa before and after the Second World War, who knew the Legion well – wrote of the relationship binding all legionnaires:

> From the highest to the lowest, there is a strong bond among legionnaires which is stronger than any solidarity of rank. A private in the Legion knows that his colonel prefers him to any officer who is not in the Legion. The Legion is like a large family that needs only itself to exist.

Bruckberger then went on to narrate a story illustrating the loyalty of legionnaire to legionnaire, regardless of rank:

> In 1945, an agreement between the French and Russian governments provided for the repatriation of all French prisoners in Russian hands, and all Russians on French soil. A Russian commission visited the barracks of the Legion. It was received with perfect courtesy. It showed the colonel a list of Russians in the Legion. The colonel recognised all the names, but the commission must excuse him for at that hour of the day all the men were out for drill. He asked the commission to return the following morning and promised that all the men would be there. That evening he called all the men together, explained the situation and asked each one what he wanted to do. They all preferred the Legion to Russia. The colonel immediately changed all their names to others that had a French ring. When the Russian commission presented itself the next day, it was received with the greatest courtesy. 'I'm terribly sorry,' said the colonel, 'but

yesterday evening I imprudently told those men to be ready to appear before you in the morning. Last night, every one of the scamps deserted.'

The Legion has made a speciality of its stories – some apocryphal – which in various ways illustrate aspects of the corps. Colin John, a British legionnaire stationed in Indochina during the early 1950s, retold the well-known account of the legionnaire who was continually falling foul of authority:

Some time or another he visited a tattooist, and printed indelibly in letters an inch high across his right hand was the one word 'Merde!' [Shit!] This had somehow escaped notice at his medical examination, and later caused quite a bit of embarrassment. He was ordered to wear a glove on his right hand so as to avoid giving offence to officers when saluting. As he liked nothing better than giving offence, he was constantly losing the glove, and each time he was sent to prison for fifteen days.

Another popular anecdote was recounted by Legion historian Erwan Bergot, relating to the White Russian cavalrymen who joined the Legion in the early 1920s:

The story is told that one day, during an inspection at Sidi-bel-Abbès, a colonel was struck by the appearance of a recruit with the moustache of a Tartar and the beard of a prophet. The colonel asked: 'What were you before you came here?'
'I was a general, mon colonel.'
This story cannot be confirmed. What is certain is that, disregarding the strict discipline of the Legion and in the secrecy of the barrack room, a certain sergeant would come each evening to kiss the hand of a simple legionnaire and address him according to the ancient Cossack tradition as: 'Monsieur le sotnik' (a Cossack rank equivalent to captain). The sergeant had previously been his batman.

Among German legionnaires the story of the Prussian royal prince who had secretly volunteered in the 1880s remained in common currency for years, his identity only discovered after a heroic death fighting tribesmen in Algeria. The idea of redemption through combat – especially by a well-connected ne'er-do-well – found its way into many Legion narratives. This, of course, is not to say that they were not necessarily true. Zinovi Pechkoff, the adopted son of the Russian writer Maxim Gorki and a Legion officer who had lost an arm in the trenches in 1915, described the actions of an Italian legionnaire – a former First World War I officer – during the 1925 campaign against Rif tribesmen in Morocco:

> Once, when we were on a long march, I saw him weary and tired, dragging along behind his section. I said to him: 'I should like better to see you at the head or your section and not behind – especially you, an ex-officer, with all your decorations.' But on the day that he was wounded I saw him at the head of his section, rushing forward, fearless of danger. Afterwards he wrote me a letter from hospital saying:

> > My foot is badly shattered, but I am recovering from the wound, and I hope to come back. The only thing I want to ask is – did you see me in battle? I would be so sad if you were left under the impression which you received when you saw me marching behind my section.

> Then I received another letter from his father [a retired general], telling me that he himself had sent his boy into the Legion.

> > Please do not think that he is a criminal or a young murderer. He is not. He is young. He misbehaved himself. His passion for cards got the better of him and he did what a gentleman should not do. I paid his debts. Then I told him to join the Legion and if he did well for five years he could come back to his family. Now he is wounded. You write me that his conduct was brilliant. I am overjoyed, I am proud of him. He is once more my beloved Enrico. He will continue his service in the Legion and after the five years he will be once more accepted in the family.

The idea that the Legion offers a break with the past and a chance to begin anew has been taken up by many writers. The French author André Maurois put it more grandly than most in his preface to Pechkoff's memoirs:

> All civilisations have their sufferers. In every country in Europe, and without doubt in America also, live men for whom life is a penance. Some have been stricken down by misfortunes or by unforeseen happenings and the sight of the places where they have been unhappy has become unbearable for them. Others have suffered by their own mistakes or they have committed some act for which their consciences reprove them; they feel that, rightly, they are despised and they know that they can reconstruct themselves only by escaping from their pasts. Others, citizens of countries which have been overthrown, cannot adapt themselves to new conditions: their only resource is to expatriate themselves.
>
> For all these beings, for all those whom Dostoevsky calls 'The Insulted and Injured', the Foreign Legion offers a refuge.

Adrian Liddell Hart developed the concept of the Legion as a psychological safe-haven:

> The Legion is a refuge . . . As such it exists in a world where it becomes increasingly difficult for the individual to find a refuge. And it may even be surer to escape into the anonymity of suburbia than the anonymity of Sidi-bel-Abbès. But many people do not want to escape into nothing – they want to escape into a community, into a tradition, into a myth. Man needs to make a gesture.
>
> Finally there is the idea that the legionnaires do not necessarily become better or wiser, but they become more integrated. In joining the Legion men do not join only an organised, disciplined institution; they enter a situation which is more or less recognised by the whole world and sanctified by its sacrifice. They belong – many for the first time.
>
> The Legion claims to be something more than a military force. This claim is essential. However much it may fall short of the fulfilment, the Legion could scarcely exist without this aspiration,

this mystique. And the strictly military exigencies are, to some extent, subordinated in practice to this human ideal.

A. R. Cooper, the British legionnaire who served during the inter-war period, provided this summary of what it was to be a soldier in the Legion:

> Many legionnaires took a masochistic pleasure in an unhappy life. Attempted explanations are complicated by the fact that the Legion is composed of men of many races, whose origins, sentiments and ideas are totally different. This in itself gives the legionnaire an indefinable personality of his own.
>
> The Legion is a refuge, a meal ticket, a place for rehabilitation. It can also be a profession. A man goes to it without identity papers, with the nationality of his choice, and shorn of criminal records. He leaves his past outside the recruiting office door. In the Legion one finds strange mixtures of good and bad, latent heroism, and sometimes a degraded soul. All these aspects, when fused together, emit an iron energy, an instructive zest for adventure, an astonishing fount of initiative and a supreme disdain for death. The composite legionnaire has all the sublime virtues brought out by war and displays virility and superiority. Yet he lives in a fantasy world, and if he is ever in trouble he will blame le cafard, a name adopted by legionnaires to mean a form of temporary madness peculiar to the legion brought about by a variety of circumstances, including boredom. But, above all, the men of the Legion religiously uphold their traditions and military integrity.

Most of today's legionnaires tend to see the Legion and themselves in less highly wrought terms, although Christian Jennings provided this modern view of the Legion's sense of itself:

> Over the decades the Legion had developed its own kind of soldiering. It was not soldiering where all hung on victory or defeat, as in other armies, but rather a stylish profession of arms, aimed at bringing greater glory to France and to the Legion. As at Camerone and Dien Bien Phu, the cost was high; but the Legion

in its purest tradition saw only merit in dying for France. Painted on the walls of a barracks in the last century had been the words, 'Legionnaires, you are soldiers in order to die, and I am sending you where you can die.'

This was the essence of its self-glorification. It was an idea based on the lifestyle of the true legionnaire, who, before his time in the Legion, had been nothing, and therefore in the eyes of the Legion, anything he had done in his past life was immaterial. He only became whole in becoming a legionnaire.

The lines of a poem were written on a plaque at the end of our corridor, *Lui qui est devenu fils de France, non par le sang reçu, mais par la sang versé* (He who has become a son of France, not through blood received, but by blood spilt.) In our history lecture I grasped only the most basic nature of this warrior creed, but it was something which I was to find permeating the Legion at every level.

CHAPTER 3

BASIC TRAINING

Even before he has reached the main training centre at Castelnaudary – or Castel, as it is better known – the recruit will have been made aware of the Legion's obsession with neatness and cleanliness. British volunteer Tony Sloane recalled: 'Everything had to be immaculate. Each morning before six we would be washed, shaved, beds undone with blankets folded, rooms and washrooms cleaned.'

Dave Cunliffe, an *engagé volontaire* from North Wales, soon found out that any form of slackness would not be tolerated:

> On the day we left Aubagne to go to Castel we had to get up very early, and I thought I needn't bother to shave because being blond and only 19 years old no one would see any stubble on me. But when we got to the camp, our instructors came over. This big German said to me: 'You haven't had a shave,' and he whipped out a lighter and burned the bristles off my chin. I learned my lesson pretty quickly after that!

Today's recruit would empathise with the experiences of American Bennett J. Doty, who discovered the uncertain delights of seemingly endless *corvée* duty on his arrival in North Africa in 1925:

> Here indeed I made my first acquaintance with the absolute cleanliness of the French Foreign Legion.

Twice a day the floor and staircases, which are of tile, were washed and scrubbed; how many times a day they were swept, Heaven only knows. The *carré du quartier* [parade square] was meticulously policed; not a scrap of paper, not a cigarette butt, not a toothpick ever was to be seen there. My first days in the Legion made me wonder whether I had not made a mistake, and turned myself into a scrub-woman, instead of a trooper in a crack corps. I washed tiles, I scrubbed them, I polished them. I swept, I swabbed. I paced the *quartier*, a hood on my back, stopping twenty times at each step to pick up infinitesimal bits of matter out of place. And there was also the kitchen police; there are no servants in the Legion. I peeled potatoes and cut up carrots and shelled peas.

It was to be thus during my entire stay in the Legion. I never saw a barracks, a post, a camp, which was not scrupulously clean and inspected twice a day. Woe to the man with dust under his bed, or dirty clothes in his pack. His number was up. He was due for four days of extra duty the first time; eight days in the *boîte*, the 'box', the prison, the second time; and a regular course of chastisement if he held to his slothful way. Cleanliness is the Legion's only claim to kinship with godliness; realising this, they make the most of it.

Doty also described the care given to such otherwise mundane duties as bed-making:

This is quite a meticulous proceeding, almost a ceremony in the Legion. The blankets are folded into perfect squares and laid at the foot of the bed. The sheets are rolled into two cylinders, one of which is laid across the right extremity of the blanket square, the other across the left. The pillow is placed between them, in the exact centre. After the beds had been made, each man swept up the floor under his bed and within his area, and then washed it carefully with a wet rag.

A recruit was expected to learn how to pack his uniform in a neat, perfectly squared-off pile. This was known as *paquetage*, a vital skill explained to German recruit Erwin Rosen by a veteran legionnaire in the early 1900s:

He rummaged in the bundle of uniform things on my bed, pulling out one by one jackets, pants, shirts etc, and folding them with astonishing quickness. I watched him in wonder. This old soldier with his big rough hands had fingers as clever as a chambermaid's. Piece after piece he folded rapidly, smoothing every crease with almost ridiculous care. Each of the folded pieces he measured, giving each the same length, from the tips of his fingers to his elbow. Finally he erected with these bundles, upon the shelf at the wall over my bed, the ingenious structure of uniforms, the *paquetage* of the Legion. The legionnaire has no clothes chest. To get over this difficulty he invented the *paquetage*, which is a work of art, solving the military problem of how to stow away several uniforms in a compact space without crumpling them.

Unsurprisingly, the standards required in the wearing of parade uniform have always been high. Recruits are expected to be able to wield an iron as expertly as a rifle. Tony Sloane outlined some of the procedures necessary for an acceptable turn-out:

We had ironed our parade uniforms to the immaculate state required by the corporals. The insignia badges had to be stitched on and creases put in the front and rear of the shirt. Each crease had to be sharp and in a straight line. No *double plis* (double creases), and no overlapping of creases. Above each front pocket of the shirt, three creases would run vertically from the epaulette. The creases had to be exactly 35 millimetres apart. The back of the shirt boasted two horizontal creases with three vertical creases joining them. These had to be 53 millimetres apart. We spent hours getting it right. Each time the corporals would measure the creases and inspect each surface of the shirt for unwanted folds or blemishes.

Besides inculcating a mania for neatness, once at Castelnaudary the Legion begins the process of turning the EV into a legionnaire. This transformation is accelerated when, shortly after arrival, the recruit is sent to the 'Farm' for a four-week stint of extreme training. The Farm is, in fact, a number of semi-derelict farmhouses dotted about the foothills of the Pyrenees mountains. Conditions are grim, as British recruit Gareth Carins revealed:

We were given a brief tour of the Farm, and what a shit hole it was. Even the most ruthless estate agent would be hard pressed to sell the qualities of this place. It was located on the side of a shallow valley and set on two floors. The upstairs was our sleeping accommodation and consisted of knackered bunk beds with damp mattresses, and a battered grey steel locker each. The washroom was one long cast-iron trough with a couple of cold-water taps, but the selling point of the whole place was the showering facilities. The bank of showers only had ice-cold water, which considering we were at the base of the Pyrenees and it was only March, would mean that getting a shower would be more of a punishment than a way of washing.

Survival training, running, long marches, meticulous cleaning routines, with minimal sleep and insufficient food, are some of the constants of the Farm experience. Like other recruits, Irishman Pádraig O'Keeffe found it tough going:

One morning, a training officer woke us up at 5.00 a.m. by throwing a 'flash-bang', a type of smoke bomb, into our barracks room. We had only been in bed for an hour after a gruelling seventy-two-hour endurance march through the mountains. There was dust residue from the explosion everywhere – in our hair, in our beds, even in our underwear. One hour later we were told we were having a full kit inspection. When we failed – as everyone knew we would – all our gear, from our socks to our bedclothes, was thrown out a second-floor window into the slime and mud of the track below. It had been raining solid for twenty-four hours and the ground resembled a muddy farmyard.

We were then told that, two hours later, there was to be a fresh kit inspection, forcing us to collect and sort our gear, fight for space in the washrooms and then iron everything – only to fail the repeat inspection and have to go through the whole soul-destroying cycle again. It was total insanity. We hadn't a hope of making any of the kit-inspection deadlines. But that was precisely the point. We were being asked to do the impossible – and the training cadre wanted to see how we reacted to pressure, exhaustion, mayhem, futility and maybe even despair.

The Farm was all about your mentality. It wasn't about whether you could make it physically as a soldier. It was about discovering weaknesses and identifying those recruits who would invariably seek the easy way out. The Farm instilled a kind of attitude, a Legion outlook on how things should be done and why you never, ever quit. For some, the Farm became a kind of living nightmare and they would never allow themselves to be put through a similar experience again. It was more than the bare concrete walls and ceilings – the whole experience became a measure of just how painful military life could be. It was a combination of physical exhaustion, mental fatigue, self-doubt and, for some, probably even a bit of fear. A few lads slammed doors on their fingers or deliberately tried to break bones just to get out of the Farm. There is only one word that can summarise the experience – hell.

The idea of the Farm, as one instructor put it, was to 'take you down to the basics and then build you up'. Nothing was written down, but at the Farm you'd get everyone at the same level, starting with lessons in how to wash, and then work upwards.

According to Carl Jackson, the idea of re-creating the individual along strict Legion lines was central to the training process:

Recruits come from all walks of life, from all parts of the world. They might be ex-military, for instance, like Spanish legionnaires, Portuguese commandos, German paras, American marines – all sorts. And everyone's got their own way of doing things. But the Legion doesn't want people set in their ways and doing their own thing, so they break you down and remould you to what they want: a person that will work as a team member and not an individual.

The NCOs who are your training instructors are expert in this field and know just how far to go before you reach the edge of breaking point. And the way they do this is mostly through sleep and food deprivation and physical torture. What they like to see are fatigued, exhausted recruits willing to fight anyone. They know when they've got you because they can see it in your eyes: you're hungry and ready do anything. Then they start rebuilding you to what they want. Legion training is psychologically draining, more so, say, than in the British Paras or the Royal Marines, mentally and physically it's a brainwashing process.

Acquiring a basic knowledge of French is also a priority. Great efforts have been made by the Legion to help the recruits, each man being assigned a native French speaker – a *binome* – for assistance in understanding instructions and, if possible, gaining a greater knowledge of the language. Matt Rake, who subsequently became a medic in the 2nd REP (*Régiment Étranger Parachutiste*), described how he came to grips with the language:

> Learning French was very hard at first, especially as I'd given up French in my third year at school. But what French I had eventually came back to me, especially when doing it 24/7. Gradually it came on and by the end of basic training I could understand all the basic drills. Although having a chat with someone was a bit more difficult; that didn't really happen until about two years in. It mainly came through going out for a beer, and having to use French to communicate with a Pole or some other nationality. By the time I got out of the Legion I was a very confident French speaker.

American Jaime Salazar recalled one teaching method adopted by the NCOs: 'The sergeants had a clever way of teaching the names of foods. At *soupe*, Sergeant Gagné strolled around asking *engagé volontaires* what various items on their plates were. Anything they could not name in French, he ate.'

To encourage the process of learning French, recruits are prohibited from speaking their native languages, especially while on duty or within earshot of an NCO. Erwin James, a British volunteer in 1979, discovered this on his first morning at Castelnaudary:

> A Chilean recruit named Garcia, with whom I'd become friendly at the recruitment centre in Lille, swore in Spanish. Two of the corporals raced at him and began screaming in his face. '*Seulment français! Seulment français!*' [Only French! Only French!] They pushed him to the ground and screamed again, '*Allez Pompez!*' Garcia was made to do push-ups while we gathered our stuff

together. Then we were ordered back to our billet to change into PE kit for the first of what were to become regular dawn runs. Garcia was still struggling with his push-ups when we returned, exhausted, an hour later. Our first lesson: on no account were we allowed to speak anything other than French, even when we swore.

Christian Jennings and a fellow recruit were punished in a more unusual way for speaking English while dismantling a tent: '[Corporal] Vigno had taken two lumps of granite from the side of the hill and made us keep them in our mouths for three hours. We folded wet canvas and icy guy ropes, sucking back streams of saliva which collected in our teeth, unable to smoke, talk or move our jaws because of a mouthful of rocks.'

Whatever the methods used, even the slower recruits will have acquired basic French by the end of their training. This has always been the case in the Legion. Recalling his time as a legionnaire in the 1890s, Frederic Martyn wrote:

> What struck me as being very wonderful was the fact that though a good percentage of recruits did not know any French at all when they joined, I never met, in all my time in the Legion, a man of six months' service who could not converse with ease in the sort of French that is spoken in the Legion barrack-rooms – which is not book French by any means.

An absence of 'book French' was still the case a century further on, as Dave Cunliffe explained: 'Until you start talking to French people, you don't realise that a lot of the words used in the Legion aren't French at all. They're adapted or taken from Arabic, or from German. It's only when you start talking to civilians that you realise that they don't understand you – that's why we call it "Legion French".'

Colin John, a British recruit from the early 1950s, described the constantly evolving Legion French:

> This is a mixture of French *argot* [slang] and German Army jargon, with a few words from Russian, Polish, Hungarian, Spanish, Italian, Arabic and Annamite [Vietnamese] thrown

in. The advantage of this medium of expression is that, since words from three or four languages are mixed up together in almost every sentence, everyone understands at least a part of what is being said, and so more or less follows the gist of the conversation.

The Legion's own songs have been used as a means of language instruction – and a way of developing group cohesion. Typically, they are combined with the slow, rhythmic parade march of the Legion. John described how they were ordered to sing as they marched:

> The Legion has a great number of marching songs. They are nearly all of German origin, with French words adapted, and some of them are very fine indeed. The Legion authorities regard the melodious, rhythmic, vigorous, and unanimous execution of these songs by detachments on the march as of the first importance. It is considered that singing in chorus does a great deal towards the inculcation of an *esprit de corps* in men who have no other universal way of communicating together.

The Legion's singing usually has a tremendous effect, both on performers and audience. Simon Murray, while undergoing training in Algeria in 1960, explained its power:

> Tremendous emphasis is laid on singing. When we return to camp after a day in the hills we march proudly through the streets of Mascara, singing our guts out as we try to break the windows with our voluminous melodies. The slow marching plod and the sheer force of the body of men singing in deep ringing tones with improvised harmony is like nothing I have ever seen or heard before.
>
> The local people stand staring, mesmerised, as they have probably done for years and will continue to do, for it never goes out of fashion to watch the Legion marching, and it is a sound that grips you and holds you while it passes. The excitement on the faces of the watching crowd produces a chill down the spine and a justifiable surge of pride. It is at moments like this that our heritage is felt, as a thousand tales of the Legion cross the faces of the onlookers, and I am indeed proud to be in these ranks.

And yet, there have been dissenting voices directed against the Legion's musical efforts. One of these came from Tony Sloane:

> I didn't really see the point in learning all these songs. I didn't understand its relevance to being a soldier. I knew it was a tradition, but why adopt a style of life from our predecessors simply because that was the way they lived? I questioned the old stuff until it proved itself to me: I didn't think singing songs brought us together. It didn't create camaraderie. Hardship, shared lifestyles and equality made us bond. Songs made us hoarse.

The ability to march long distances has always been a cornerstone of Legion training – as it is for other elite infantry units. The concept of hard marching had been established as soon as the Legion developed into a fighting corps in Algeria in the 1830s. Erwin Rosen described the rigorous discipline of the march in the early 1900s:

> The legionnaire can march. Forty kilometres a day is the fixed minimum performance. He must be able to do that, day by day, without interruption, without a day of rest, for weeks on end. That is the object of his training from the very beginning. Several times every week the men must make practice marches over a distance of at least twenty-four kilometres, with full equipment, at the Legion's pace of five kilometres an hour. The only object of the practice marches is to teach the recruits steady quick marching.
>
> The '*marches militaires*', as the practice marches are called, usually commence at midday when the sun is at its hottest, after a hard morning's drill, so as to represent a practical exercise. On one of the military roads which branch off from Sidi-bel-Abbès in all directions, the march goes on until the twelfth kilometre is reached, and then the men are marched back again.
>
> On the march a legionnaire may carry his rifle as he pleases, either shouldered or by the strap, just as is most comfortable for him; he may take off his knapsack if it hurts him, and carry it in his hand; he is not ordered when to open his coat or when to shut it. The officers do not worry the marching legionnaires with paltry orders, and they are allowed to sing or smoke as they

please. The marches are regulated by the one principle: march as you like, with a crooked back or toes turned in, if you think that nice or better, but – march!

It is always being drummed into the legionnaire that he is intended for nothing else in this world except for marching. If the pangs of hunger are gnawing at his stomach or thirst parches his tongue, that is so much the worse for him, but it is no reason for his not marching on! He may be tired, dead tired, completely exhausted – but he must not stop marching. If his feet are bleeding and the soles burn like fire, that is very sad – but the marching pace must not be slackened. The sun may burn till his senses are all awhirl, he must go on. His task in life is to march. The greatest crime he can commit is to fail on the march. There is no such thing as an impossible marching performance for the regiment of foreigners. Each individual is inoculated with the one idea, it is hammered into him, that he has to march as long as he can control his legs. And when he can no longer control them, then he must at least try to crawl.

It is a merciless system, which, however, produces wonderful soldiers.

The hard-marching tradition carries on in contemporary Legion training. At the Farm it begins with a combination of runs and marches with full kit. The four weeks culminate in the 'kepi blanc march' – a 120-kilometre epic conducted over two or three days. Once successfully completed, the recruit will be awarded the coveted white kepi and become a legionnaire.

Chistian Jennings' Farm had been based at Canjeurs in the Alps – rather than the Pyrenees – and his 'kepi blanc march' was made from Canjeurs to the Legion cavalry base at Orange:

We marched fast and by noon had covered twelve miles. We stopped at the side of the road outside a small town for lunch. One of us made a fire and we brewed coffee and lay in the autumn sun. Down from the mountains the weather was warmer, without the snow and wind of Canjeurs. All of us had sores and infections on our hands and arms from the cold and dirt. My knuckles and hands were a mass of windblown cuts and boils which meant that whenever I clenched my fists the gashes opened. Our faces were red and raw and most of us had blisters.

We moved off two hours later, through a town with white buildings with red shutters and dogs asleep in the road. The locals sat in cafes and stared at us as we passed. We moved through the town and up a hilly field covered with vines before we entered a forest where the branches grew close above the path. We had to fight to make our way through as rifles, packs and radio aerials snagged on bushes and branches. It was a relief to reach the edge of the wood and come out into bright sunlight again.

We stayed that night in an empty holiday home we discovered on the edge of a village. [Sergeant] Ninez saw no reason to complain or criticise so long as we marched fast enough. We carried on. Through the morning and the sun of the afternoon we marched, thirty-five miles across the departments of Savoie and Vaucluse, through woods and towns, up hills and across vineyards. We were filthy, our uniforms, our hands and faces covered with a mixture of mud, wood smoke, sweat and dust. We stopped at a shop and bought apples and beer, which we guzzled on the march, assault rifles and ammunition belts swinging around our necks as we used our hands to prise off the tops of the beer bottles. We spent that night in a field full of asparagus seedlings.

We crossed the wide River Rhone the following morning on a huge suspension bridge, then moved up a main road, poplars and plane trees to either side of us. We reached Orange before any of the other groups and went into the barracks. They were hot and dusty. I had a shower, scrubbing off the dirt of a month in the open. My hands stayed brown and cracked, the knuckles swollen and bleeding.

When the trucks arrived we unloaded them, watching those who had fallen out of the march as they disembarked. Nineteen of us [out of thirty-six] had made it to the end.

Gareth Carins described the ceremony in which they were awarded their kepis:

We dumped our kit, and I hobbled over to the back of the truck where we were given a bottle of beer and a handful of peanuts.

And thirty seconds later I was pissed and enjoying the atmosphere. For the first time in two months we were relaxed and sat around waiting for the other two groups, just enjoying the feeling of being free and the sense of achievement that had come with pushing ourselves further than any of us had ever done before.

Once we'd all arrived we formed up in three ranks on the side of the mountain. We each had our kepi blanc in our hands, waiting in anticipation for the order to put it on for the first time. In a simple ceremony we were ordered to place our kepis on our heads and at that moment we became legionnaires. We sang '*Soldat De La*', which made the hairs on the back of my neck stand up, and then headed back to Castel in the trucks, where we stopped just outside the main gate and formed up again.

My feet were in bits, but I was determined not to hobble and end up looking like a twat. We marched the Legion's slow march, singing our sombre anthem, through the main gate and past a guard of honour that saluted us as we went past.

It was incredibly moving to be acknowledged and accepted in this way, and although only the first of many hurdles to overcome in the next five years, it was one of the most important.

After the white kepi ceremony, the new legionnaires continue training at Castelnaudary. Some of them have, however, questioned why they were awarded the white kepi so early in the training process, as Carl Jackson explained: 'After just four weeks I didn't really feel I was a legionnaire. It gave you a false sense of security because you got your balls broken afterwards.' Indeed, any sign of arrogance or even complacency is ruthlessly stamped on by the instructing NCOs.

The Legion's basic training is, perhaps surprisingly, less 'military' than that of other armed forces. For the many recruits with previous military service, basic training can be disconcerting, as David Taylor explained when talking of the experiences of British former servicemen:

A lot of the lads, who were ex-British Army, found basic training very non-military, with less of the usual technical background, small-arms training and such like. And a lot of the British lads found that hard to cope with: they wondered what they were letting themselves in for, and some of them even deserted, believing that the Legion was a bunch of muppets. What they didn't realise was that the first four months was, basically, making sure you could adapt to the Legion style of discipline, learn French and become physically fit to cope with the military training, which you then got in your regiment. But for the ex-military guys this seeming lack of military expertise was very frustrating.

The main function of basic training has been to teach every recruit the Legion way of doing things, as Simon Jameson confirmed:

It may not be the most logical way or the simplest way, it may seem like the most stupid, ridiculous method in the world – but it is done that way and you are going to do it that way – even if it takes all night and all the next day. They may send one man to do the job of ten or ten men to do the job of one. It will drive you to insanity at the time but what it is doing is re-affirming military discipline into your new way of life. If you can prepare yourself for this and accept their way of getting the job done, then you'll be well on your way to becoming a 'bon legionnaire'.

CHAPTER 4

INTO THE LEGION

At the end of his four months of basic training the new legionnaire is assessed and then assigned to one of the Legion's regimental formations where his training continues. The better the legionnaire does in his basic training so the greater are his chances of going to the regiment of his choice. In addition to the training and headquarters regiments, the Legion deploys two infantry regiments (one stationed in mainland France, the other in French Guiana in South America), an armoured cavalry regiment, a parachute regiment, plus combat engineer units and detachments in Djibouti on the Horn of Africa and on the island of Mayotte in the Indian Ocean.

Pádraig O'Keeffe, the former chef from Cobh in Ireland, was initially sceptical about joining the 6th REG (*Régiment Étranger Génie*), a combat engineer regiment, but when told by his officers that 'the type of engineering they had in mind was more to do with demolition than construction', he allowed himself to be persuaded:

> I quickly learned that my initial preconceptions about the engineers and sappers couldn't have been more wrong. We were trained in all aspects of high-explosives: how to position charges, how to defuse mines, how to judge a fuse so that you didn't blow yourself up, how to trigger a defensive perimeter with anti-personnel mines – and all the while learning the ropes as combat infantrymen as

well. The REG insisted its members be fully trained in amphibious warfare and also be able to support helicopter assault teams.

It may sound idiotic but, to a 21 year old fresh into one of the world's elite fighting forces, there is nothing quite like the thrill of getting to blow shit up in training. In Ireland, the most expensive piece of equipment I worked with was a €500 cooker – here I was entrusted with military hardware that cost millions.

Arguably the most intense continuation training takes place in the 2nd REP (*Régiment Étranger Parachutiste*), based at Calvi in Corsica. Not only are new legionnaires given parachute instruction, they will complete ever-more gruelling forced marches, on the basis that a heavily equipped paratrooper must be able to get away from the landing zone in double-quick time. The newly arrived legionnaires also find it disconcerting that they are again at the bottom of the food chain, and are treated with considerable contempt by their fellow paras until they have earned their wings and settled into the regiment.

On arrival in Calvi, Erwin James recalled that, 'our new teachers were fiercer and even less forgiving than those a Castel. Getting us out of bed in the early hours to don parachutes and jump off bedside lockers was a favourite jape. Loading our Bergens [rucksacks] with rocks for the eight-kilometre run with full pack was another.'

Also at Calvi, Christian Jennings described his initial parachute training:

> We spent hours on the training area learning about parachutes and how to pack them, fold them, carry them and put them on. We sat in a mock-up of a Transall [aircraft] in the training area, swung on the wires and cables which simulated the feeling of being under a parachute, and we learned the hundreds of technical details connected with jumping. We ran our eight-kilometre battle run again, which I managed in 36 minutes, and we climbed ropes in the gym.

The first parachute drop is an unforgettable occasion, which some find terrifying and others find exhilarating. Simon Low was one of the latter:

This was the adventure I craved – my dream come true, my match-winning goal at Wembley, my lead-guitar solo at Hammersmith Odeon – and, thankfully, I had the good fortune to know it. During [the] five-minute journey to the airstrip, I was granted a transcendent experience, a unique personal moment in my life that was unsurpassed then and remains so to this day.

After boarding the C-160 Transall transport aircraft, the paratroopers arranged themselves in preparation for the jump, with Low third in his stick. He recalled the jump:

The Transall accelerated hard down the runway for take-off. The vibrations ceased as we left the ground and were replaced by a more relaxed drone. We climbed steeply for about 20 seconds, then banked hard right. The plane levelled out and we were ordered to 'Debout, levée le siège, accrocher, série vers l'avant' [Stand up, lift the seats, clip on, dress forward]. With this task accomplished, I found myself next to a gaping hole as the door slid away to reveal clear daylight – a violent rush of air filled the interior. I was feet away from nothingness, an utter void that I would fling myself into a few seconds later. Wild excitement was coursing through me. This was it! Eyes wide open, I looked out and saw that it was not quite empty space, catching glimpses of the greenish-blue sea below. Any second, the red light above the door would flick from red to green and a buzzer would sound, signalling us to 'go, go, go'.

The Spaniard [first in the stick] was now in position with his arms braced either side of the hole, ready to launch himself out. As soon as the light changed he was gone. Without thinking, I pushed forward close behind Carrière, who also slipped silently away a second later. It was now my turn. I moved into the space left by Carrière and threw myself out with my eyes screwed shut and arms automatically crossed, my hands grabbing hold above the elbows. A violent wind seemed to be sweeping me off down a tunnel, shaking me roughly about and lifting my legs up as my torso was thrown around. The sensation came to an end with an almighty jerk, and instead of flailing uncontrollably around I was sedately swinging to and fro. My parachute had deployed, the static line hooked on in the plane doing its job!

On opening my eyes I was surprised to see the lumbering Transall was now quite far off, its underbelly still spewing out bodies. The fading drone of the distant Transall and the bird's-eye view of the slowly approaching ground signalled to my well-programmed reflexes. All was OK. I then did a *tour d'horizon*, checking that none of the other jumpers around me were too close – good. The ground was getting rapidly closer. I prepared myself for landing: legs together and slightly bent to absorb the impact. Bracing myself for the impact, I tried not to look as the ground raced up, concentrating instead on letting my legs tell me when I'd made contact. Crunch! I hit the ground hard, knocking the wind out of me and jarring my head back painfully.

Low gathered up his parachute and made his way to the camp and then back to the airfield to carry out another jump. Once six jumps have been successfully completed, the newly qualified paratrooper receives his wings.

One major test open to all legionnaires when assigned to their regiments is the commando course, which can be taken at a number of centres, including the one at Mont Louis in south-west France. Pádraig O'Keeffe described his time there:

Mont Louis, located high in the mountains, was used by the Legion to fine-tune the military skills we had started learning at the Farm and then at regimental level in the various Legion bases. As a commando training centre, Mont Louis was unsurpassed. It pushed men to limits they never thought they'd reach. But it also fostered the ideas of team work and operating as a tight-knit military unit. If the Farm was a blunt object, Mont Louis was the precision instrument which sculpted soldiers into Legion specialists. Mont Louis honed the skills the Legion so prized – that nothing was impossible to a well-motivated legionnaire and his unit. We scaled cliffs that a person would normally be nervous simply to look at. We climbed obstacles and barricades using nothing but muscle, sweat and blood. We crawled through fields of barbed wire and undertook forced marches with full packs. We hurtled down the death-slide, a rope abseil system that truly lived up to its nickname.

And when we left Mont Louis, we walked that little bit taller and felt the kepi sat that little bit prouder on our heads.

The intensity of training at the commando course can be seen in this passage from Tony Sloane, describing instruction in unarmed combat:

We learnt how to sneak up on a sentry from behind and break his neck. We were careful to ensure that our heels touched the ground first, rolling forward on our feet as we crept behind our opponent. Once within a few centimetres of my victim I sharply wrapped my right arm around his throat, ensuring that I hit his trachea to stop him screaming. I then clenched the inside elbow of my left arm with my right hand, put my left hand behind his head and pulled back. He fell to the ground. In a combat situation we were told to jump back to land on our fronts. The momentum would break our enemy's neck.

We began with no weapons but soon I was carrying a length of rope with which we routinely strangled each other. We learnt how to defend ourselves from punches and kicks while taking advantage of our opponent's weight. We trained on each other, beating each other with relish. There wasn't any 'wimping' out. The corporals made sure of that. Picking us out individually for a sparring session they would punch and fight us with all their strength and we would fight back. This was my first taste of *corps à corps* (unarmed combat).

French Guiana provides legionnaires with a superb environment to develop their skills in jungle warfare. Carl Jackson of the 2nd REP described his training there:

We went as a parachute company to Guyane (French Guiana) for six months, and went on the jungle commando course. When you get there they acclimatise you to the area, orientate you to the animals and other things, so that, for example, we went to a zoo run by an ex-legionnaire where there were lots of dangerous reptiles such as an anaconda which you had to walk up behind and pick up by grabbing the head. Anacondas move very slowly on land but not in the water where they are very swift, effective killers. So I remembered that every time we were doing a river crossing, the anaconda issue was always on my mind.

I was at the forest school in Régina, where they taught us forest bush craft and those sorts of things. The assault course there was absolutely fantastic, the hardest I've ever done – a pure mud bath. Getting over the wall on this assault course was an exhausting process, as it was absolutely enormous, we had to climb up on each other's shoulders, sometimes taking up to four legionnaires to reach the top of the wall, with the poor guy at the bottom screaming in excruciating pain because of the weight factor – this was something else.

While we were at Régina we had the 2nd Division Recon' from the US Marines training out there too, as well as some Canadian Special Forces. As a section we did the assault course in about 47 minutes but the Americans took quite a while longer, up to seven hours. While we were out there we would carry one water bottle on our webbing, with a jerrycan for topping it up, but the Americans had four, five or six bottles attached to their belt webbing and you could always hear them crashing through the jungle. On their T–shirts were the words 'Swift, Silent and Deadly', and in the foyer when we saw them come in, one of the boys said: 'Swift, Silent, Deadly? More like, Slow, Noisy and Harmless!' That went down like a lead balloon and a major scrap occurred. My colleague was right, they were harmless.

Once the legionnaire has been with his regiment for a couple of years and proved himself a reliable soldier he is typically offered the chance to become a corporal (although there are other, quicker ways to gain this rank for those who do well in basic training). The corporals' course – the *peleton* – is exceptionally testing, as Matt Rake explained:

In some ways, the corporals' course is a step backwards. When you are an experienced legionnaire you tend to get left alone by the corporals, and have a cushy lifestyle, but when you're on the corporals' course, you're all suddenly back to square one – head shaved bald, running around night and day, and so on. And you think, I should be past all this, especially when you see the guys who are going through basic training are getting treated easier than you. Yes, it's a tough course – but there again nearly all the courses are tough!

As is usual in the Legion, emphasis is placed on physical strength and stamina, although the student must also become proficient in the technical and tactical aspects of his profession. Tony Sloane took his corporals' course in Djibouti:

We learnt all the characteristics of all the weapons. I could recite weights, lengths, maximum and minimum ranges. I knew all the frequencies, all the antennas, all the part names and numbers. We learnt every minute detail; we learnt battle first aid and practised putting drips into each other. When we weren't in the classroom we were patrolling or learning how to position mines and traps.

Before each meal we had the *aperitif* . . . the rope . . . pull-ups . . . sit-ups . . . and press-ups. It was too hot to work in the midday sun. In the afternoon, when the sun was still high, the instructors would have a little siesta while we carried rocks up and down a 200-metre hill to the rear. If at any time someone messed up we would all have to run up and down it – which I found annoying – but we soon learnt that we had to work as a team to get things done. I resented the people who messed up, but soon I helped them for my own ends. I didn't want to run up and down the hill, so I made sure they didn't mess up. In the evenings we marched each other around singing songs or wrote our reports, which would take us to the early morning.

When Simon Murray started his corporals' course in June 1963 he was a battle-hardened legionnaire, but he was the first to admit that it was 'murder' and his basic training at Mascara 'a holiday resort by comparison'. In his diary he wrote:

Objective one of the NCOs is to keep us short on sleep. This is the quickest way to break resistance and they mean to break us.

Each day one of us is appointed as the corporal of the day. It is his job to prepare the duty rosters and get the *peleton* on parade at the appropriate time and to make sure we are ready for *appel* [roll call] in the evening. The night before he has to prepare numerous charts with the order of the day, the guard roster and other things, and this has to be presented to [Sergeant] Delgado after *appel*. It is an exercise in perfection. Everything has to be to millimetre precision; the spacing between the lines and the width of the margins. Very few people get it right much before three in the morning. Delgado sees to that.

Our daily programme is not dissimilar in content to that which we had at Mascara except that before we were coming to it for the first time, learning it. Here we are learning how to teach it to other people; we are learning how to be instructors of others.

We spend the afternoons in the hills. Combat training and practical map reading are priorities and in the evenings we return to camp at a forced march. In the Legion if you cannot march further than your men you will never have their respect and you will never lead them.

The NCOs devised various 'punishments' to test the resolve of the *peleton* candidates, as Murray explained:

On one occasion earlier this week [Sergeant] Schmidt found a mosquito in my helmet at *appel*. Six of us then carried the mosquito outside on a blanket, we were the pallbearers, and I had to dig a hole five feet deep in which we buried it. I then had to make a cross for the grave and paint on it '*Tom Dooley est mort*' [Tom Dooley is dead]. Schmidt thought the whole episode hysterical and I suppose I might have done too if it had not been one in the morning by the time we were through. We are in the hands of madmen.

They have another little punishment for us too, which is to send us after *appel* to the coast where we fill our water-bottles with sea water which we bring back to the sergeant for inspection to prove that we have been there. The sea is five miles away and at night the journey takes five hours. We return at three in the morning. I have had to do this only once so far, but it again hits at the vulnerable spot of tiredness.

On one occasion, a legionnaire called Piva managed to turn the tables on the NCOs, as Murray explained:

> At *appel* [Sergeant] Winter sent him to collect sea water in his water-bottle, for having dust on the underside of his boots. He told Piva to wake him on his return in the early morning.
>
> Piva went off into the night but returned ten minutes later and declared he was damned if he was going to get sea water and instead peed into a bottle, added some cold water from the tap, set his alarm for two o'clock and went to bed. At two in the morning he reported to Winter. Winter put his finger in it and tasted it to make sure it was sea water and that was that. Winter has drunk Piva's pee and Piva becomes immortalised among us all. It was a major coup and morale has been uplifted a mile.

Despite the attempts by the instructing staff to break the legionnaires' resolve, Murray and a hard core of candidates refused to be cowed, and excelled in a round of examination tests. In the course of the *peleton*, the legionnaire who comes top normally graduates as a *caporal-chef* [chief corporal], a rank considerably higher than that of corporal, and with many attendant privileges. Competition is correspondingly intense. Murray, to his surprise, finished first in his *peleton* and was subsequently awarded the black *caporal-chef*'s kepi.

The corporals and sergeants form the backbone of the Legion, and are given more responsibility that is usual in other armies. This was remarked upon by Frederic Martyn in the 1890s, when he compared the Legion's system – in which the NCO was accorded considerable disciplinary powers – favourably with that of the British Army:

> The system is no doubt responsible for a certain amount of petty tyranny, but, even with that drawback, it is, I think, much more conducive to military efficiency than the milk-and-water methods of dealing with private soldiers that obtain in our army. It makes

the French non-commissioned officer a much more important personage than his English prototype, for men who have the power of punishment must of necessity have more influence than those who have not, and the sense of responsibility it engenders makes the *sous-officer* [NCO] a very dependable quantity when left to his own initiative in a tight corner.

American legionnaire Bennett J. Doty enthused over the importance of sergeants within the Legion during the 1920s:

Their prestige, their power, make them nearly commissioned officers. And they do command. They are the cement and the rock of the Legion, devoted, tireless, bearing the brunt of the training and the fighting. They glory in their work, they are the priests of the traditions of the Legion, they are the mainstay of the regiments. They are rough, of course, most of them. They roar a great deal. They are martinets as to discipline, bitterly critical judges of the niceties of the manual of arms. They are of all nationalities, and in character, some are good and some are bad.

No one doubts that discipline in the Legion is severe – and always has been. Whether this discipline is too severe remains a matter of ultimately irresolvable debate. Many writers – including some former legionnaires – have condemned the Legion as a school for sadism. Others have offered more benign views. George Manington, after five years of service in the 1890s, claimed to have suffered no 'real inconvenience', although he wrote: 'A regiment of men is not like a girls' school, and it is impossible to maintain discipline in a corps composed, as mine was, of so many "hard cases" unless a certain amount of severity is used.'

A century later, the Legion takes a similarly robust view towards discipline. The training NCOs believe they are placed in an unusually difficult position, having to control men from so many different nations and backgrounds. As a corporal in the 2nd REP, Matt Rake considered himself to be firm but fair:

The Legion mentality is that everyone is lazy and you have to push them to do everything. I was quite laid back with a lot of the lads:

I didn't come down on them like a ton of bricks. But when you've got 25 lads all sharing a dormitory and you are duty corporal you have to make sure that everything works. To take an example: a guy comes in drunk at five to ten, just before the sergeant comes round to make his inspection. He's standing there swaying around, gobbing off, so what are you going to do – tell him to shut up or give him a dig? You can't handle a drunken Polish guy who's about 6 foot by simply telling him to sit down.

David Taylor – another corporal – believed in a juicy carrot and a big stick:

When I was an instructor in basic training, I used to carry a crate of beer at the bottom of my rucksack – 20-odd bottles of Kronenbourg – as well as the basic weight. And during runs I made sure that the first guys back got a beer. It was a way of showing them: 'Keep up, do your job and there's a reward at the end.' Hopefully, I always tried to be more a good guy than a bad guy. But if necessary I'd give them a proper kicking; even send them to the infirmary. There's nothing like a couple of broken ribs to give somebody something to think about!

Taylor provided an example of the sometimes uncompromising inducements offered to 'encourage' wavering recruits:

You pushed them as hard as you could. We had a Turkish kid on the kepi blanc march who literally sat down and said he wasn't going to walk any more. You'd do the normal sort of cajoling, and then give him a few slaps around the head, and you'd make sure that his team understood that if he was holding them back they were in for it as well. But this didn't work. Then the *caporal-chef*, a German called Sauer who was as hard as nails, came over. Once it became obvious that this Turkish kid – blubbering his eyes out – definitely wasn't going anywhere, Sauer handed him his nine-mil [pistol], and told him, 'If you aren't going to march any more, you might as well shoot yourself in the head!' And what was crazy was that the kid pulled the trigger. Now Sauer had made sure that the weapon was clear, but the very fact that the lad could sit against the tree, in tears, and pull the trigger was too much. We told him to take his pack off, get in a jeep – and he was shipped straight out of the Legion.

Instructing raw recruits – with little or no command of French – was a trying business, as Sergeant Dave Cunliffe recalled:

> You're trying to do lessons, and a lot of it is done by imitation, so if you're doing basic weapons you have to pick the bit up and show them. It is no use just talking to them. If you talk too much you're completely wasting your time. It can be frustrating for the recruits too, because a lot of the time they think this is pointless. And *you* get frustrated because they're not doing what you want.
>
> The corporals used to get frustrated because of the language problems, and they weren't slow to lash out – and the sergeants the same. There were a lot of group punishments as well, such as the *marche canard*, having to squat down and walk about like a duck.
>
> There's a very big gap between being a sergeant and being a legionnaire recruit, and when you're a sergeant you completely forget what it's like for the little man on the ground. It's just the way it is; you can't help it. If you've had a bad day, you end up punishing everyone.

No matter how tyrannical the behaviour of the instructing staff, it was always unwise for a recruit to attempt to retaliate, as Carl Jackson discovered to his cost:

> Some of our training NCOs were psychopaths and would carry around with them little aerosols of CS gas which if sprayed in the face could incapacitate an elephant. This was used as back up if they felt threatened by a larger-than-life recruit who they thought they might not be able to handle. I know, as I was one of those recruits. One evening we were at a roll-call and one of our section sergeants was in a really bad mood; you could see it in his eyes and from the tone in his voice. So he started moving down the line punching and hitting the occasional recruit in the

stomach or face a few times. He did exactly the same thing to me and in a matter of seconds I set about him, offering my brand of punishment with a head butt and a few blows to the face.

The next thing I remember is being sprayed in the face with CS gas and my legs falling from under me as I panicked due to my respiratory system being all over the place. Then I remember being punched and kicked by what felt like around 20 people and then waking up on my bed, which the lads had carried me to after the NCOs had left. Later that night when I was in bed I was paid another visit by three NCOs who just wanted to reaffirm that I understood the situation by giving me a further kicking. So it shows it didn't matter how good or how big you were, the Legion would always win in the end.

Although brutal, such punishments were less dangerous than some of those meted out to miscreants during the Legion's more distant past. Although there has been exaggeration of these punishments, they tested men to the full, and sometimes beyond. Erwin Rosen described the *silo* punishment that had been employed in the nineteenth century for serious crimes; although it should be remembered that Rosen was merely repeating what had been told to him by old legionnaires:

The *silo* consisted of a funnel-shaped hole in the ground, broad at the top and pointed towards the bottom. A regular funnel. Into this hole, used as a cell for solitary confinement, the misdoer would be thrown, clad only in a thin suit of fatigue clothes, without a blanket or any protection at all against the rain or against sun, at the mercy of the heat by day and the cold by night. The poor devils would be left for several days in this prison. They could not lie down, for the bottom part of the hole was only one or two feet square. They spent day and night alternately standing and crouching, now in pouring rain, now in burning sun. They very soon became ill from the foul vapours. When at length they were taken out of the *silo*, they could neither walk nor stand and had to be carried into hospital. Now and then a *silo* prisoner died in the hole.

VOICES OF THE FOREIGN LEGION

As a legionnaire in the 1892 Dahomey expedition in West Africa, Frederic Martyn witnessed the infamous punishment of *crapaudine*, apparently common throughout much of the 19th century but by the 1890s only used in extreme circumstances. The march into Dahomey had come to a virtual halt at a place called Sabovi due to a desperate shortage of water, and tempers had become frayed, as Martyn recalled:

> On this night at Sabovi during the search for water an Italian who belonged to the Legion got at loggerheads with a sergeant and struck him. When they returned to camp the sergeant reported the occurrence, and it was decided to punish the man with the *crapaudine*. It must be remembered that in most armies he would have been tried by a drum-head court-martial and shot.
>
> He was stripped naked, his hands were pinioned behind his back, and his ankles tied together. Then his ankles were lashed to his wrists, and he was thrown on the ground looking very much like a trussed fowl. The agony incidental to this constrained position must have been almost beyond human endurance after a time; but in this poor man's case the punishment was intensified by the fact that in no long time after he was tied up his body was literally covered with a swarm of black ants – and any one who has been in tropical Africa will know what that means. After this man had been in this position about an hour his cries were agonising. To stop them a gag was placed in his mouth, which had the effect of reducing his cries to much more distressing moans. The man was eventually released after about three hours of it, and he was so ill that he had to be taken to the hospital, and did no more duty during the campaign.

Crapaudine has long gone from the Legion. Today, the main form of constraining punishment is solitary confinement. David Taylor – disciplined for failing to take part in a parade – described the experience:

> In solitary, they literally opened the door once a morning in your cell, which was about four foot by seven foot, with a blanket and a bucket of water to shit and piss in. They took

out the previous day's food tray, gave you another food tray, exchanged the bucket and shut the door. And that was it for 10 or 12 days. There was no light, no heating, no clothes – you were stark naked – no cigarettes, no communication whatsoever. Once every three or four days, they took the blanket out and hosed the place down.

There's only so many times you can bang your head against the wall or punch the door and get irate. In a way, this was a life-changing experience for me. Up until then, I could always say I had an anger button – I was never scared to use my fists. In solitary you calm down.

A common punishment is pack-drill – known as *pelote* – where the wrongdoer is force-marched around in circles with full equipment and a pack filled with stones or sand, while made to do press-ups at regular intervals. During the 1920s, Jacques Weygand described a group of legionnaires carrying out a *pelote* session in the midday heat:

They are promptly marched off to a far corner of the camp by an NCO whose good humour is not noticeably increased by the work in hand at this hour of the day. They come to a circular track in the dry, bare earth, where the pebbles seem to have been churned up by the eternal round of some beast of burden, dumb and damned; and this is the stage where the *pelote* is played. This is where the defaulters, fainting under the heat, bent under the weight of their equipment, will go round and round for two hours, jerking forward or flung to the ground by the harsh voice and whistle of their tormentor.

'Double-march! Faster! Faster! . . . Halt! Down! Up! . . .'

The packs are back-breaking; the braces cut into the men's shoulders; elbows and knees are bruised or bleeding from repeated contact with the stony ground. No matter; chin-strap braced, watch in hand, implacable, the sergeant threshes his human grain.

Sweat runs in dark runnels down faces that are clotted with dust; and a lesson never to be forgotten is stamped into the most rebellious spirits.

Not all spirits were broken by this punishment, however; some fitness fanatics have even enjoyed it, as David Taylor recalled after his release from solitary confinement:

> I ended up getting a further 30 days' hard labour, but hard labour for me was a doddle. We got knocked out of bed at about half-four or five in the morning to run 8 or 10 kilometres around the parade square with a pack full of wet sand. I thought to myself, this is great endurance training! Then after breakfast we did the assault course with sacks of sand, and I loved that too. Then we were sent to dig ditches. And if a ditch didn't need digging, we filled one in. I loved it in a bizarre sort of way.

A last comment can be left to Bennett J. Doty, which for him, at least, summed up the Legion's approach to training, discipline and punishment: 'Hard the Legion certainly is; cruelly hard I found the life there. But it is just.' Few would disagree with the belief that the Legion is hard, but many might have problems with the idea of it being just. For the Legion, the concept of justice is not of such great importance, when set against its requirement to produce 'cruelly hard' soldiers.

PART II

LIFE IN THE LEGION

It is thanks to you, gentlemen, that we are here at all. If I ever have the honour to command another expedition, I shall ask for at least a battalion of the Foreign Legion.

(General Charles Duchesne, Madagascar)

CHAPTER 5

BARRACK-ROOM CULTURE

Away from the drill square, training ground and seemingly endless *corvée* duties, the legionnaire has been allowed a certain amount of free time to spend with his comrades. And he soon discovers that his fellow legionnaires can be as tough as his NCO instructors. The Legion has never been for the faint-hearted and violence or the threat of violence has been a constant factor in its world. The usually mild-mannered Legionnaire H., formerly a music hall artiste in 1930s Paris, simply stated that 'you must fight or otherwise your life would not be worth living'. For the middle-class 'gentlemen rankers', who provided many of the accounts of life in the Legion, this realisation came as a profound shock. But for the vast majority of recruits, drawn from the working classes, or even under-classes, of Europe, the dog-eat-dog life of the barracks came as less of a surprise.

Fights could be savage. Frenchman Antoine Sylvère – writing before the First World War – described an encounter between a former seaman called Van Lancker and Leborgne, a new arrival who was throwing his weight around in Sylvère's section:

> Leborgne charged. The ex-sailor dropped down in a quick movement, to simulate a head butt, rose up and threw two fists forward, powdering the eyes of Leborgne with a double jet of sand which he had picked up in his first feint. Leborgne swore and lowered his head, just enough to receive a terrible kick in the

face, which put him on his backside. A second kick, more violent, threw him backwards. In the blinking of an eye, Van Lancker was on him and with hard kicks of his hobnailed heels in his face, forced his head into the gravel. The ex-sailor continued to roll over his adversary who no longer reacted. He began to work him over in detail, on the ankles, the knees, on the tibias, with angry and destructive relentlessness. After breaking a couple of ribs in passing, he stretched out the arms to smash the hands, the elbows, the forearms. 'Don't kill him completely,' Garrigou warned. 'No fear,' Van Lancker said. 'I've done enough so he won't bother us any more.'

Levels of conflict have not been moderated by the passage of time. In 1984, new recruit Christian Jennings observed his first brawl within days of his arrival at the Legion's headquarters in Aubagne:

A Spaniard and an Englishman were arguing over some duty, when the Englishman head-butted the Spaniard between the eyes; as the latter stepped backwards clutching his face, the Briton executed a curious hopping movement as he placed both hands behind the Spaniard's head and wrenched it down to meet his upcoming knee. There was the squashing noise of bone meeting flesh as the Spaniard's upper lip and nose was split all over his face. A sergeant-major witnessed this from his ground-floor office and leapt out to pull the two apart; he slapped the Englishman and pronounced the Spaniard ready for the infirmary. He was accompanied there by two recruits, his face pouring blood. The sergeant-major's attitude to violence was catholic so he kicked the Englishman once before letting the matter drop.

As long as good order is not seriously prejudiced and injuries not life-threatening, NCOs have tolerated fighting among the men, accepting it as a means of sharpening their aggressive instincts. Beyond the simple motive of self-assertion in an often hostile environment, men have fought for a multitude of reasons, exacerbated by a plentiful supply of alcohol.

The Legion's policy of minimising national distinctions in favour of the concept of '*Legio Patria Nostra*' (the Legion is our Country) has occasionally broken down and national rivalries have re-emerged to become a source of conflict. Writing of the period just before the First World War, French legionnaire Jean Martin noted:

> Because the Legion is French, and the Germans are the most numerous, the differences of race come back to this Franco-German antagonism. The majority of Russians or 'candle-eaters', the Poles, and in general those from northern and central Europe are with the Germans. The Latins, the Belgians are Francophile. The British, when there are any, don't give a damn. One mustn't think that this makes for perpetual conflict, but it gives rise to niggling problems, to preferences of NCOs for their nationals, and on payday, often fights between drunken legionnaires which have no other cause.

National groupings – or '*mafias*' as they are known in the modern Legion – have been based on linguistic rather than strictly national lines, providing off-duty soldiers with a chance to relax with those of the same tongue. Speaking in anything other than French is prohibited during training and discouraged after that, but it is usually tolerated in off-duty moments. This has been especially true of the traditionally monoglot English-speakers (*la mafia anglaise*) sometimes known to French-speaking legionnaires as '*les fuckings*' – this being the word heard most often in English conversations.

With their obvious language advantage, French legionnaires have had an easier time than their non-French speaking comrades, which in turn has led to resentment. Former Royal Navy seaman Kevin Foster – whose contract began in 1983 – claimed that the French 'thought themselves above everyone else. The common denominator in the Legion was that everyone hated the French.'

Jaime Salazar, an American assigned to the 2nd REG (*Régiment Étranger Génie*), echoed this view after arriving at his new base at Saint Christol in the early 1990s: 'The French wasted little time organising the inevitable *mafia francophone*, making the non-French further resent their exclusivity and arrogance. The Legion was supposed to be for foreigners, for Chrissake!'

But not everything went the way of the French. When British legionnaire Dave Cunliffe achieved the rank of sergeant, he was allowed a certain amount of latitude in his dealings with French officers: 'We Brits liked to needle them a bit. The Legion had this big celebration on 18 June when General de Gaulle had made his call to arms to the French in 1940 – the same date as the Battle of Waterloo. On the day, the officers used to see us celebrating too and ask us about Charles de Gaulle, and we'd say, "Oh no, we're celebrating the Battle of Waterloo!"'

And yet, at the same time, individual legionnaires have forged close friendships with men of all nationalities, French included. And whatever their differences, legionnaires have always presented a united front to outsiders. The legionnaire's sense of his superiority over others – especially over other non-legionnaire soldiers – has led to many garrison-town brawls. Jacques Weygand related an account of a pitched battle between the Legion and transport drivers in a North African bar during the inter-war period:

> By now every one in the hall was standing up; a ring had formed round the struggling bodies. A number of legionnaires, who took a personal interest in the result of the mêlée, were watching developments closely.
>
> 'Look out!' cried a voice. 'They've got knives!'
>
> That was a foul; such a breach of the rules that no further consideration need be shown. Crespi disengaged himself a little from the scrum, and, with a voice of thunder, gave the cry for which everyone was waiting:
>
> 'A moi, la Légion!' [To me, the Legion!]
>
> Heard on the battlefield, in the middle of a hostile mob, or in some cataclysm of nature, this summons always produces the same magical effect – a galvanic reflex on all muscles of all those who wear the seven-tongued grenade on their collar, whatever their rank, whatever their momentary occupation. Instinctively and without hesitating for a split second they fling themselves to the rescue of their comrades in distress.
>
> Already the first rank of spectators were in the fight; from the back of the hall other legionnaires were rushing up, jostling every one out of their way. Their enthusiasm was not unmixed with a secret desire to extend the area of conflict; soon every one of the two hundred persons present was involved in the swirling, shouting, crashing inferno. The drivers were knocked out and

thrown into the street; a few discontented soldiers took the same road, but were handled somewhat less roughly. At last came the turn of a dozen Jewish merchants of Bou-Dénib. Fat and very pale, the unfortunates had gathered trembling in a corner of the hall as soon as the row had started; in accordance with local tradition they too were beaten and thrown out.

Theft from one's own comrades was a divisive force undermining barrack-room harmony; while apparently commonplace, it was the most despised of crimes. Evan McGorman, a Canadian volunteer in 1989, spoke with the deep feeling of one who had repeatedly suffered at the hands of thieves:

> Theft is rampant within the ranks of the Legion and I could recount dozens of tales where people had their entire pay or large portions of it stolen by the two-faced bastards that infest every single formation. Allow me to vent for a moment. There can be no lower form of human life than a thief. This contemptible personality trait is reprehensible at the best of times, but in a close military environment it is unforgivable. It can collapse the spirit of trust and confidence that is critical to the members of combat unit where lives may hinge upon whether or not you can depend on someone. The Legion does act with a vengeance when someone is caught with their hand in the cookie jar, but most larcenists are not apprehended.

If caught, the thief's life would be misery. Stories abounded – only possibly apocryphal – of the traditional Legion punishment of nailing thieves' hands to a table using bayonets. In the early 1900s, Erwin Rosen witnessed a thief caught and severely dealt with in his barrack-block. The criminal, a man from another company, had been found going through a legionnaire's belongings under cover of darkness:

> '*Voleur!*' [Thief!] cried the bugler.
> The word acted like a signal. All at once fists were clenched, a bayonet gleamed, a struggle arose, and a dozen men rolled on the ground. The scene lasted for perhaps a minute. Then all was still

– the man from the tenth company lay there gasping and covered with blood. His face was black, so terribly was it bruised. A blow from the bayonet had split his cheek and a stream of blood flowed over his blue jacket. The guard came up and the fellow was carried into hospital. The man lay in hospital for weeks. That was the end of it. The night's lynch-law in our quarters was not inquired into. The punishment of the thief rests in the hands of his comrades. So decrees the custom of the Legion . . .

Even border-line infractions could elicit a severe beating. Following a bout of heavy drinking, Christian Jennings had managed to mislay his dress-uniform trousers and with an inspection in the offing he had taken a pair from another, absent British legionnaire in the next room. On his return, the British legionnaire was reprimanded by his superior, Sergeant Garcia, for the loss of his trousers. 'After Garcia had hit him two or three times, they found them on my hanger,' Jennings wrote.

Lying on his bed following minor dental surgery, Jennings became the target for their wrath:

When they found me on my bed, the Briton walked over, ignored my comatose post-anaesthetised state and bleeding mouth, and started to systematically beat the shit out of me. He swung his fists into my mouth, eyes and jaw, kicking me on the ground and shouting at me. Other members of the Section watched from the doorway. He finished by picking up a stool and hitting me across the chest with it. Garcia then told me that when I recovered from my dental treatment there was another beating coming from him too. I wished I was somewhere else. My face hurt and in one move I had completely and justifiably lost any sympathy I might have had from the rest of the group. My face swelled up dramatically, my eyes yellow and purple, my lips cut and my cheeks bruised.

Technically, Jennings was guilty of 'decorating' – a term derived from the German, 'dekorier dich', literally meaning 'decorate yourself'. Walter Kanitz, a legionnaire during the Second World War, explained its true significance:

For the legionnaire, however, the term *dekorier dich* has a distinctive meaning. There is no equivalent in the English language. The closest we can come would be 'help yourself' but this term does not carry the same spirit as *dekorier dich*.

If the legionnaire comes too late for soup and his stomach is angry with emptiness and there is no food left, the advice is *dekorier dich*! He will tax his ingenuity to obtain food somehow, even if he has to steal it. If he is assigned to guard duty the night of pay-day when he wants to go into town to get drunk, he looks for a substitute; he 'decorates himself'. If he finds himself without money for '*pinard*' [wine] he looks for a sucker to buy him a litre. Or he sells his labour in washing legionnaires' togs or he touches a green recruit for a few francs, pretending to obtain a desired favour for the man from a sergeant. All this falls under the general classification of '*dekorieren*', but the application of the term is so vast, the scope so great, and the varieties so colourful that it is impossible to list them all.

Over time '*dekorier dich*' became modified into the French '*demerdez-vouz*' (or '*demerdez-toi*') which, in effect, meant: 'Get yourself out of the shit.' During the First World War, the American David W. King indicated the subtle gradations between out-and-out theft and '*demerdez-vous*': 'There are certain hard and fast rules in the Legion. To take money or valuables is stealing. To sneak equipment or any government issue from your own section or squad is neither etiquette nor healthy. Otherwise you can shift for yourself. This is called System D (*Demerdez-vous!*).'

The expression remains to this day in the Legion, with the emphasis on being able to solve any problem through improvisation.

Existing alongside what was always a tough and sporadically violent environment was a fierce sense of comradeship forged by shared hardship. This was especially true while on campaign, where legionnaires put aside the squabbles of the barrack-room to face a common enemy. An instance of selfless behaviour among legionnaires was provided by George Manington during the conquest of Indochina in the 1890s, as malaria and yellow fever swept through a Legion outpost:

The able men not on duty – they were generally but a few – neglected their own comfort, and sacrificed their rare hours of rest to attend, without murmur, to their stricken comrades, and did their best, in their rough but kindly way, to lighten their sufferings.

It was a quaint and touching sight to watch one of these bearded mercenaries, as he passed from cot to cot, and note his efforts to repress his own impatience and clumsiness, as he piled blanket after blanket on a shivering sufferer, changed the damp linen of another, or calmed with a voice which he had tried to render gentle, the ravings of a delirious friend, standing the while to change every few minutes the wet bandages on the burning brow of the stricken one.

Not all behaviour was quite so altruistic, however. More typical were the dealings and transactions of everyday life. Pay was traditionally abysmal in the Legion, and a man who was able to prevail upon friends or family to courier money out to him had many advantages. Englishman William Stamer joined the Legion in 1854, and as a gentleman of leisure he was able to buy the services of his comrades:

Having money in my pocket, I soon became popular; half-a-dozen hungry-looking, ill-clad Germans introduced themselves to me as aspirants, like myself, to military renown in the ranks of the second regiment of the French Foreign Legion, and I cannot say that I felt proud of my future brothers in arms, rather the reverse. However, I gave them something to eat and drink, and thus made them for ever my most obedient slaves.

According to Erwin Rosen, the situation in the early 1900s had changed little when money arrived: 'Then there is joy in the land. For a day, or a few days, or even a week, the prodigal son with the postal order lives like a king. He has his boots cleaned for him, and would not dream of making his own bed as long as the money lasts. A comrade does that for him, and in reward is graciously permitted to share a drink.'

NCOs generally permitted such practices, and many were not against benefiting from small, discreet payments made to them by the better-off legionnaires. Adrian Liddell Hart discovered its advantages while stationed in North Africa in the 1950s, prompted by the activities of a fellow legionnaire called Klaus: 'Klaus lent money to the corporals and bought them drinks and though I had inhibitions about this practice at first, I followed suit with Sergeant Molnar and others. After all, it is an old Legion tradition. Soon we were paying each other in kind or in cash, to escape duties and fatigues. Even a few hundred francs made a big difference in Africa.'

Although the practice of payment for services rendered began to die out in the 1950s, a regular postal service provided a lucky few with a variety of comforts that were the envy of their less fortunate fellows. Simon Murray recounted the arrival of a food parcel: 'A parcel from Anskie stuffed with food. It's the labels on the chocolate and the stamps on the brown paper and the realisation that this was wrapped by friendly hands in a warm home in England that feeds my system like no other feast has done.'

Many legionnaires had little or no contact with the outside world, however, and the tradition of sharing letters and parcels around was commonplace, as Christian Jennings explained while stationed in Aubagne at the end of his basic training:

The mail was waiting for us. Among it was a parcel for Mike [an ex-Rhodesian soldier] from Harare. It contained a letter and some food. There were biscuits, sweets, chocolate and cigarettes. The Corporal who was with us at the time immediately awarded Mike 2,000 press-ups. This was the usual practice when mail was given out; a recipient of a letter would normally get 150, two letters 300, and the penalties for a parcel were 500 and above depending on its contents. The parcel which Mike received was a perfect target.

In an organisation where a lot of people, through necessity or personal choice, were cut off from their families or friends at home, mail and letters took on special importance. Most people would share their letters, reading them out to everybody else. We were all conversant with the problems of each other's friends and relatives. The Corporal had given Mike more press-ups than he could possibly hope to do, so the penalty had to be shared out among us all. We did 100 each and Mike shared out his parcel.

> We ate the biscuits and cake, and smoked his cigarettes, trying to
> swap things with him in return for the photo of his girlfriend.

A striking example of the Legion's positive side is to be found in
its celebration of a series of festivals throughout the year. Among
these are New Year, Easter, Bastille Day (14 July) and special unit
celebrations – such as St Michel's for the paratroopers – but the
two key festivals have always been Christmas and Camerone Day
(30 April).

The commemoration of Christmas is an opportunity for the
Legion to express paternal sentiments over its rough-and-ready
family of legionnaires. Preparations for Christmas are taken to
great lengths, with a special meal and entertainments laid on, and
– adding an almost surreal touch – the building of extremely detailed
nativity cribs or crèches to be judged by the regimental CO. Jennings
described crib-building during his first Christmas at the Cavalry
Regiment's base at Orange:

> The cribs were not the usual constructions of shoe boxes and
> straw, with small religious figures and matching sets of the
> Magi; they were a challenge to the ingenuity and imagination
> of each section and would often involve large amounts of gravel,
> stones, concrete and other building materials. Some would fill
> half a room, and the themes were normally an interpretation of
> the nativity in military terms. The mountain troop of the 4th
> Squadron were devising a crib which involved a lifelike figure of
> the baby Jesus abseiling down a mock-up of a cliff face towards
> a rock grotto containing an edelweiss, the symbolic flower of
> [German mountain] troops.

Despite the cribs' obviously kitsch nature, NCOs could gain
considerable prestige by winning the competition and they put
pressure on the men of their section or company to perform well.
Jaime Salazar's section chief, the near-psychopathic Corporal
Diagana, was given overall responsibility for crib construction:

> We went to great lengths to produce a scale-size model of the
> Legion's last stand at the battle of Dien Bien Phu, complete with

a silty river. The tedium didn't bother me much, and I spent entire afternoons quietly twiddling cardboard into a red-green Buddhist temple, which should normally have taken a half hour to make.

Noticing that I was underemployed, Corporal Diagana put me on to building a bunker with 2x4s, in which we placed a figure of the Virgin Mary cradling the Christ Child in *tenue de combat* and *kèpi*, with an Indochinese assistant in black spray-painted pyjamas and Adidas shower sandals. The bunker was reinforced with sandbags and camouflage netting. Jungle sounds were broadcast by a hidden cassette player. It took a month to assemble but when it was finished it was breathtaking.

To Diagana's pleasure – and Salazar's relief – the crib won 'undisputed first place' in the competition.

Jim Worden joined the Legion during the late 1950s when its headquarters was still at Sidi-bel-Abbès. He was unprepared for the sumptuous dinner prepared for Christmas Eve, the centrepiece of the festival, where rank was reversed so that officers and NCOs served the men:

We were not marched to the dining-room but drifted there in small groups, immaculately attired in our newly pressed uniforms, as if wandering to some elaborate social gathering.

I found it difficult in believing my eyes on entering. The tables had been arranged in a large U-shape, with beautiful white linen tablecloths, adorned with shining glasses, cutlery and plates. As straight as legionnaires on parade, the centres of the tables were lined with bottles of wine, champagne and beer. A stage had been erected, and a crèche had been constructed in the corner with far more care, attention to detail and devotion that I had seen in my own church in London. The whole room was ablaze with light, with Christmas decorations festooning it. The walls were decorated with carefully painted posters on which were Christmas greetings in a dozen languages, the largest of which, suspended over the stage, read 'Merry Christmas' in English.

We were greeted upon our entrance by the captain and other officers, with a handshake and the murmured greetings in the recruit's own language of 'Happy Christmas'. Even the sergeants were lined up to shake hands, greeting me with big smiles, as if the bastards had been using my arse as a football only in the line of duty. Christmas being Christmas, I forgave them all and shook hands.

Lobster and turkey in the Foreign Legion? They were cooked to perfection. I enjoyed a cigar presented to me by the most feared German sergeant at the base, the one who had given me the hardest kick up my butt. Then the entertainment began. Legionnaires were being invited – repeat, invited – to the stage to sing in their own language.

After the entertainment came the distribution of Christmas presents. Each legionnaire received a gift handed to him by the captain. The gifts themselves provided further shock, for there was nothing cheap or shoddy. Some received watches, and very good watches, with faces inscribed *Légion Étrangère*; a couple received small portable radios. I found a first-class sleeping bag, lightweight, red in colour, of oiled silk and kapok stuffing, a much valued gift in the mountains.

At midnight the solemn voices of all in the room joined in 'Silent Night', all singing this most moving hymn in German.

Worden's description of the Christmas festivities was borne out in many other Legion memoirs, although not all celebrations were as well organised as those at Sidi-bel-Abbès or Aubagne. And, for some, an aching homesickness could undermine the occasion. Henry Ainley, shipped out from Oran to Indochina in 1951, encountered a Christmas entertainment organised by his company commander, Lieutenant Baudoin, and the Vietnamese madam of the local Legion brothel:

It was a memorable and curiously lamentable affair. Around eleven the curtain went up and the show began. During the intervals Baudoin handed out Christmas presents of wristwatches to the men – several of which caused instant interest and hilarity by running through twenty-four hours in about as many seconds. Just before midnight the bugler sounded off with a fantastic call of his own invention, the lights went out, the curtain up and there on the stage were the Madame and her girls prancing around in every variety of undress, carrying out enormous cut-out paper letters, spelling out 'Happy Christmas To You', and 'Yours Who Are Far Away'; the whole to a weird cacophony they were singing which vaguely resembled a mixture of 'Holy Night' and 'Auld Lang Syne'. The effect on the majority of us was appalling – somehow the sight of those raddled over-painted old bags touching on Christmas and home life was so unbelievably sinister and obscene that it killed the evening.

Wherever legionnaires were stationed, Camerone Day followed a set pattern, beginning with a morning parade and a recitation of the official account of *Capitaine* Danjou's defence of the Mexican farmhouse. A series of entertainments followed. 'The Legion goes mad on Camerone Day,' Simon Murray recalled. 'Officers and NCOs do all the *corvée*, including serving the food. There will be sideshows and a parade of floats through the town.' On a subsequent Camerone Day, Murray related how Legionnaire Nalda and some other Spaniards organised a bullfight to supplement the parade:

We had a big parade in the morning. Lots of brass arrived and we were inspected by a four-star general. Senior officers from regular army units in the area came with their wives to see how the legionnaire animals lived. The main event, the bullfight, got under way just after lunch in front of a huge crowd. The bull ring was surrounded by bales of straw, behind which the crowd were pressed four deep. Nalda was dressed immaculately and after several vodkas he eventually staggered into the ring. A roar went up from the crowd and the bull promptly charged. Nalda panicked and, having seen the bull, I didn't blame him. Twenty Spaniards jumped into the ring to save the honour of Spain and attacked the bull with bottles, brooms and pickaxe handles. The bull went berserk and charged headlong through the straw bales and was last seen going for its life down the main street.

Since the Legion's move to France, Camerone Day has been used to showcase the Legion to the French people: the gates are opened to the public who, for once, are able to inspect the Legion at close quarters. The legionnaires remain on their best behaviour while the public are in the barracks.

The physical conditions of the modern legionnaire have improved over the years but they remain modest to the point of austerity. The men sleep in small dormitories, the bunks of training days typically replaced by single beds with a locker for their uniform and equipment, within which is a single shelf for personal possessions. Old sepia-tinted prints of Legion barrack-rooms from the late nineteenth century, with boots neatly stacked under beds and uniforms carefully folded on a shelf above the bed, are remarkably similar to recently taken photographs, all of which reveal the Legion's obsession with tidiness and cleanliness.

The Legion has provided some facilities for its men in their spare time – such as gyms, cinemas and swimming pools in the larger bases – but effective organised recreation has generally been neglected, with legionnaires generally left to their own devices. Card playing is officially discouraged, on the basis that gambling encourages theft, but as in other armies it goes on nonetheless. Jim Worden described the establishment of poker schools throughout his battalion following pay day:

> It became almost habitual that, month after month, at least fifty per cent of the pay made to any one company would find its way into the hands of that company's expert poker player. By some coincidence, these were almost invariably Italians. The only exception was myself.
>
> I made it a strict rule not to play poker until at least a week had elapsed after the distribution of pay. This allowed a sifting process of the big winners of one section or company, playing against other big winners. Only then would I commence playing poker. I did not play with any of my own section – I played with their money! We formed a monthly syndicate, and I would play on their behalf, profit being distributed equally. During two years of playing, I lost all our pay only once; at all other times we made a profit. During December 1960, after playing over 20 hours continuous poker, our food brought by various well-wishers, I arose from the table having won more than £2,600. As we were

near Algiers at the time, all members of the syndicate had a very merry Christmas.

But in the garrison towns and far-flung outposts inhabited by the Legion the mass consumption of alcohol has been the legionnaire's chief recreation. Half-hearted attempts have been made to curb excessive drinking but they have invariably failed. At one time temperance posters were put up in Legion barracks displaying a skull and crossbones, under which was the caption: 'Alcohol is Deadly'. The posters were withdrawn, after barrack-room wits responded with their own addition: 'But the legionnaire does not fear death.'

The French hold a fairly relaxed view towards alcohol consumption, and new legionnaires – especially from America and northern Europe – have been surprised by the availability of beer and wine throughout the day. Traditionally each legionnaire has been entitled to his daily '*quart*' (quarter-litre) of wine, but during the course of a day more generous measures supplement this modest tipple.

The canteen or foyer within the barracks has always been a first port of call. A decidedly prim Erwin Rosen, recently arrived at Sidi-bel-Abbès in the early 1900s, was invited for 'a litre' by a fellow legionnaire:

> The regimental canteen was in a small building in the corner of the barrack square. We opened the door and I, at least, must have looked very much surprised. There was an awful noise in the little room. A great many soldiers were talking and laughing and singing and yelling in many languages; in German, French, English, Italian and Spanish – there was the jingle of many bottles and glasses.
>
> With wondering eyes I surveyed the men in the canteen and the canteen itself. The smoke of many hundreds of cigarettes filled the place with a heavy bluish vapour. The noise was indescribable. One had to yell to be understood by one's neighbour, a quietly spoken word would have been lost in the turmoil. Everybody was yelling and everybody seemed in high glee. The legionnaires were having what they considered a good time. They jumped on the tables, kicking and dancing, jingled their glasses, threw empty bottles about and made fun of everybody and everything. Every minute the uproar increased. These hard-faced, hard-eyed men were like

children at some forbidden game, trying to get as much fun as possible while the teacher was away.

If they had gained permission to leave the barracks for the evening, legionnaires preferred to sample what was on offer in the local town, although certain procedures had to be observed. The Legion has always expected the highest standards of turn-out when its men are in public. In 1914 American volunteer David King was made aware of these standards:

> Every man has to pass the inspection of the sergeant-of-the-guard at the gate. Brass button must shine, boots, if not polished, be neatly greased; the broad blue woollen belt of the Legion must be wound around without a crease, and, as it was 9 feet long, this was quite an accomplishment. If the sergeant happened to be in a bad humour a man might be told to go back two or three times to make good minute defects. Coming back was easier, as all returned together. But even so the lynx-eyed sergeant was on the watch for any men he considered sufficiently drunk to shove into the *boîte* (prison).
>
> Regarding this, it was an amazing sight to see some of the old-timers. They would reel up the street roaring obscene songs at the top of their lungs. Twenty yards before they came to the gate the songs ceased, shoulders went back, and they would march through the gate, saluting smartly like automatons. Out of sight of the guard the singing would break out anew, as they zig-zagged across the yard and lurched up the stairway to their barrack-room.

While the Legion was still based in North Africa, wine (*pinard*) was its preferred drink, occasionally supplemented, if supplies could be found, by absinthe or, in Indochina, a rice-based drink called *choum-choum*.

> Wine is cheap in Algeria [wrote German legionnaire Fritz Klose in the 1920s], and wherever he may be an old legionary always continues to get a plentiful supply of it. Without wine it would be impossible for the Legion to carry on. It is the legionary's medicine for all physical and spiritual ills.

In the last few decades, beer has replaced wine as the drink of choice, the Legion closely involved with the Strasbourg brewer Kronenbourg. In the early 1960s, Jim Worden wrote approvingly of 'the magical Kronenbourg beer, the life-giving sustenance without which the Legion would not have survived'.

The heavy-drinking culture continues. Tony Sloane – from the 2nd REP (*Régiment Étranger Parachutiste*), based in the Corsican town of Calvi – described his and his comrades' drinking habits:

> The town was small. There were a couple of discotheques but it was mostly small family-run bars. The 'Son des Guitaries' was where the British would generally hang out, drinking and fighting as soldiers do. I tried to have a mixture of friends from all nationalities. I often saw a giant of a man at the bar who would be holding a dwarf he considered to be his property. Each time he entered the bar he would grab the dwarf and tuck him under his arm like a schoolboy with his swimming stuff. The dwarf would protest initially but he was helpless in the arms of this monster of a man. At the bar it would be 'two bottles of Kro' – always one for the dwarf who would eventually be released in a drunken stupor at the end of the night.

The Legion's levels of alcohol consumption could on occasion undermine operational efficiency. In 1925 Bennett J. Doty was assigned to the *Vingt-neuvième* company of the First Foreign Regiment, which had orders to sail from North Africa to suppress a tribal revolt in Syria. An enthusiastic Doty was looking forward to the ceremonial dockside send-off organised by his company commander, Lieutenant Vernon. Despite the lieutenant's best efforts to the contrary, the legionnaires secured and drank copious amounts of wine as they waited to embark:

> When the ship had finally docked, and time came for our planned departure with full panache, the *Vingt-neuvième Compagnie du Premier Régiment Etrangère* was unable to rise to the occasion. The massed bands of the Tirailleurs struck up the '*Marche de la Légion*' once more, the guard of honour presented arms.
>
> But half the company could walk only in zigzags and lurches,

and fully twenty men could not walk at all. To those of us who could walk it fell to get those who could not walk aboard. Instead of marching briskly up the gangplank in single file, we went by threes. Two, more or less sober, would start up the plank with that third one between them. Sometimes he would be completely inert, and went along with feet dragging, like a dead man; sometimes he harboured signs of life, and, in the firm grasp of his comrades, gestured like a puppet in wild farewell gestures toward the shore. A fine sight it was. Lieutenant Vernon was tearing his hair out at the result of all his efforts. Thus it was that the *Vingt-neuvième* went off to war.

From the point of view of the officers and senior NCOs who had to lead their men, alcohol was an enduring problem. Zinovi Pechkoff, when a commander of an outpost in North Africa in the 1920s, despaired of his men's thirst for Algerian *pinard*:

There are no distractions in the outpost. One is confined to its four walls. But outside the post, built against its wall, there are three canteens. The men go there on the days after they receive their [fortnightly] pay and they spend all their money. For about two days every fortnight almost everybody is drunk, and one has to have untiring energy in order to control these men.

Because of the legionnaire's enthusiasm for alcohol, other drugs have played a relatively small part in providing him with a form of internal escape. The prevalence of marijuana in modern Western society has led to the consumption of this drug in the Legion, but no more so than in other armed forces. The only sustained exception was opium smoking in Indochina, a common practice among French colonialists until the Second World War. One old legionnaire recalled in 1913 that 'in our post, almost everyone smoked, despite formal orders to the contrary. It was the custom of the country.'

George Manington, campaigning in Indochina in the 1890s, befriended Sergeant Tho, a Chinese auxiliary who, assisted by his wife, enjoyed an evening opium pipe:

She threw a glance at Tho which meant, 'Are you ready?' He nodded and started drawing at the bamboo [pipe]. A gentle movement, and the skewer pushed the ball of opium onto the tiny hole, and it was held just over the lamp. There was a frizzle as the drug began to burn, continuing under the steady suction of the smoker. Presently all was consumed; the smoker opened his mouth and allowed the black smoke to escape slowly from between his lacquered teeth, which shone like ebony in the dim light of the tiny lamp. 'Biet!' (good) he exclaimed, and then prepared for another. The air in the tiny room was now heavy with the odour of the drug, which at first seemed acrid and unpleasant, but it improved on acquaintance, and soon became soothing and enjoyable.

[After several attempts Tho managed to persuade Manington to try opium himself]: I consented one evening to make the experiment, and smoked four pipes. I was rewarded by the most violent headache, prolonged nausea, and a sleepless night crowded with waking nightmares. It is hardly necessary to add that I didn't repeat the experiment.

Sexual relations in the Legion have traditionally been confined to prostitutes. The Legion's unsavoury reputation as well as the average legionnaire's lack of money and prospects – along with draconian restrictions on marriage – did little to attract women looking for a husband or a long-term relationship.

Throughout most of its history, the Legion has served outside Europe, and sex has taken a correspondingly exotic hue. Despite his poor pay, the legionnaire invariably held an economic edge over the impoverished colonial populations he lived alongside. While stationed at a desert outpost on the Algerian–Moroccan border in the inter-war years, German legionnaire Ernst Löhndorff described sexual encounters with local Arabs:

The oasis-dwellers are blessed abundantly with children, especially girls, and they do not scruple in the least to sell us their half-grown daughters, who are about thirteen years old but already mature women. For a few hours spent alone with the daughter of an Arab in his tent, we pay five boxes of wax matches or a tin of sardines.

In larger towns there were recognised red-light districts. The most infamous was the *village nègre* in Sidi-bel-Abbès. Before the First World War the area was out of bounds to legionnaires, but the prohibition was widely ignored, and during the 1920s the Legion accepted the inevitable and lifted the ban. A visit to the *village nègre* was a rite of passage for a legionnaire, even if he were just a sightseer. Löhndorff provided this picture of the *village nègre* after nightfall:

> There are girls hardly fifteen years of age who beckon with their henna-dyed hands. Then negresses with bodies of enormous girth, against whose bluish-black skin the broad silver ornaments show up sharp and dazzling; Frenchwomen, worn out and painted as though they were on the warpath; Spanish women, and one or two fair-headed Kabyle girls with blue eyes, all sit in a long row, beckoning and gossiping, or motionless like barbaric statues beside the flickering candles – while a stream of Spahis, Legionnaires and Tirailleurs and Arabs surge up and down – and high above all, the moon in a cloudless sky sheds an inexhaustible fountain of bright light upon the alley of the painted women.

During the latter part of the nineteenth century, the French authorities worked hard to regulate sex to minimise the incidence of venereal disease. Simon Murray described the system, still in operation in the 1960s:

> I went into Mascara this evening and visited the military brothel, known as the *bordel militaire controllé* or just BMC. It was not a particularly inspiring establishment and having seen some of the talent, enthusiasm was rapidly extinguished. I must say that the French attitude to military brothels is enlightened. Every regiment in the Legion has its own brothel which goes with it on operations into the interior.
>
> The brothel has a bar and there is always plenty of atmosphere. There is no obligation to get involved just because one goes in, and the bar enables one to have a few drinks and inspect the merchandise at leisure without necessarily making a commitment. The bar does however in time contribute to the lowering of one's

standards, and this can lead to a plunge which might not have been taken in a more sober environment. Costs range from about one pound (sterling) for a quickie to five pounds for the night.

The situation for the legionnaire was better in Indochina, where many of the native Annamese women were more accommodating. Known as *congaïs* ('young girls'), they effectively acted as mistresses to the legionnaires. A grizzled old legionnaire told the German writer Ernst Jünger (an underage Legion enlistee in 1913):

> When the worst of the heat was over we went into the village to drink wine and everyone had an Annamite woman who washed his clothes. They aren't any bigger than girls of twelve at home – they were light on our knees when we sat in the gardens and smoked and drank rice-wine until the great fireflies rose out of the bushes.

Henry Ainley described how the *congaï* system worked in 1950s Indochina:

> The *congaï* formed an integral part of military life out there. Whenever a unit changed sector, with it went not only the military brothel but also the chattering swarms of *congaïs* with their mothers, sisters, cousins, children and the whole lot. Often an official order came through that the *congaïs* were forbidden, that a unit leaving an area should leave the local fauna behind and so on; on arrival the men would find the *congaïs* waiting for them, already installed in shacks and rented rooms, and life went on as before.
>
> The hierarchy of the *congaïs* was rigid and easy to follow, their importance being based on their incomes and, since the tariff was in strict proportion to the rank of the husband, a *congaï* automatically assumed his rank. A comic note crept in when a man left for France. The captain commanding B company left, and Mrs Captain having had her cry and stayed out of sight for a day or two for decency's sake, started with delicate eagerness to hunt for a new man – the captain's successor had brought along a *congaï* of his own and had no use for his predecessor's

grass widow. After a few days of useless search and snubbing of the lecherous common soldier she wound up making the best of a bad job and went back to work in the brothel. There amongst her colleagues she was treated with all the deference to her past rank and did a roaring trade with the men who got a vicarious kick in bedding with the old man's wife.

The official military brothel (BMC) in Ainley's battalion comprised 20 girls under the charge of a madam:

> The girls were a merry, raddled lot, though their duck-bottomed gait and generally tawdry appearance were rather nauseating. Cheerful and hardworking, they knew, biblically, very nearly everyone in the battalion and gave not one damn for rank. The fact of being so intimately acquainted with the personnel of the battalion developed in them a curiously acute *esprit de corps*: invariably invited to the officers and NCOs' messes for celebrations, they participated equally in those of the men promoted and decorated and wept bitterly over the dead or repatriated who had been good customers. Frequently the better-looking or more skilful left the BMC for a spell to become somebody's *congaï*; in which case the man bought up what was left of her contract from the Madame and the two set up house together.

Since the Legion's move to France, sexual horizons expanded beyond just the use of prostitutes; increased pay and prospects have made legionnaires more attractive, especially to female tourists holidaying in Corsica and southern France. But traditions die hard in the Legion, including the brothels in the remnants of France's colonial empire. Prostitution thrives in Djibouti, with the Legion's sexual needs being served by young women from Somaliland and Ethiopia. Kevin Foster described the system operating in Djibouti City in the 1980s:

> We had a good brothel, with nine prostitutes – or *niahs*, as they were known – for the whole regiment. After three months the *niahs* were changed around. If you wanted to go with one of them you had to see a medic to make sure that anyone who had the clap didn't go through the door. You'd then get a chit, which

cost 1,500 Djiboutian francs, about £25, from the corporal at the bar in the brothel, which you handed in when you chose one of the women you were going to go with. Each chit or pass got you about 15 minutes.

Not all legionnaires used the local BMC. After a heavy night's drinking, Christian Jennings found himself in Djibouti City's 'Bar de Paris' at 4 a.m.:

> The mixture of beer, wine and Somalian gin inside me had leant softer proportions and gentler attractions to the grizzled face of the middle-aged barmaid, and I accompanied her home. The woman unlocked the door made out of metal sheeting and we entered an area of beaten earth, open to the sky, where a family of goats slept, limbs intertwined. The bedroom led off this area, and consisted of a double bed, a scrap board table and a cassette recorder. The uneven floor was well-trodden earth, and through gaps in the roof you could see the stars. The barmaid's mother was asleep, and complained bitterly at being turfed out to sleep with the goats merely so her daughter could entertain one drunk legionnaire.
>
> I took off my uniform carefully, looking for a clean surface on which to lay it. Despite my partner's adept advances and wily tricks, she was no match for the effects of 16 hours' drinking, and I passed out. Coming to an hour later I witnessed the extent that alcohol can disrupt one's perceptions.

The reckless consumption of alcohol and the enthusiastic pursuit of sex are commonplace activities for young men, although in the French Foreign Legion they have been taken to extremes. But the Legion is an extreme organisation, whether in its training regime, in its rest-and-recreation activities, or in the way it marches and fights on the battlefield.

CHAPTER 6

THE LEGION ON CAMPAIGN

The ability to march long distances with full kit has always been central to the Legion's tactical philosophy. Hard marching also had a special importance for colonial troops, and the famous Legion exhortation 'March or die!' simply reflected one of the brutal truths of campaigning in Africa and Asia: those men who fell out were liable to be hacked to death by native tribesmen.

The legionnaire's pride in his marching prowess has been revealed in many memoirs. Writing of his time in the Legion during the late nineteenth century, Frederic Martyn recalled:

> When we came to a village or a town we straightened ourselves up, the bugles blared out a striking march, and we stepped out jauntily, as if we would say, 'Yes, we are the Legion! Look at us! We don't feel the weight on our backs, and the farther we march the better we like it.'

A company commander in the 1920s, Zinovi Pechkoff was impressed by the performance of his men on a march to the Moroccan town of Tadla:

> Our men in the Legion are really aces. Many of them have no shoes, and they march barefoot. Many are sick. Notwithstanding that, everybody goes ahead. There are a few men who cannot keep up the pace, but, on the whole, everybody marches well. The month

of rain and extreme cold has been a great experience for troops equipped only with protection from sun and heat. The commander of the region has sent ten wagons to meet us, in order to bring in those who cannot walk, but not one legionnaire of the battalion has taken a place in the wagons and we have sent them away.

Simon Murray, newly arrived in a company of the 2nd REP (*Régiment Étranger Parachutiste*) in June 1960, discovered the importance of clambering up and down the Algerian mountains as a means of acceptance within the regiment: 'This seems to carry tremendous significance with everybody. It makes or breaks; there are no half measures and you're not one of the boys until you have proved yourself in the field. I am myself reasonably fit and I cannot see how it can be so bad. However, life is full of surprises.' A couple of weeks later, Murray was put to the test:

> We covered many miles today on a trek that would have flattened a mule. We climbed to 6,000 feet. As *section du jour* [forward platoon], we took the lead marching in extended formation upwards at the head of the company. Marching in extended line, particularly at the pace of [Corporal] Hirschfeld, is of course twenty times worse than marching in column. One has to gallop to keep the line straight. The terrible ache in the legs and back is surpassed only by the frantic strain to get breath into the lungs. The taste of blood at the back of the throat is slightly terrifying as one literally drags air down into the lungs. I don't know how I made the top at all, but somehow staggering and stumbling, with Hirschfeld bellowing to keep in line, I kept on my feet. Dead from exhaustion and on the last verge of resistance, we eventually arrived at the top. I would have welcomed a bullet.

The gruelling terrain and extreme climate always made campaigning in North Africa an arduous business. Provisions were usually in short supply; what could not be taken from the local population had to be carried by the troops themselves. This had been the case from the very outset of the Legion's involvement in Algeria. Clemens Lamping – a German officer serving in the Legion – described the legionnaire on campaign in the 1840s:

Besides what is loaded on mules, each soldier carried nine days' provisions consisting of ship-biscuit, rice, coffee, and sugar. Bread and wine are not given on a campaign, owing to the very limited means of transport. Cattle are driven, and during an expedition each soldier is allowed double-rations, that is, one pound of meat daily.

This meat ration was an official figure, however, and after the depravations of commissariat and cooks, considerably less would find its way into the legionnaire's *gamelle* or mess tin. Lamping also described the legionnaire's equipment:

Besides his provisions, which are replaced from time to time, each soldier carries sixty rounds of ammunition and a linen sack into which he creeps at night, and which stands him instead of both and upper and under sheet. His only outer garment is the grey *capote* [coat], which protects him against the summer's heat and the winter's rain; his stock of shirts is usually limited to the one on his back, which he washes in the first stream near his bivouac, and which is considered dry in ten minutes. The French set but little store by other articles of dress, but before they set out on a march they take care that each soldier be provided with a good pair of shoes, for shoes and arms are the first necessaries of a soldier on active service.

The relaxed attitude of the Legion towards standards of dress while on campaign was noticed by journalist G. Ward Price, who accompanied the Legion into Morocco in 1933:

The most marked impression I received was that legionnaires were the untidiest soldiers I had ever met. The stubbly beards on the chins of most of the men were inevitable in a country where water was so scarce, but it was astonishing to find troops that had only left their barracks six weeks before in such ragged and nondescript clothes. I learnt that it is one of the unwritten traditions of the Legion that on campaign considerable license is allowed in this respect. Scrupulous though the standard of smartness is on garrison duty, a legionnaire is not worried by any kit-inspections on active service. Providing a man remains fit for military duty his external appearance is considered of secondary importance.

Any attempts at parade-ground smartness would have stood little chance in North Africa. Ernst Löhndorff, a German legionnaire campaigning in Morocco during the inter-war years, described the ground they were forced to fight over:

> I have already seen plenty of mountainous country in the world, but none that gave such a gruesome impression as these Atlas ranges do! Vegetation is found only in places in a few ravines where the waters rush down in winter. In such places grow stunted oleanders, fig-cacti, scraggy oaks and tall grasses . . . Otherwise there is nothing but cold, naked stone everywhere.
>
> We pant for miles in disordered ranks across immense *warrs*, where the ground is littered with enormous boulders and stones. If the Moroccans were to attack us at such moments, they could easily wipe us all out, for we are too exhausted and breathless to be able to fight at all.
>
> Marching, stumbling, falling, marching! There is never an end to it! There is no path, at most there is a wide gulley, a dried-up stream, whose waters consist of round stones as big as heads. It is icy cold at night and scorching hot in the day time.

In the desert regions the legionnaires faced terrible heat in summer, with the ever-present threat of sandstorms. Alfred Perrott-White – who had volunteered for the Legion shortly before the outbreak of the Second World War – provided this account of the elemental ferocity of a sandstorm:

> A wind had sprung up accompanied by a peculiar moaning sound that made me uneasy. I could still see the sun, now blood red in the thickening blur of the wind-blown sand. In an incredibly short time the wind rose to a shrieking fury, so strong I could not stand upright against it. It became as dark as night while the almost solid wind-blown sand lashed against my face. It was now too late to do anything except lie flat on the ground and cover my head over with my *shech* – a long muslin wrap worn expressly as

a protection against sandstorms. Every few minutes I had to rise up a little to heave the sand off my body to avoid being buried. Seven hours passed before I felt the wind pressure letting up, and the storm ceased as suddenly as it started.

Leading a column of legionnaires into the desert, Pechkoff was forced to retreat in the face of a relentless sandstorm:

We had been marching about two hours when the wind began to blow harder and harder. Already the men were advancing with great difficulty. My horse, restless and blinded by the sand, became almost unmanageable. It began to whirl around and envelop us, like a mist, and we could not see the sky or where we were going. We no longer walked on firm ground but on moving sand.

When we could not advance further, we gathered together in a circle and waited. As soon as it was possible to move we went back to the fortification. The return journey was very painful. We marched as close together as possible, and the men at the rear kept watch to see that nobody was left behind. An additional glass of wine compensated the men for their efforts during the day.

The terrible sirocco had not stopped whistling, and continued to throw itself against the fortification with all its weight. It battered the walls and windows with terrific force, throwing wave after wave against them. We were like people besieged in a fortress. The enemy was bombarding us – only in this Algerian desert the enemy was the sand storm and the wild hurricane. For two days the wind blew, bringing with it the sand from the desert, and life became almost unbearable. No one dared go out. Not until the third day was everything calm again.

Despite or, perhaps, because of the extreme conditions encountered in North Africa, many legionnaires developed a fondness for the terrain. The mountains of Morocco and Algeria impressed almost all who struggled across them, including Prince Aage, a Danish officer who had volunteered in the 1920s as part of an expedition into the Middle Atlas: 'The country through which we marched was exceedingly beautiful. The fields were a riot of multi-coloured wild flowers growing in lush luxuriance; ahead towered the mountains, their slopes grown thick with cedars, the heights crag-crowned, with occasional patches of snow reflecting the sun's rays in patterns of deep blue and white.'

Pechkoff, in his turn, was captivated by the mystery of the desert:

> What silence envelops me when I ride out from the little town near where the battalion is located. I am in the middle of a desert of sand. The changing dunes are buffeted by strong, whirling winds which are ever moving from here and there. They are never the same. From afar these hills resemble the waves of a sea whose motion has been suspended by a magic spell.
>
> When you stop your horse in the middle of this ocean of sand, covered by the magnificent blue of the sky, when all around there is nothing to break the silence and peace, when the circle of the horizon seems to touch the Infinite, you are overcome by feelings of admiration, of surprise and wonder before the greatness, the magnitude of nature . . . of life . . . of existence.

Pechkoff was an unabashed romantic, but other, more down-to-earth types were similarly affected by North Africa. They included Jim Worden, a British legionnaire fighting Algerian *fell* (nationalist rebels) in 1961:

> I discovered that I had fallen in love with the natural beauty of Algeria, even though most of that discovery had been made while marching through it. The awe-inspiring depths of the Aurès, the rugged windswept peaks of the Atlas mountains, the high plateaux found where least expected, the ever-changing flora and fauna, always with the breeze bringing the sweet smell of the yellow Algerian flower, standing on the edge of an escarpment and admiring the view of the magnificent gorges and ravines – a sight that can be equalled only by the Grand Canyon in the United States: I had learnt to love all this, despite the uncertainty, whilst admiring the beauty, that some stupid *fell* might be aiming a rifle at my head from the other side of the gorge.

While North Africa was always considered to be the home of the Legion, Indochina was held in special regard by many legionnaires. The first Legion units arrived in Indochina – modern Vietnam, Laos and Cambodia – during the 1880s to support the French conquest of these territories. At first sight, Indochina seemed a genuine hardship posting: fatal diseases were commonplace and the extreme humid heat debilitating. Of the climate, George Manington wrote:

> In July the heat became tremendous; the afternoons, which were the hottest part, averaging 110 degrees in the shade. The men were kept indoors from nine in the morning until three in the afternoon, and operations were restricted to short reconnaissances, which took place either in the early morning or in the evening.

But better pay for overseas service, easier discipline and good opportunities for combat and looting were undoubted inducements for an oriental posting. Yet it would also seem that the legionnaires enjoyed the country for its own sake. One German commented that 'Indochina is a second fatherland'. The thick jungle and jagged limestone cliffs – common in northern Vietnam – caught the legionnaires' imagination. Manington recalled a march towards the garrison town of Lang Son on the Chinese border:

> The road passed through a stretch of scenery wild and magnificent. By a succession of loops and curves the route rose and passed round the flanks of one mountain after another. Sometimes the convoy crept slowly over small bridges spanning mountain torrents, overhung with dense, tropical vegetation. Now the road would wind through beautiful thickets of bamboo, so dense that it would have been impossible to penetrate it.
>
> We halted the night at Kep, Sui-Ganh and Bac-Lé, and passed the night in the forts at these places. Here the convoy was packed in the enclosure surrounded by a high bamboo fence, fires being kept burning all night to scare away tigers and panthers, as there were many in the jungle along the road.

Although the going was tough and, at times, painfully slow, the legionnaires were usually able to call upon the service of local coolies to help transport food and basic items of equipment. Manington described the native helpers:

> The coolies, on their arrival, were told off into squads, and the daily ration of rice and salt and fish was served out to them. This they cooked in copper pots, and the men of each squatted around the fires awaiting their evening meal, while one of their comrades, who acted as the cook for the occasion, kept stirring the stew with a bamboo stick.
>
> The meal finished, the majority indulged in a few pipes of cheap opium, locally known as *Sai*, and the surface of the compound was starred over with the numerous tiny twinkles of their little lamps. These went out one by one, and before midnight the camp was plunged in silence and slumber, the naked limbs of the sleeping coolies having the appearance of old ivory or new bronze in the flickering glimmer of the watch-fires, round which they reclined. Then the stillness of the night would be broken only by the song of the cicadas, the crackle of burning wood, the occasional call of sentries, and the far-away cop! cop! cop! of a tiger hunting in the hills.

As well as being great marchers, legionnaires were great builders, taking part in the construction of both military and civil projects. While on campaign in Indochina, the building of simple field works was commonplace, and much of the fighting in Tonkin revolved around attacks on forts and outposts. Frederic Martyn took part in a raid through heavy jungle towards a hidden enemy stronghold:

> Working parties chopped away at the undergrowth under the protection of squads of their comrades fully armed and on the alert. As soon as a space was cleared a temporary fort was made to hold it, and the men garrisoning these forts got what sleep they could as they sat down with their firearms in their hands. Look-out platforms were fixed in the tops of tall palm trees, which were ascended by means of primitive ladders formed by joining thick bamboos on to one another and passing short lengths of bamboo through holes so there was a foothold on each side of the pole as it was fastened upright against the tree-trunk. Officers or non-

commissioned officers, generally the latter, kept watch on these platforms day and night for any thread of smoke appearing above the trees, any sudden flight of birds, or any other sight or sound that might give an indication of the whereabouts of the enemy.

George Manington was impressed by the effectiveness of bamboo as a building material in the construction of field works of all kinds:

> The [Tonkinese] *tirailleurs* laboured with us at this task; and it was while watching them at work that I was struck by the diversity of uses to which these natives are capable of adapting the bamboo. They used it for almost everything. Roof-beams, doorposts, window-frames and rafters were obtained from it for building purposes, and also beds, tables, chairs, matting and blinds. The whole of our position was surrounded by two barriers of bamboo, and in the space between them, about 20 ft, thousands of small pointed stakes of the same wood, boiled in castor oil to harden them, were planted in the ground. The native troops were undoubtedly cunning workmen, and were of great assistance in the construction of the fort.

But the type of fortification that came to characterise the Legion in the popular imagination through books such as P. C. Wren's *Beau Geste* (and its many spin-offs) was, of course, the stone-built fort of North Africa. These fortifications – ranging from small outpost-towers holding a few men to complete walled towns – were dotted throughout Algeria and Morocco. G. Ward Price described Fort Timli in the Moroccan Grand Atlas, perched on a ridge some 6,500 ft above sea level:

> The fort was of the regulation type, and consisted of a square enclosure with walls 9 ft high and each side about 200 yards in length. Projecting towers at the corners rose to a height of about 15 feet, and the platform behind the parapet at the top of them was sufficiently roomy for a 3-inch mountain gun to be posted on it. The walls of the fort were a yard thick, of loose stones plastered and whitewashed. At intervals there are embrasures for machine-

guns. The centre of the enclosure is filled with low stone buildings that house the three or four officers, 10 non-commissioned officers and 160–200 men who form the garrison. Store houses, a cook house, a hospital and a telephone and wireless room lie along the inside of the parapet. Sometimes a pigeon cote for carrier pigeons is provided as well. And, 20 or 30 yards further out, the fort is surrounded by a broad barbed-wire entanglement through which the only exits are by zigzag passages closed at nightfall with *chevaux-de-frise*.

In the larger posts wireless is the main form of communication with the outside world. The field telephone lines connecting other forts are so frequently cut by the Berbers as to be seldom reliable. In the smaller posts, where there is no wireless, external communications depend upon optical signals alone, the heliograph being used by day and flash-lamp apparatus by night.

Throughout the winter the little garrison lives isolated among the savage hills and the aggressive tribesmen. The nearest post of a similar kind may be 10 or 15 miles away over rough and pathless slopes, and it is generally impossible to leave the fort, even by day, except in a strong party capable of resisting attack, while after sunset all emergence from the wire-entanglements is forbidden.

Zinovi Pechkoff took over command of an outpost in June 1923 with a garrison of about 60 legionnaires:

The commander of a post has many things to do. He has a thousand duties – he is commander of the post, commander of his unit, manager of the commissariat and the supply of armaments for the entire region. All the troops in this section of the country are supplied by me. I am a grocer, a bread maker (we have two ovens to make bread for the troops in this region), and a butcher. Not only must meat be furnished, but I also have to make contracts and buy livestock. I have to deliver sugar, flour, lard, wine, and oats and hay for the animals. Construction material must be delivered also.

Each day is full, and one does not have a moment to oneself. Everybody comes to the commanding officer with every little thing. The nights are not very calm, either. There are brigands around the post. In these first days, when men of every rank are unfamiliar with the place, everything has to be organised and shaped.

While Pechkoff and other officers had the advantage of being kept busy, for most legionnaires outpost life lacked the variety of campaigning. Ward Price described a typical day in Fort Timli:

Reveille at dawn opens the monotonous day of these isolated garrisons. The night-sentries are relieved by other lookouts, who have powerful field glasses so that they may report any suspicious movements on the horizon. The water-guard then moves out to reconnoitre the neighbourhood of the stream whence the day's requirements are to be drawn, for it is the habit of the Berbers to [lay in] ambush there during the night, in the hope that by lying up they may get a shot at point-blank range and be able to make off with the stolen rifle of their victim. After the water-fatigue is over, the animals of the fort are taken down to drink.

Meanwhile, the commanding officer inspects the walls and wire-entanglements, and the legionnaires of the garrison are set to work on construction and repairs, which last all winter. A quarrying-squad will be sent out under escort to extract and bring in the stones that are required for building, while others are employed in shaping them, in mixing mortar, or as carpenters. A fatigue-party collects the rubbish of the post to be burnt in an incinerator 100 yards outside it, and manure from the stables is buried in warm weather for the avoidance of infection. The drinking water has to be filtered and purified with chemicals. Other members of the garrison have their allotted duties as butchers, cooks, tailors or clerks.

At 10.30 the midday meal is ready. The fort contains six months' supply of food, consisting of flour, rice, beans, peas, lard, tinned meat, coffee, sugar, wine and barley for the animals.

No green vegetables are available unless the relations of the garrison with the local tribesmen are sufficiently friendly for them to be obtained by purchase, and in order to avoid the danger of scurvy through the constant consumption of preserved food, regular rations of lemon juice are distributed.

After dinner comes a rest until 12.30, when work is resumed until 4.30 p.m. At that hour the *Rompez* [break] is sounded and the day's leisure begins. In fine weather, and under peaceful conditions, a game can sometimes be played outside the fort or a bathing-party allowed to go down to the stream. At six the evening meal is served, and half an hour before dark the bugle sounds the 'Retreat', when all must come inside the gates and the passages in the wire are closed.

There is a foyer or large room in each post where the men gather in the evening to play cards, read or sing. Some posts even have wireless reception sets which are supplied by the French Red Cross Committees. At 8.30 p.m. there is a roll-call and at 9.00 p.m. comes 'Lights out'.

While the construction of military works, such as forts, has been accepted by the Legion as part of its work, labouring on civil projects such as road building has been viewed in distinctively ambivalent terms. One German NCO complained: 'What most recruits have never realised when they join the Legion is that we are not primarily a fighting corps, but a militarised labour corps.'

As a cavalry officer, Jacques Weygand was able to view the Legion's road-building exploits in the inter-war years from the point of an impressed onlooker:

What surprised [the cavalry] was the work the infantry got through. In the narrow part of the valley the only possible method was to hang the track along the side of the cliff. At certain places the cliff-wall presents a hump into which a road can be terraced. More often, it is necessary to raise enormous walls from the very bottom of the *Wadi* to the appropriate height. Finally, at one memorable point, the track demanded nothing less than a tunnel through one of the rocky spurs of Foum Zabel. Months were required for the task. The Legion had no tractors, no excavators or mechanical shovels; it had to rely on the strong arms and broad backs of its men, and most of all on its indomitable will and its pride in the accomplishment of the impossible.

When the [mile-long] tunnel was finished a stone carver from [Major] Tscharner's Battalion hewed this inscription at the entrance:

VOICES OF THE FOREIGN LEGION

THE MOUNTAIN BARRED OUR WAY
AN ORDER TO GO THROUGH IT WAS ISSUED
THE LEGION CARRIED IT OUT

At a later date, however, Weygand found himself reluctantly supervising his own men in building a road through rough country:

Twenty days without a Sunday among them, twenty days without a rest. Every morning at six o'clock the whole force was on parade with a carbine in one hand and a pick or crowbar in the other. In small detachments officers and men drifted to the edge of the *Kreb* [hill], where they were swallowed up by the enormous gaping hole of their own digging. In the first rays of the sun they could see the outposts of the [native] *Goum* on duty, placed so as to protect the work from hostile interference. Then work would begin under the whip of a wind so icy that iron tools stuck to the hands that held them.

Mining was necessary to make any impression on the rock cliffs, and dozens of two-man teams were occupied continuously in drilling holes for explosive charges. Farther down, among the fallen boulders, masses of stone which had fallen across the trace of the road had to be removed. Clusters of fifteen or twenty legionaries would make a ferocious attack on masses of rock weighing several tons and, with ridiculously inadequate equipment, break up or remove them; and at the very bottom, among the sand dunes, a stone causeway was being built. To watch the long lines of men bent almost double under the weight of the blocks they were carrying made one think of the construction of a pyramid.

Even in the modern era legionnaires have had to rely on brute human strength. In January 1993, Pádraig O'Keeffe and his engineer unit was despatched to Cambodia to provide humanitarian relief to the war-ravaged Cambodian people:

For the next few months I felt more like a construction worker than a soldier. My REG [*Régiment Étranger Génie*] was assigned to reconstruction projects, and that meant legionnaires swapping combat fatigues for work clothes as we repaired roads, rebuilt bridges, helped dam paddy fields and generally did whatever strategic 'Good Samaritan' work the local communities needed.

The heat and humidity of Cambodia made any outdoor work extremely strenuous. Usually I was with a four- or five-man construction team working on bridges and culverts. Most Cambodian bridges were made of heavy timber frames and each had to be lifted into place using nothing more than sweat and brawn. We had no access to heavy construction equipment, which would have made such jobs pretty straightforward. So we did it the old-fashioned, muscle-and-sinew way.

The work was long, hard and tedious, yet we slowly but surely got the bridges repaired and re-opened. You could see the difference such work made to the lives of ordinary people. A simple task like moving from one village to another had suddenly become much easier. Farmers hauling fodder or rice didn't have to negotiate huge caverns in the road or ford a river where a bridge once stood. People were grateful for the improvement, and the smiles on the villagers' faces spoke volumes about what we were doing. The work may have been back-breaking but it was also inspiring.

For most legionnaires construction tasks brought little pleasure, however. Simon Murray and the men of the 2nd REP were tasked with rebuilding their own camp – formerly a collection of tents – during the winter of 1962. Murray wrote:

The work goes on day in and day out with no change in the routine. The main road, which is 25 feet wide and 18 inches deep, is already two miles long. The drainage system throughout the camp is beginning to be effective and our tents are gradually being replaced by steel-framed barracks.

So we have more comfort but at what cost? Bashing rocks, digging ditches, shovelling sand and gravel, loading and unloading rocks onto lorries, pushing wheel barrows of concrete endlessly along planks all day. Back-breaking work, soulless enterprise yielding no satisfaction. Every day is the exact replica of the one that preceded it. The prospect of doing this for another two years fills me with total despair.

VOICES OF THE FOREIGN LEGION

Although the versatility of the Legion – with men coming from a wide variety of backgrounds with many useable skills – made it handy for construction duties, there was a price to pay with a deterioration of morale and military efficiency. And this encouraged the twin evils of *cafard* [depression] and desertion.

CHAPTER 7

DEPRESSION AND DESERTION

While war has always energised the Legion, the rounds of outpost and construction duties have tended to blunt military efficiency and lower morale. At its worst this has caused a form of depression legionnaires call *cafard*, after a small beetle that metaphorically eats away at a man's brain, apparently devouring both mind and soul.

Many legionnaires have talked up *cafard* as being something unique to the Legion, highlighting its potentially destructive qualities. One of these was the German Erwin Rosen, who wrote of his experiences in the early 1900s:

> I myself lived in a state of continual irritation. The least trifle put me into such a rage that I can hardly credit today. Often enough I would tear down my *paquetage* from the shelf, destroying what had been wearisome work, just because some trousers or jacket did not seem to be folded correctly. My vexation, my irritability, my brooding was the madness of the Foreign Legion.
>
> The rest of my comrades in the room all had at different times the *cafard* more or less seriously. Crowded together like horses in a bad stable the men became dangerous. They fought over the quarter of a litre of the Legion wine that was apportioned to us every second day, and watched with ridiculous suspicion that the next man did not get more than he did; one quarrelled over a piece of bread; one took one's neighbour for a thief who

wanted to steal a bit of black wax for leather polishing. If one man got more work to do than his neighbour, he cried murder and roared out about protection and favouritism, and vicious preference.

This was the atmosphere in which the Legion whims were developed. It was really strange how many legionnaires had a screw loose, often only harmless peculiarities, but which could increase to madness.

All idiocy in the Legion is called *cafard*. A legionnaire is gloomy, sitting sullenly on his bed for hours, speaking to no one. If you ask him what is the matter, he will answer you with a gross insult. He sits thinking all the time and does the queerest things. He has the *cafard* . . .

His madness may turn into a senseless explosion or a fit of fury; men suffering from *cafard* will run a bayonet through their comrade's body, without any reason, without any outward cause. Sometimes they rush out into the desert, sometimes they tear every piece of their outfit into rags, just to vex themselves and others thoroughly.

Ernst Löhndorff wrote of the deadly tedium of life in a desert outpost in the early 1930s, and what he described as an outbreak of *cafard*:

The oasis of Hadsherat-M'Guil consists of a few palms and a pool. The bed of the Oued-Dermel is waterless and overgrown with green sedge. The fort is a clay affair with high walls, flat-roofed buildings with loopholes and a wooden, scaffold-like watchtower. And now we are alone underneath the African sun, in the desert. The nearest fort lies a good many hours of stiff riding behind us. Life has already grown monotonous, and I think that the *cafard* will not be long in breaking out amongst us.

It does not take long. From the way the men are staring from the fort at the desert or glaring at one another in a dull and hostile manner over the eating utensils at mealtimes, or slouching about, it seems to me as though the garrison of Hadsherat-M'Guil has gone mad through the heat, apathy, and repressed passions. Yes, we are mad, including the officers, who lie all day on their beds and read yellow-back novels over and over again . . . we are all crazy and rabid!

The mantle of monotony has descended upon us. We try to get out of one another's way, and listen to the howling of Feddersen, who had a sudden attack of delirium and had to be locked up in the dark cell. We clean our weapons, although they shine already like silver and in the evenings we listen to the stories told by the [Moroccan] *Goumiers* on their return from reconnoitring.

The views of Rosen and Löhndorff were, however, contradicted by Frederic Martyn, who suggested that legionnaires themselves tended to be intrinsically more mentally unstable than the average soldier:

A great deal of nonsense has been written about the Legion being of a sort that drives men to madness, and the number of men invalided out of the corps on account of insanity is pointed to as proof of the assertion. I say that a better reason for it can be found for it than the hardness of the life. A large proportion of legionnaires are eccentric – if they were not so they would not be in the Legion at all – and a good many are distinctly 'queer in the upper storey'; but almost without exception they were so when they enlisted, and the Legion is in no way responsible for their condition.

As to the *cafard*, or *soudanite*, as the doctors call it – a form of mania supposed to be peculiar to the Legion – it is nothing more nor less, according to my idea of it, than a sort of hysteria set up by the action of a monotonous regime upon restless active natures in that climate. It is nature calling out insistently for change. It is but rarely that manifestations of the *cafard* end in tragedy; in ninety-nine cases out of a hundred they simply assume the character of an ordinary drunken quarrel or an extraordinary drunken spree.

In addition to the inevitable boredom of peacetime soldering, the Legion has generally treated its men in a distinctly heavy-handed manner, whether in training or afterwards in the regiments. The tensions caused by this high 'bullshit' factor – which remains part of the Legion – was explained by Gareth Carins during his basic training:

> Many times I had wanted to punch the walls in frustration or do some damage to something or someone. This place had that effect on people. With its constant insistence on doing things that are completely pointless and the frustration of orders that much of the time seemed designed only to keep our motivation at rock bottom and suppress any sense of at least trying to enjoy our training, or even just making the most of it, there were times when you thought you were about to explode. Just when you think you are starting to understand the rules of the game, they go and change them just to piss you off and to let you know who is in charge.
>
> Our frustration was at times a constant struggle to control and huge personal effort was required to try and stay level-headed. Whether this meant thinking of home, or counting the days until the end of instruction, it didn't matter as long as you had something to keep your sanity in check. Much of the time it felt like you were in a pressure cooker and with no avenue to vent off steam. It usually boiled over in the form of fighting amongst ourselves. I have forgotten the number of minor punch-ups we had between one another, but normally they were over the most irrelevant of things and they never lasted more than a few seconds at most. I remember having a punch-up with a Romanian recruit one time about not wanting to pick up a football. One second we were having a friendly kickabout and the next we were tearing chunks out of each other. Stupid thing was, we were actually good mates.

Men who were unable to adjust to the Legion's way of doing things had a particularly difficult time. Although Christian Jennings had secured a place in the elite 2nd REP (*Régiment Étranger Parachutiste*) he was too much of an individualist to be suited to life in the Legion, where he found himself coming under constant pressure from his immediate superior, Corporal Garcia. Jennings wrote frankly of a growing disillusionment with the Legion during a posting to Djibouti in the Horn of Africa:

There was nothing that was demanded of me that wasn't demanded of everybody else; I was not the only one to find ironing, cleaning, sweeping and 'coat-hangering' the shithouses a pain. We all took turns performing the most mundane, boring tasks, and adjusted ourselves and our own routines to coincide with what we had to do. The older soldiers, and those who had served in the regular army before, were used to the ball-breaking process of military discipline and didn't complain. Slug [a fellow legionnaire] had been fucked around too much in the Royal Marines not to able to cope with the demands made on him by the Legion. He knew when to shut his mouth and carry on with things, and he knew when it was acceptable to moan. I was lazy and thought too much about everything we did, tending to analyse and dramatise the smallest incidents. I was also a constant complainer, whinging wildly about any extra task that came my way. So the corporals reacted in the most predictable fashion and unloaded more fatigues on me. By now I was getting disenchanted with the Legion fast, and Corporal Garcia's mission to make my life a misery only served to increase my frustration. I hadn't the experience or age to realise that most soldiering, in a regular army anywhere, consists almost entirely of performing countless, small menial tasks. The logistics of organising and maintaining a group of men in a foreign country in a hostile environment meant that there were many occasions when the things we were ordered to do seemed absolutely pointless.

At its most extreme, the oppressiveness of the Legion has forced men towards suicide. Whether the Legion has a higher rate of suicide than other military formations is difficult to ascertain, but within the Legion itself the belief is commonplace. John Patrick Le Poer served during the 1880s, maintaining that men sent to far-distant outposts were especially vulnerable:

These are the 'suicide stations', if I may call them so – the stations where a shot rings out at night and all rush to arms, fearing an attack of Touregs or Kabyles, but when dawn comes there is only a dead sentry making black the yellow sand at a post. When one man shoots himself an epidemic seems to set in; men hear every day in hut or tent or guard room the ill-omened report; soon they go about looking fearfully at one another, for no one knows but that he is looking into the eyes of a comrade who has made up his mind to die. The corporal counts his squad, 'fourteen, fifteen – ah! there were sixteen yesterday', so he says; he thinks: 'How long until I have only fourteen, and who will be the next man to quit *la gamelle*' [mess tin]?

The belief that suicide is 'contagious' was confirmed some 50 years later by Legion officer Jacques Weygand:

The first was a corporal of No. 2 Troop called Artenbach, who shot himself while on a night patrol. Then, one after another, two legionnaires in an infantry company; finally Corporal Morris, who had been attached to Signals on account of his proficiency in wireless. He was found hanging in the Signals Office; at the end of his record of messages received during the night he had written: 'I am fed up. I am killing myself.'

One of the infantry suicides chose the death of an Epicurean. He was a Russian about forty, of whose past history nothing was known. One day he went to the *Coopérative* and bought a bottle of the best wine and a tin of *foie gras*; he sought out a quiet corner and, having enjoyed his last meal, shot himself in the head.

Tension grew worse every day; the fear of being awakened suddenly to learn of another death began to give the officers sleepless nights. They all did what they could to make the men think of something else, to shake them out of their dreadful apathy which had laid hold even of the best among them. The sealed confidential bag of the north-bound courier carried exhaustive reports in which each of the officers responsible – squadron and company commanders and the Commandant – described the progress of the epidemic and suggested possible remedies.

Although the Legion has obviously been unable to employ sanctions against successful suicides, it has punished those who have failed in the attempt. Tony Sloane described one such attempted suicide during basic training:

Schmitt looked like a pig. He had a round full face and small demon eyes. He was a little overweight for his 20 years, I didn't really like the man, there just seemed to be something not right. He was with us for a few weeks. After reveille at around 5.30 in the morning we shaved. Ray arrived first one morning to find the toilet floor covered in a huge pool of blood. The cubicle door was locked so he climbed over the top to find Schmitt slumped on the floor. He had sliced his wrists. Of course, the medics were called and he was taken away. I mopped up the blood that had been trodden around the room. Fortunately, or unfortunately for Schmitt, he didn't die and so once he was patched up he was sentenced to the usual month in prison before being released back into the streets.

Sloane continued the story, suggesting some ambivalence towards suicide on the part of the Legion:

The company was paraded by the sergeant-major, who was not happy. Stern words were said but the interesting part was the explanation of how to kill oneself correctly. He didn't care if you wanted to finish 'it' (whatever 'it' was) off but just make sure you do it properly so as to not waste people's time. 'Don't cut the wrist; cut down the inside of the elbows deep – there are bigger veins and you will have more success.' He demonstrated with elaborate hand gestures so that we were all sure.

Only a little way apart from suicide itself are outbreaks of suicidal behaviour. One such manifestation was the 'game' of cuckoo, described here by Weygand:

The 'cuckoo' is a Legionary institution, which appears to have been introduced by Russian members of the Corps, and which is practised only in times of extreme boredom. A group of NCOs – or even of officers – carefully darken the windows of their mess with blankets and draw lots for a victim. Each, with the exception of the 'cuckoo', is armed with a revolver loaded with a single round. They stand in line with their backs to one of the walls of the room. Lights are then put out; the victim enters, feeling his way as best he can, and starts to move about in the dark. After a certain length of time, having done his best to confuse the marksman, he stands still and utters the fatal word 'Cuckoo!' Whereupon everybody fires, to the best of his judgment, in the direction of the sound.

Cuckoo was still being played during the Legion's final days in Indochina: as the garrisons along *Route Colonial* 4 awaited destruction by the Viet Minh in 1950 it became a diversion, reflecting the Legion's nihilistic attitude to both life and death.

Another extreme manifestation of dissatisfaction with the Legion is, of course, desertion. This has become something of a tradition, spawning its own brand of escape/desertion stories. Adrian Liddell Hart explained its appeal:

> Almost all legionnaires have run away to the Legion for some compelling reason – or they are excessively restless. Almost inevitably they get homesick, disillusioned, bored, often upset by small incidents. What do they do?
>
> In the first place, many try to desert from a force to which, after all, they owe no special natural allegiance. Observers have often wondered at the contrast between the legendary reputation of the Legion for endurance and gallantry and yet its indisputably high record of desertion, even to the enemy. The authorities accept it as natural. 'We expect these young legionnaires to try and desert in the first few months,' a commandant remarked.

Many legionnaires, of course, regard desertion itself as an adventurous challenge, faced with the difficulties and hardships in North Africa and elsewhere. And at the end of the adventure, moreover, is the possibility of safety in familiar surroundings – a possibility which does not open to the deserter from a national army.

Many desertions have been spontaneous actions and often poorly planned. To effect a successful desertion requires sound preparation and a good deal of luck. Location is also important. In colonial times, the best places to desert were from the towns of the North African seaboard or in transit to Indochina, where transport ships passed through the Suez Canal or re-coaled at Singapore – both British possessions that offered the deserter sanctuary from

French authorities. Those attempting to get away from deep within Algeria or Morocco had little hope of success, as Jacques Weygand explained of the legionnaires who deserted from Bou-Dénib during the late 1920s:

> Although there may be an even chance of success in deserting when passing through a port or when stationed in a town, only the unbalanced would attempt it from a starting-place like Bou-Dénib. The only patch open lay in the direction of Colomb-Béchar, and that was neither easy nor safe. The rest of the surrounding country for many miles was either desert or rebel territory.
>
> Journeys of pathetic folly, most likely to end in the lock-up of a Native Affairs Office, whose informers are always on the alert, with the alternative of a slow and painful death; for even the strongest cannot fight thirst. Yet these tragic examples deter no one. Those who undertake them are gamblers, adventurers; desertion is a new adventure, and the stake is high.

The sense of adventure in deserting the Legion has continued to the present. Christian Jennings made an impromptu attempt to desert from Djibouti, which, given the harshness of the terrain, the hostility of the local people and lack of a suitable sanctuary, almost inevitably ended in failure. He discussed the reasons for deserting and some of the methods used by deserters:

> When most people deserted, they subjected themselves to a much worse experience than the one they had left behind. Two people had deserted from Corsica by swimming across the straits of Bonifacio to Sardinia. This was across miles of rough sea, where the currents which swept around the sides of the two islands met in a jumble of waves and confusing tides. From Sardinia, they would have to make their way on to mainland Italy, leaving behind wetsuits and flippers on a remote beach, changing into civilian clothes they had bought with them in their waterproof bundles.
>
> In Djibouti or Guyana, the methods of escape were even more dramatic. Two legionnaires had stolen a jeep, stuck the badge of rank of a captain on their chests, and simply driven out of the front

gates and into the desert. They dumped the jeep when it ran out of fuel, and from there had headed off into Ethiopia, eventually arriving in the Sudan. They had caught a plane home to London, arriving broke and suntanned at Heathrow on a rainy autumn afternoon. In Guiana, two legionnaires had worked their way through the Amazon jungle, across the border into Suriname and on to the West Indies in a stolen fishing boat. The adventure and risk of setting sail in a fishing boat from a mangrove swamp on the South American coast, or of roaring across the desert at night in a stolen jeep, were almost ends in themselves. The adventure was exclusive. It had little to do with anything which had preceded it, or anything which would come after it. It combined all the risks and physical daring which people had been looking forward to in joining up, but which had been absent because in the 1980s the French Foreign Legion was an organised peacetime outfit. Within its confines of brutality, discipline and curious tradition, it was almost sedentary.

Among other legionnaires, desertion produced mixed emotions. Some sympathised with the deserters, others condemned them. Carl Jackson, a paratrooper in the 2nd REP, was one of the latter:

I always said to myself that I would finish my time. I've got to admit, though, during the first two years I felt like going over the wire many a time. I thought, what the fuck am I doing here – I don't need this shit, and I'm off, but, on the other hand, I thought, no, hang on a minute, I signed the contract, I gave my word, so what sort of guy would I be if I didn't fulfil my pledge of five years in the Legion? At the end of the day, they fed me, they clothed me. They didn't ask me to come; I went looking for them. So then to say, I'm going to run away, is a bit of a discredit to them, really, and to yourself, because I wouldn't be a man of my word, and I believe your word is your bond. So I'm not big on deserters.

The belief in staying the course, regardless of conditions, was shared by Tony Sloane:

The little pointless things in the Legion made me question if this was really what I wanted to do. Once during my five years I had thought of deserting, of returning back to England because of the seemingly meaningless jobs. However, it was my personal pride that kept me for the duration. I thought, how could I return and hold my head up high or even mention the Legion if I deserted? I would not be able to without having the feeling that people would think that it was too difficult for me: that I was not tough enough.

But for those deserters caught in the attempt, the attitudes of their comrades counted for little when set against the punishments meted out by the authorities. Christian Jennings was beaten up by two Spanish corporals on his return to the main camp in Djibouti, thrown into solitary for five days and then given his official punishment of 40 days' hard labour. At the height of the Algerian War of Independence, Simon Murray described the fate of two deserters called Lefevre and Aboine, who received a particularly savage punishment:

> Lefevre and Aboine deserted this afternoon during the siesta and at about seven o'clock this evening news came through that they had been caught by a regular army cavalry regiment. I was on guard duty at the time and was ordered into the jeep which was sent to collect them. The collection committee comprised the company adjutant, Chief Sergeant Westhof, [Sergeant] Wissman and myself. On our arrival at the regular army camp, the two prisoners were dragged forward and Westhof staggered everybody including myself by pulling out his pistol and dropping both of them to the ground by a blow to the head with the butt of his gun. Lefevre's head started to bleed like hell. They were bundled into the jeep.
>
> The mixture of horror and astonishment on the faces of the French soldiers was something to see – my own face must have looked a bit dazed too. We returned to Sully and the two prisoners were paraded in front of Captain Glasser in his office. I was on guard outside the room. He beat the living daylights out of them and since then they had a terrible time.

The two deserters were forced to perform a particularly strenuous three-hour session of pack-drill (*pelote*). Murray continued his account:

When they were exhausted, with not an ounce of strength left in their bodies, they were made to crawl through an open sewer, and finally as the last indignation, they had to crawl on their bellies around the barrack room, gasping and grunting while we stood to attention, each man beside his bunk. They crawled past our feet, covered in slime and filth, and they no longer resembled human beings. This was the punishment for deserters and it was to be a lesson to all of us. There was not a man among us who had not considered desertion, and there was not a man among us now who, for all his feelings of revulsion and hatred against this meaningless barbarism, was not only secretly afraid at what he saw – afraid at such brutality; that it could be administered by a sadist like Wissman, with no control and no appeal to any authority except that of the Legion – and in the Legion there is no appeal, and the authority is in those it is vested, and it starts at the rank of corporal.

The Legion has always made an example of deserters to new recruits, to act as a suitable deterrent against further desertion. A legionnaire in the 1990s, Gareth Carins witnessed this brutal philosophy first-hand. While in training at the Farm a recruit called Schuhmann was caught deserting. Carins described how he saw Schuhmann slumped at the bottom of a flag pole: 'His wrists had been bound together behind the flag pole, as had his ankles, so that it was impossible to stand up, and he was forced into a sort of kneeling position. I could see blood on the side of his face.'

Schuhmann was left tied to the flag pole overnight. Carins described the next stage in his punishment:

Later that morning we stood in silence in front of Schuhmann, an unwilling audience to the [Sergent] Chef's twisted version of Legion discipline which was based on fear of your superiors. And he was soon demonstrating the power that came with his position, randomly grabbing individuals by the collar and asking them if they too were wanting to desert. He paced up and down shouting out words like honour, courage and camaraderie as if they somehow justified the treatment of Schuhmann. On and on he ranted before stopping by the flag pole and kicking Schuhmann in the bollocks which forced him to try and curl up to protect himself. This had been made impossible, though, due to his ankles and wrists being tied behind the pole, which left him incapable of turning away and completely exposed the front of his body.

One side of his face was already swollen from a punch the night before and it was heartbreaking to watch him making futile attempts to dodge the fists, feet and knees of the *Chef* – which came raining down until he had satisfied his anger.

Schuhmann was eventually cut down to be taken back to Castelnaudary by the military police. The effectiveness of such deterrent 'lessons' is debatable, as desertion remains a constant of military life in the Legion – in the case of Carins' section, another recruit successfully deserted the following day. But the authorities would justify their harsh treatment of deserters on the basis that it is all part of the toughing-up process that has made the French Foreign Legion such a potent fighting force, from its origins in the 1830s to the present day.

PART III

THE LEGION AT WAR

The grandest assembly of real fighting men that I have ever seen.
(Field Marshal Lord Alanbrooke)

CHAPTER 8

AN EMPIRE IN AFRICA

The origins of the French Foreign Legion as a fighting unit were less than auspicious. The Legion was formed by royal decree on 10 March 1831, as an infantry force composed of foreign nationals to be deployed for service overseas. One of the prime reasons for its formation was to round up the many foreigners considered by the French government to be trouble-makers and potential revolutionaries. Some seven battalions were hastily raised and then sent to the French colonial enclave in North Africa centred round the city of Algiers.

Poorly trained and led, the local French commanders initially refused to accept the Legion as a combat unit, and its men languished as common labourers. They were stationed in some of the more unhealthy spots around Algiers; disease was rampant and deaths frequent. But renewed attempts by the Arab population to eject the French brought a demand for front-line troops and a change in the Legion's fortunes. Yet, no sooner had it demonstrated that it could fight, than the bulk of the Legion was despatched to Spain in 1835, 'loaned' to Queen Christina in a brutal war with her brother-in-law, Don Carlos. Of the 5,000 or so legionnaires sent to fight in the Carlist wars, a mere 159 front-line soldiers returned to France in January 1839.

Meanwhile, what remained of the Legion in North Africa soon found itself engaged in a full-scale war with the Arab leader, Abd el-Kader. In June 1835 the French were defeated at the Battle of Macta, and to maintain the now tenuous hold over their North African possessions, reinforcements were rushed to Algiers. The Kabyle tribes were among France's fiercest opponents and the mountainous stronghold of Constantine became a focus of opposition.

In 1837 the French laid siege to Constantine. Surrounded on three sides by near-vertical cliffs, it could only be approached from the south. And it was here that the massed French artillery was able to make a breach in the city's walls. Among the French troops waiting to attack the breach was a Legion battalion under the command of Major Bedeau. One of Bedeau's company commanders, Captain (subsequently Marshal) Achille Leroy de Saint-Arnaud was an ambitious officer determined to make his mark in the North African campaign. In a letter to his brother, Saint-Arnaud described the legionnaires' assault on Constantine:

> We had just arrived at the breach when there was a shattering explosion, followed by the silence of the grave. Those still on their feet were staggering, blinded by gravel, powder, momentarily suffocated. In a matter of seconds, however, a terrible spectacle was enacted before our eyes. Those wounded but still capable of walking appeared, crying out with pain, from the debris. I was amazed that our men stood firm. Combes [a fellow officer] and Bedeau raised their swords. I heard them shouting 'Forward! Forward!' I took up the cry myself, calling out to my men, '*A moi la Légion!*' [To me, the Legion!] At them with the bayonet! Forward! Forward!' and began to run towards the swirling clouds of smoke expecting to be blown to bits, convinced as I was that a second mine would go up at any moment.
>
> Seven Turks were firing at us from loopholes in the walls. They discharged their muskets in our faces, but we bayoneted them as they were trying to reload. There was no question of taking prisoners.
>
> I then doubled my men in the direction of the heaviest firing, and arrived outside the house of Ben Aissa, the Bey's lieutenant. Major Bedeau was there already and, as we looked for the best way to penetrate still more deeply into the town, bullets rained down on us, bouncing like hail off the cobbles.

While Bedeau and Saint-Arnaud rallied their legionnaires, news reached them of the erection of a barricade at the end of an alley, where the Kabyle defenders were going to make their last stand. Saint-Arnaud resumed the story:

> Advancing towards the end of the alley, I saw that we were being held up by a barricade consisting of wrenched-off doors, beams and mattresses, everything one could think of, defended ferociously by the Kabyles. Going back to my men, I told them that by charging with the bayonet they would lose far fewer than by creeping forward and firing ineffectually into a pile of mattresses. I then put my marksmen into houses from which they could fire over the barricades down to the defenders and, sword in hand, shouting 'Forward the Legion!', charged.
>
> I reached the barricade, climbed it and fell flat on my face in the middle of a group of Arabs. The fall saved my life, as the shots fired at me were too high. Even so, I was so near the musket barrels that my overcoat was singed and my scabbard holed. It was while I was still on the ground that I heard a soldier call out, 'Save the Captain. He's wounded!' But I got to my feet and started to carve up Turks with my sword, as my men destroyed the barricade, opening up a passage into the very street that the first column had been repulsed.

Once again Saint-Arnaud reorganised his troops and then pressed on along the street:

> My first action was to establish my sharpshooters on either side, firing crossways. But men were dropping all the time. After not more than twenty paces we were stopped by a really intense fire coming from a big house on the right, which seemed literally aflame, so continuous were the flashes coming from it. I learned later that it was the barracks of the Bey's guard!
>
> There was nothing to do but take it by storm. We battered in the doors and plunged into the courtyard, broke into the rooms, climbed the stairs. What a sight! What slaughter! Blood everywhere! Not a murmur from the dying. One killed or was killed in that state of frenzy which makes a man grit his teeth and stifle a groan from the very depths of his soul.

After the house was cleared Saint-Arnaud and the legionnaires advanced deeper into Constantine:

> I was attacked by the Turk whose *yatagan* [light sword with a curved blade] I sent you. His pistol was jammed and he threw himself on me, blade raised. I parried his cut, lunged, and my point entered his neck. One of my men, Keller, who was just behind me, leaped forward and plunged his bayonet into the body. At that moment he was hit by two bullets and the poor boy died for me, since it was at me that the bullets were aimed. A third bullet hit the greatcoat I was wearing slung bandolier-fashion.
>
> We advanced slowly against redoubled fire. In vain I tried to charge, crying 'Forward!' My men were mown down, and it was in this unhappy position that Sergeant-Major Droze, at the head of a handful of volunteers, captured a banner, killing all its defenders, and thus earned the cross for which I recommended him.
>
> Again I rallied my men, and they followed me, bayonets levelled. But at last the Turks had had enough. They fled and the street was cleared. We chased them down a number of alleys, until we arrived at a small square where I found Major Bedeau, the battalion commander. Happy to see each other alive, we shook hands warmly.
>
> I was just going to advance down another alley, when an Arab suddenly appeared waving a piece of paper and crying, '*Carta. Carta.*' The man was a son of a sheik. It was all over. The town had surrendered unconditionally.

Saint-Arnaud was decorated for his gallantry and exemplary leadership, while the banner captured by Droze was transferred to Les Invalides in Paris, where it remains today. The fall of Constantine did not end Kabyle resistance, however, and fighting was to continue for the next two decades.

The German officer Clemens Lamping was soon in action against the Kabyles. Bored with garrison duties in his native Oldenburg, Lamping had resigned his commission in 1839 and joined the Legion to see active service. He described his posting to the 3rd Battalion, based in the Algerian port of Dschigeli: 'The battalion is composed of men from all nations: Spaniards and Italians, Germans and Belgians,

Dutchmen and Poles, only no English. Most of them had joined the service out of mere folly, some from political or civil offences, and a few from misfortune. These men are for the most part brutal and ill-disciplined, but ready to encounter anything. They form a band who, under an energetic leader, might do great things.'

Within a week of Lamping's arrival in Dschigeli in August 1840, the legionnaires were called upon to do 'great things' when a Kabyle war band assaulted the fort, which at that time comprised little more than a series of interlinked blockhouses:

> They attacked with unusual fury and pertinacity. Some time before sunrise we saw a large party of Kabyles coming down from the mountains; as far as the eye could see the place swarmed with white burnouses. Every blockhouse was attacked at the same moment. Our well-directed fire was insufficient to keep off an enemy which pressed upon us in dense masses, and in a moment they were close under the walls. Here they could no longer do us any damage with their shots; but in their rage they threw huge stones over the walls upon our heads. We made a rapid retreat into our blockhouses and barricaded the doors. In one moment the Kabyles climbed the outer walls, and attempted in their blind fury to storm the blockhouses. Some of them tried, but in vain, to throw the cannon over the walls; and now they had the worst of the fight.
>
> The half of the party who were in the upper story removed a plank that was left loose for the purpose, and poured their fire down upon the heads of the Kabyles, while some canoneers who were with us threw a number of hand-grenades, of which we had a good store, among them. This was rather more than they could bear, and they dispersed in all directions, yelling fearfully; they however carried off their dead and wounded, for the Mohamedan never leaves his comrades in the hands of the foe.

Once attacks on the coastal settlements had been repulsed, the French pushed deeper into the mountainous interior of Algeria. It was a harsh, unforgiving land, where bitter winters contrasted with blazing, brain-frying summers. The Kabyle tribesmen were finally defeated when their mountain stronghold of Ischeriden fell to the French in 1857. A brigade of the regular French Army under General Charles Bourbaki led the main assault on the Kabyle fortifications but it was the Legion who gained the laurels of victory:

> A hundred and fifty yards from the enemy and [Bourbaki's] 2nd Zouaves and the 54th of Line were completely in the open. At that very moment a sinister death-clamour rose from the ramparts obscured by the smoke of a murderous fusillade. The French column, literally mown down, was halted. In vain some of the Zouaves tried to worm their way forward on their bellies; in vain a few officers shouted, 'Forward!' They were blasted out of existence as the Kabyles' fire redoubled in fury.
>
> It was then, to the left of Bourbaki's brigade, that I saw a Legion battalion begin to move up, its officers on horseback at the head of their companies, its veterans, superbly disciplined, indifferent to the whistling bullets. A withering fire was directed on them. They advanced unflinching, without replying, and in a few minutes had reached the trenches, swarmed into them and exterminated the defenders with the bayonet. The surviving Kabyles fled. Where the courage of the Zouaves and the 54th had failed, the silent scornful bravery of the Legion succeeded.
>
> 'It was an attack from your *grandes capottes* [greatcoats],' said a prisoner, 'which drove us from our positions. But for them we would have annihilated you. But when we saw these *grand capottes* moving forward without even bothering to return our fire, our nerves broke.'

By the 1860s Algeria had become a well-established French colony, although the Legion remained on active service subduing periodic revolts and extending French rule into the Sahara desert. The nomadic Touareg people of the Sahara proved both redoubtable and elusive opponents. John Patrick le Poer, an Irishman who had signed up in the early 1880s, had his first taste of combat as his company advanced to the edges of the great desert. Le Poer's section was part of a piquet line guarding the main company position during a night time halt. Just before dawn, le Poer, peering into the darkness, began to suspect an enemy attack:

As I gazed I fancied that there was a movement in my front. I could not at the time, nor can I now, though I am a man of wider experience today, swear that I actually saw anything, but that an impalpable, strange, indefinite change was coming over the blackness of the desert, I neither doubted nor misunderstood. Raising my rifle to my shoulder, quietly and cautiously as one does whose own body may be in a second the target for countless bullets, I aimed steadily at the blackest part of the blackness and fired. As I turned to run to the picket an awful shriek rang out, telling me that my bullet had found a billet, and then, while I ran shouting: '*Aux armes, aux armes!* [To arms, to arms!],' a hideous, savage cry ran in a great circle all about the camp.

When I closed on the piquet the corporal was giving his orders: 'One volley, and run for the camp.' The volley was fired, and we all ran madly back to the entrenchments, crying: '*Aux armes, les ennemis!*' not, indeed, to warn our comrades of their danger, but to let them know that we were the men of the outlying piquet fleeing to camp and not the mad vanguard of the attack. We got inside the little rampart, helped over by willing arms, and at once the crash of musketry began. Our men had their bayonets fixed; for a double purpose this – for defence if the Arabs came home in the charge, to lower the muzzle if only shooting were necessary. Luckily our firing became so successful that the Arabs stopped to reply, and, you may take my word for it, when a charging man halts to fire he is already weakening for a retreat.

Well, we kept the enemy at a safe distance till the blessed sun sprang up and turned the chances to our side. Yet still they hung around and a dropping fire was maintained on both sides. They did not now surround the camp; they had all collected in almost a semi-circle on the southern side. While the desultory firing went on our commandant eagerly turned his gaze from time to time towards the north, and he was at last rewarded. He sent orders to give the ration of brandy to every man – the rascal! He had seen the glint of lance-heads on the horizon, and he wanted to take a little of the pursuer's glory from the cavalrymen. Glory, glory! What follies are committed in thy name!

The brandy was given out, the news went around that the horses were coming up at the gallop, the men looked with blood-lust in their eyes at the lying-down semi-circle to the south, the commandant flung off jacket, belt, scabbard, keeping only sabre and pistol, and with a wild cheer and cries of 'Kill, kill!' we rushed from the camp straight at the enemy. They were not cowards. They gave us a wild, scattered fire, and then, flinging away their rifles and flintlocks, came daringly, with loud cries of 'Allah!' to meet us. And in their charge they covered a greater distance than we did in ours, for they came along every man at racing speed, and their line grew more and more irregular, whereas we, disciplined and trained to move all as one man, fell easily into the regulation *pas gymnastique* [fast march], and so went forward a solid, steady, cheering line, officers leading, and clarions at our backs sounding the charge.

As we neared one another a great shout went up from us. Nicholas the Russian, who was my front-rank man, dashed forward and stabbed a yelling demon rushing at him with uplifted spear. I ran into his place, and saw almost at once the dusky madman, with a short, scanty beard, coming straight at me with murder in his eyes. I remembered the advice given by the *vieux soldats* [old soldiers], and as he raised his sword I plunged my bayonet with all my force into his face. He half reeled, he almost fell, and as he recovered again I lunged and struck him fair and full on the breast bone. Again he reeled, yet still he tried to strike; I thrust a third time, and now at his bare neck; the spouting blood followed out the bayonet as I drew it forth and back to strike again. Before I had time to do so the Arab fell, a convulsive tremor passed over his body, the limbs contracted, the eyes opened wide to the sky, the jaw fell, and for the first time I saw my enemy lie stark and cold in death before me.

The Touareg and other Saharan warriors found hit-and-run tactics most effective, using the desert and nearby Morocco as a sanctuary. In the early 1880s Colonel François-Oscar Negrier introduced mounted companies, consisting of legionnaires equipped with mules, to improve French mobility and catch the enemy while on the run. Frederic Martyn was a recruit:

The company was not cavalry – we were simply infantrymen mounted on mules in order to enable us to get over the long distances we had to traverse in patrolling the Moroccan border or hunting the marauding Arabs in the desert to the south of us. We were kept pretty hard at work, and as we were continually having brushes with somebody it was more or less like campaigning in a mild sort of way.

Typically, two men would share a mule, with one mounted and the other marching alongside. The mounted companies became an elite within the Foreign Legion, combining mobility with firepower that overwhelmed the Touareg war bands. The hard marching that was such a feature of the mounted companies' war is revealed in this entry in the War Diary of the 12th Mounted Company:

The fifty men of the 12th Company, which included several young soldiers who had joined only a few days previously, left Oudjda on Saturday at 11 o'clock in the evening, and joined up with Colonel Felineau's column at six o'clock the following morning. On the march at 7.30, they took part in a brush with the Beni Snassen. By the time they bivouacked at five in the evening, they had covered 50 kilometres (30 by night) with only a cup of coffee and a tin of sardines in their bellies. They had a meal at six, another at eight next morning, then were on the march again, covering another 50 kilometres with only one stop – another brush with the enemy. At six in the evening, they were back in Oudjda. Not a single man had fallen out. Next day, exchanging their rifles for picks and shovels, they were at work on the Marnia–Oudjda road.

The fighting and marching qualities of the Legion began to be appreciated in a wider sphere in the early years of the twentieth century, as foreign journalists began to accompany French military forays in North Africa. Reginald Rankin, who was part of General D'Amade's expedition into Morocco in 1908, was impressed by the ordinary legionnaire's fortitude in the line of battle. While admitting they were a 'difficult lot to manage in peace time', he believed they were 'first-rate' on active service: 'Their chief characteristic is their coolness under fire, which promotes good shooting and prevents waste of ammunition.' He provided an example of legionnaire sangfroid:

At the second battle of Settat I saw a legionary hit in the hand as he was in the act of firing. He asked a comrade to bind it up, and then went on shooting. Five minutes later he was hit in the other hand, rather badly, and again begged his friend to bind him up, remarking that if the Moors [Moroccans] fancied they'd stopped his work for the day they were jolly well mistaken. Such is the spirit and temper of the Legion in action, and finer fighting troops it would be impossible to find in any army.

Although the Legion was inextricably bound up with the occupation of North Africa, it also played a part in French conquests of other parts of Africa, including Dahomey and Madagascar.

The French protectorate of Porto Novo on the West African coast had come under attack from the warlike peoples of Dahomey (modern-day Benin) under their new king, Behanzin. In 1892 the French organised an expedition to subdue the Dahomeyans. Dahomey had grown rich through the slave trade and was able to put as many as 12,000 warriors into the field. Among the elite of Behanzin's army was a corps of female warriors, inevitably known as Amazons by the French. Veteran British legionnaire Frederic Martyn was both intrigued and impressed by the Amazons:

These young women were far and away the best men in the Dahomeyan Army, and woman to man were quite a match for any of us. They were armed with Spencer repeating carbines, and made much better use of them than the men made of their rifles; and for work at close-quarters they had a small heavy-backed chopping sword or knife, very much like a South American machete, with which they did great execution. They fought like unchained demons, and if driven into a corner did not disdain the use of their teeth and nails.

The uniform of these female warriors was a sort of kilted divided skirt of blue cotton stuff. This garment barely reached to the knees. It was supported at the waist by a leather belt which carried the cartridge pouches. The upper part of their bodies was quite nude, but the head was covered with a coquettish red *fez*, or *tarboosh*, into which was stuck an eagle's feather. These ladies were all exceedingly well developed, and some of them were very handsome.

In September 1892 the French forces under Colonel Dodds were divided into three columns that advanced northwards into Dahomey. Martyn's company was assigned to the second column, and as day broke on the 19th it came under attack:

> We rushed to our arms and formed up; there were a few more shots, and then the piquet came bounding into camp with thousands and thousands of black shadows close at the men's heels – the Dahomeyans had surprised us. As fast as we could ram the cartridges in and loose off we fired into the moving black shadows and saw them topple over like corn falling under the sickle.

Another legionnaire recalled the same dawn attack:

> Our first salvoes mowed down the enemy, who left mounds of corpses on the ground. But it was a nightmarish experience being attacked by these yelling savages in the half-light of early dawn. The least weakening could have resulted in our destruction. Three minutes after the assault had been launched, however, we were joined by two other Legion companies, and our Lebel rifles exacted a heavy toll on the shrieking hordes surrounding us.

Once the impetus of the Dahomeyan assault had begun to slacken, the French went over to the offensive. Martyn described the ensuing bayonet charge that made the Legion so feared in colonial warfare:

> We were on the run towards the threatened side of the camp, and in a few seconds we were in the thick of them, ramming our bayonets into their bodies until the hilt came up against the flesh with a sickening thud, and then throwing them off to make room for another, like a farm labourer forking hay, until we had to clamber over the dead and dying men piled two or three high to get at the living.
>
> For the moment there was no question of those enemy who were receiving our special attention running away. They couldn't run away, for the great mass behind was pushing them onto our bayonets. It was a terrible slaughter.

VOICES OF THE FOREIGN LEGION

As the French advanced deeper into Dahomey, shortages of drinking water became an increasingly acute problem. A legionnaire wrote of how he and his men hacked their way through thick vegetation towards a water hole:

> In spite of our exhaustion and killing heat, in spite of the dense clouds of mosquitoes biting and biting till our hands and faces streamed with blood, we had to reach the water point. We charged into the thick forest and soon came to a glade in which was a hollow of clear, pure water. I won't attempt to describe the troops' reaction. Let him who has never been dying of thirst throw the first stone!
>
> It was at this moment that the Dahomeyans attacked, but were held at bay while water bottles were filled, as well as the water containers, before the battalion fell back through the forest, being sniped at the whole way, to a bare ridge on which we dug in for the night.
>
> The following day, a half-platoon, returning to the water point, was attacked by two thousand of the enemy, and only saved from annihilation by a company bayonet charge. Even so, the legionaries were constantly attacked, the Dahomeyans realising only too well that, without water, the column would be forced to retreat.

Martyn was one of the legionnaires involved in saving the men at the water point:

> When we at last came in sight of our hard-pressed comrades we found them beset by a large body of the enemy, whom we had to charge with the bayonet three times before they would give way. Then the order was given to retreat, and back we went, without a drop of the much-desired water, picking up our dead and wounded as we receded under a terrible hail of bullets.
>
> An old legionary of 24 years' service was grumblingly criticising our officer for ordering us to retreat instead of forcing our way to the water, saying he would rather be shot than be thirsty, when he suddenly stopped and fell to the ground badly wounded, remarking with a curse that he was now both shot and thirsty.

Colonel Dodds decided to temporarily withdraw his troops to await reinforcements and a re-supply of munitions and rations. On 24 September he resumed the offensive with French forces pressing on Kana, in preparation for an advance on the Dahomeyan capital of Abomey. King Behanzin's warriors made a determined stand, but the French forced them back towards the walls of Kana. A legionnaire outlined the assault on the city:

> Kana is made up of several scattered groups of buildings. The houses are of cement. The outer walls, high and wide, are flanked by six bastions, altogether a most formidable obstacle.
>
> The attack was opened under a blazing sun. Our artillery rained shells on the city. The enemy artillery was as numerous as our own and, judging by its accuracy, was obviously being served by Europeans. One enemy shell wounded one of my comrades in the leg, another blew up a case of Lebel cartridges.
>
> At three o'clock the bugles sounded the 'assault'. Firing as they advanced, our troops stormed through the breeches, shooting or bayoneting anyone who stood in their way. This hand-to-hand battle lasted till sunset. Our dead and wounded amounted to 250.
>
> The following day Colonel Dodds visited the Legion battalion. 'I am very proud,' he said to us, 'to have commanded the world's finest soldiers.'

Martyn was also present, and remarked: 'It was no news to us that we were the finest soldiers in the world – we had all known that since our first week in the corps – but we liked being told so, and we swallowed this incontrovertible fact just as greedily as if it had been the rankest flattery.'

After the fall of Kana the heart went out of the Dahomeyan army. The capital of Abomey was abandoned and Behanzin subsequently surrendered to the French. The Dahomeyans had demonstrated great courage but lacked the disciplined firepower of the French. The French small-calibre, high-velocity, smokeless Lebel rifle – which replaced the old black-powder Gras model – had proved devastating. Martyn discovered three Dahomeyans killed by a single bullet that passed through them all and a tree they had been using for shelter.

VOICES OF THE FOREIGN LEGION

As part of the European 'Scramble for Africa', the French established a protectorate over the island of Madagascar in 1885. Opposition by the indigenous Hova peoples to French rule was suppressed by a French expedition into the interior of the country in 1885 that included a battalion of the Legion. The much-vaunted Hova army – apparently 40,000 strong – collapsed when it encountered French military force, and by the end of the year the revolt was effectively over. But the terrain, climate and tropical diseases took a fearsome toll of the invaders. A diary entry from Legionnaire 'X' summed up the prevailing conditions endured by the French as they toiled through thick jungle into the mountainous interior:

> The legionnaires got to work with pick and shovel. They showed themselves to be as skilled and tireless at this labour-corps job as they were tough fighters, whenever a surprise attack obliged them to down tools and reach for their rifles. But continual hard work under the most terrible climatic conditions began to tell. They were as keen as ever, but exhaustion was overtaking them; there were some deaths. Faces grew paler, cheeks more hollow.

The *Times* correspondent E. F. Knight was taken aback at the state of the legionnaires he saw arriving at the Hova capital:

> The flying column that marched from Andriba was composed of picked men who had not suffered so much as the others from fever and dysentery; nevertheless a large proportion of these poor fellows entered the capital in the most miserable condition possible, fearfully anaemic and emaciated. I met, for example, a straggler tottering into the city, almost bent double, his knapsack on his back, his rifle on his shoulder, while from the top of his helmet down to his feet he was covered with black flies, clustering on him as if he were already a corpse.

Although there was another revolt in 1896, and some sporadic fighting that continued for a further nine years, Madagascar was never a true test of the Legion's fighting ability. The conquest of Indochina was a different matter, however, and was to leave a lasting impression on the history of the Foreign Legion.

CHAPTER 9

THE CONQUEST OF INDOCHINA

The French developed trading interests in southern Vietnam during the mid-19th century, which subsequently extended to Tonkin in the north, as well as into Cambodia and Laos. As part of the great imperialist surge in the late nineteenth century, France decided to incorporate these countries into its own empire in the East – French Indochina – although in Tonkin, at least, it would encounter bitter resistance. While nominally a Chinese protectorate, Tonkin was ruled by rival war lords and their piratical Black Flag armies.

To provide military support for the conquest of Tonkin, a Legion battalion left Algeria for Indochina in 1883, to be joined by a further two battalions. Landing at the port of Haiphong, the legionnaires became part of a column advancing into the Tonkinese interior. The French expeditionary force – under the command of Admiral Amédée Courbet – was brought to a standstill at Son Tay, a well-built bamboo and earth fort manned by Chinese regulars and Black Flags. On 16 December 1883, after a breach had been made by French artillery, Courbet decided to assault the fort. Leading the attack was a battalion of Algerian *tirailleurs* (Arab colonial troops). British legionnaire George Manington described the assault by the *tirailleurs*:

> Notwithstanding the fact that these men were seasoned troops and born fighters, they were beaten back with severe loss, which speaks much for the desperate resistance offered by the Chinese

garrison, some of whom were daring enough to dart out through the gap in the walls and decapitate the dead and wounded left in the track of the retreating column. The bleeding heads, placed atop of bamboo poles, were planted on the crest of the ramparts amid the shrill, triumphant yells of the *Celestials* (Chinese).

The Arabs, reformed and stiffened by two companies of French marines, rushed once more to the assault, but with no more success, and indeed with greater loss than the first time. Now the white-faced, gory-necked heads of some of the French marines balanced side by side with the dusky bleeding features of their African comrades. The Chinese, howling drunk with success, and heedless of the fire from the French artillery, which was covering the retreat, stood on the wall to yell defiance and invective at their enemy. Indeed, so greatly was the garrison encouraged that a sortie was made which threatened to develop into a strong attack on the flanks of the expeditionary force.

The Admiral then played his last and trump card, and a battalion of the Legion, which till now had formed part of the reserve, rushed at the breach with the band playing and colours flying.

These troops advanced at the *pas de charge*, and were met by a terrible fire; many fell, but they were not to be denied. In a few minutes the first ranks reached the edge of the ditch, and leaping down onto the slope of *debris*, formed by the stones and earth detached by the cannonade, they scrambled up to the breach, tore away the bamboo palisade, rushed, or were pushed, through it, and gained the crest.

The legionnaires suffered fearful loss; and it is to be feared that, excited by this and the cruel murder of their wounded comrades, they gave little mercy to those who opposed them. Among the first to gain a footing were a subaltern bearer of the colours, and big Mertens.

The first was immediately shot dead, whereupon the sapper seized the flag, and, rushing to the ramparts, stood on them in view of the whole army. Waving the bullet-torn, powder-stained tricolour above his head, he shouted: '*Vive la Belgique! Vive la Légion!*'

There was something grimly comical, but truly typical, in the conduct of this mercenary, who, forgetting the country for which he was fighting, and after just risking death a hundred times, coupled in his shout of triumph the name of his motherland and that of the corps to which he belonged.

Mertens received the *médaille militaire* for his bravery; and it is reported that Admiral Courbet, when complimenting him on the courage he had shown, said: 'And you would have had the Legion of Honour had you cried, '*Vive la France!*'

This last, however, is probably a soldier's yarn.

By 1885 much of Tonkin had been conquered by the French, who were now advancing towards the mountainous Chinese border. Establishing a forward base at Lang Son, the French commander, Colonel François-Oscar de Négrier, crossed the border in March 1885 towards the Chinese position at Bang Bo. There, the French were suddenly attacked by a large and determined Chinese army and were forced back in confusion to the strong position around Lang Son.

During the fighting, Négrier had been severely wounded and command passed to Lieutenant-Colonel Herbinger, who inexplicably ordered a withdrawal from Lang Son. Supplies were hurriedly destroyed to prevent them falling into Chinese hands. Lieutenant Bôn-Mat, a Legion officer, described the scene: 'An unbelievable spectacle awaited us. Barrels of wine and tafia [cheap rum], cases of biscuits and meat, sacks of coffee, flour, open, gutted, overturned, lay over the floor.' Given the free availability of alcohol, many men were drunk, some even insensible. Bôn-Mat continued:

In the town there was chaos, and it seemed that this decision to leave Lang Son had unsettled everyone. Here one threw artillery pieces into the water, as we had neither coolies or mules to transport them, despite the protestations, the supplications of the commander who promised to have his men drag them. Further on, the brigade chest, which contained as much as six hundred thousand francs which arrived two days ago, was also sacrificed [thrown into the water]. It would have been easy to save this money by giving a few pieces to each man. In the citadel, we opened boxes of cartridges and threw them into the lakes.

Legionnaire John Patrick le Poer, who had taken part in the retreat, suggested reasons for the Chinese victory:

> Now let me try to show you how our defeat came about. But first let me again say that the enemy beat us fairly and squarely in the engagement; that we retreated is good enough proof of that. Well, in the first place, the generals and the other officers firmly believed that the Black Flags and their allies would never be able to stand up against either our rifle fire or our charge.
>
> When the fight was going on we were surprised at the gallant manner in which our foes stood up against us. After a time, when more than once we had hurled them back with the bayonet, we recognised that we were dealing with the most formidable force that we had yet encountered. They gave us bullet for bullet, thrust for thrust. They were good men, and when the bayonets crossed they fought quietly and earnestly, and died without a murmur, almost without a groan. They could never hold out long against us in a charge – they were too light – and, another point to be noted, though the Asiatic will face death by the hands of the executioner with far more stoicism than the European, in the press of battle the white man's enthusiasm is infinitely better than the yellow man's contempt of death. But in the firing they more than held their own, they were more numerous, their ammunition was evidently plentiful, and to tell the plain truth, in spite of our bayonet charges they fairly shot us off the field.

The French managed to fall back towards Hanoi in good order. While overall French control over Tonkin remained decidedly uncertain – with the Vietnamese recruiting new forces to support the Chinese – a dramatic change of events transformed the strategic situation in favour of the French. Instead of following up their advantage, the Chinese proposed a ceasefire in April 1885 that led to the Treaty of Tientsin in which China ceded its claim to Tonkin. This left the French with a free hand to suppress the Black Flags, although they continued to resist the French.

The Legion was left in little doubt that they were faced by redoubtable opponents. In 1891 Frederic Martyn was part of an expedition sent to suppress a Black Flag band, under the command of a celebrated rebel called De Nam, in the Yen-The district. A combined force of legionnaires, locally raised Tonkinese *tirailleurs* and French Marine infantry were ordered to take a Black Flag fort which had repelled two previous attacks:

> It was now two o'clock, and high time that we should be making some headway if we were to achieve any success on that day. The word to advance was no sooner given, then, than we rushed at the job as if we wanted to get it over. We dashed through the stream which stood between us and the redoubt, regardless of the fact that its bottom was thickly set with pointed stakes, but when we had got that far we had to cross a flat piece of ground that was swept by the enemy's fire, and then get through the palisades before we could get to close quarters at all. We got within about a couple of dozen yards of the defences, but the enemy's fire was so hot and well-sustained that we went down like ninepins and had to retire in a hurry and take shelter from the bullets by getting into the stream.
>
> Further reinforcements were sent to us, and we got the order to try again. Back again we rushed, bayonets at the 'charge' and a man toppling over at every step. This time we actually got near enough to make thrusts at the pirates through the loopholes they were firing from. Next to me in this final rush was the lieutenant commanding the half-company of Tonkinese which originally formed the storming party, and as our powder-blackened faces were close together as we ran he shouted gleefully that we looked like winning the race and being first in.
>
> When we had got up, and he was emptying his revolver into the loopholes whilst I was making lunges into them with the bayonet, a bullet coming from my right passed so close to me that it actually tore a hole through the bottom of my jumper. I thought for a moment that I was hit, and then I saw the lieutenant drop to the ground – it afterwards transpired that he was shot through the thighs, and it was probably the bullet that gave me such a narrow squeak that found him.

Unable to make any headway, Martyn organised a stretcher party to take the mortally wounded lieutenant to the rear:

As we lifted the wounded officer onto the stretcher a strange thing happened: a bugle in the pirates' redoubt sounded the 'ceasefire', and a pirate got up on the top of their wall and shouted through a megaphone that they would not open fire again until we had removed all our dead and wounded. It was, in fact, only when we made another movement to assault half an hour afterwards that the pirates opened fire on us and drove us back with heavier loss than ever.

The pirates now began to take the offensive, for other bands had come up and were making a diversion in our rear, and as we seemed to be on the edge of disaster the colonel gave the order for us to retire. Including the officer mentioned above, we lost nine killed and twenty-four seriously wounded in this skirmish.

This was the third attempt we had made on this stronghold, and the pirates had every reason to be satisfied with the result in each case. It must be remembered that these men were really better armed than we were, for the bulk of them, thanks to the enterprise of the English and American gun-runners, were in possession of Spencer repeaters, while the majority of us were only armed with the old Gras rifle, the Lebel rifle at that date only being issued to the Marine Infantry. Further, they were fighting behind fortifications that would have been a credit to any military engineer, and as far as courage was concerned they could clearly claim to be second-to-none in the world. All the same, we felt bitterly humiliated by these successive failures, and we hoped that the next attempt would be made under better considered conditions. Our repulses were due to the fact that the French officers persistently refused to recognise the military ability of these pirate commanders and consistently under-estimated the fighting power of their men.

After this setback the French dragged up sufficient field artillery pieces to smash the fort to pieces. But just before the next French assault, the Black Flags slipped away into the night to fight another day. Martyn concluded: 'I think that the honours of this brief campaign rested with the pirates, for they had stuck to their part as long as any troops in the world could have stuck to it, and had then faded away almost before our eyes without leaving us anything to boast of. We scoured the country in all directions during the next few days, but we could find no trace of them.'

Assaults on forts and outposts were one of the main features of the war in Tonkin. Both sides became adept at defence and attack, developing complex fortifications and equally complex siege techniques. These forts were usually constructed from a combination of stone, bamboo and earth. If a fort could not be taken by a straightforward assault, then siege operations would begin, complete with trench lines, saps, mines and counter-mines. The siege of the French outpost of Tuyen Quang became a classic of Legion endurance, when its predominantly Legion garrison held out against a Chinese army in 1885. The Chinese had completely surrounded the fort by 20 January and began pushing saps towards Tuyen Quang, while digging mines to destroy the walls of the fortifications. Whenever a mine was exploded a Chinese 'Forlorn Hope' would race forward into the breach, only to be repulsed by the defenders.

One such Chinese attack on 22 February was described by Pastor Boissot, the garrison's chaplain:

> The legionaries were not discouraged. In the twinkling of an eye they were on the spot like lions, on that same ground bespattered with the torn flesh and watered by the blood of their brothers. They mowed down the Chinese, hurling back their mass. Once more they taught the enemy to respect the flag of France, for each of these gallant men knew as they rushed forward into the breach that he must conquer or die.

During the attack the Chinese had set off three mines that caused serious French casualties, including Captain Moulinay who had led the Legion counter-attack against the Chinese Forlorn Hope, as Boissot recorded: 'At the sound of the first detonation, Moulinay was on the rampart at the head of his men. Like the rest of his soldiers he was blown up by the second explosion. His body described a monstrous parabola in the air and, as he landed on his feet, his thighs were wrenched out of joint and the bones driven into his groin.

When the French relief column arrived on 3 March, it encountered a scene of utter devastation: shattered walls and trenches littered with the bodies of the dead from both sides.

As part of a legion company defending a fort, John Patrick le Poer, newly promoted to sergeant, was witness to a subterranean encounter. Having failed to capture the fort in a night assault, the Chinese and Black Flag attackers dug a mine towards the fort. Aware of this, French engineers began digging a counter-mine to disrupt the Chinese excavation. Le Poer descended the counter-mine pit out of curiosity:

> While I was holding a whispered conversation with a sub-officer [senior NCO] of engineers, a cry from a worker drew our attention. In a moment the engineer saw what had happened, and cried out: '*Les Chinois, les Chinois!* [The Chinese! The Chinese!]'
>
> As a matter of fact, the Chinese miners and we were separated only a by a thin wall of loose earth; a blow or two struck by I know not which party tumbled this down, and we were all mixed up together, French and Chinese, in the tunnel. All struck out at random. I drew my bayonet, which, of course, I always wore, and dashed the point in the face of a yellow man from outside.
>
> The lamps were extinguished in the struggle that ensued; we were all striking blindly about with pickaxe, shovel and bayonet; no man knew who might receive his blow. It was a horrible time. In the darkness I heard oaths and groans; I shoved forward my bayonet, it met something soft; I drew it back and lunged again; again it met the soft, yielding substance, or perhaps the blow was wasted on empty air. If I struggled forward, I tripped over a body; if I went back, surely a miner would knock my brains out with his pick. This went on for a short space that seemed an eternity. At last hurrying footsteps and shouts of encouragement and a welcoming glean of lights told of the arrival of aid. When our comrades came up, we found that all the Chinese able to flee had fled; fourteen of them, however, and eight or nine men of ours, were lying pressed against and on top of one another in a narrow space. All, dead and wounded alike, were carried out; the place was blocked up at once, and the counter-mine that had taken so much time and work on our part was filled in.

As well as being involved in formal siege operations, the French were engaged in counter-insurgency warfare, attempting to pin down and destroy the Black Flag bands in their jungle and mountain hideouts. This was no easy task, given the skill and determination of the Black Flags, who knew the terrain far better than the French. The three Legion battalions were in the forefront of these operations, sending columns deep into the jungle. This was back-breaking work, often with little or nothing to show for it. German volunteer Jean Pfirmann expressed the legionnaires' frustration: 'Despite our marches and counter-marches along the river or in the forest, the bandits continued to terrorise and pillage the poor natives in the region. And often, after many nights spent in the unhealthy and humid forest, we had to return to the fold without having seen the shadow of a Chinese.'

The Black Flags certainly terrorised the local population, exhorting taxes and ruthlessly punishing collaboration. Frederic Martyn recorded the destruction of a village that had apparently provided intelligence to the French:

> When we were still some considerable distance from it we came across two rows of human heads, one row on either side of the road, stuck up as if they had been placed there as a sort of mocking guard of honour. On the faces of all there were looks of agony that caused those heads to haunt me for many a long day. Farther along, on the slopes of the little hill, some distance from the village, the ground was strewn with dismembered, disembowelled, and unmentionably mutilated trunks of men and women, and arms and legs which looked as if they had been literally torn from the bodies from which they belonged. This human debris bore marks of fiendish torture which cannot even be indicated in print, and the general effect was so indescribably nauseating that several of us strong men were made physically sick by it.

Any legionnaires captured by the Black Flags could also expect a slow and painful end, and the threat of such a death kept many men from dropping out of a column deep in enemy territory. Officers did their best to encourage stragglers but if a man refused or was unable to march, his rifle and ammunition were taken from him and he was left to his fate. On some occasions the ordinary legionnaires took things into their own hands. Antoine Sylvère described the 'assistance' given to those unable to keep going:

> The worst thing about Tonkin was that the Legion organised light columns; nothing but a canteen, a haversack and some bullets. There were no wagons, so if there were sick or wounded it was awful. It was often in the worst spots where, if we left a chap, we would find him butchered by the pirates who came to play at cutting him up or to stick a pug up his ass until it came out his shoulder. Now we didn't approve of that. So when there was one who was on his last legs, we gave him a drink of *tafia* and then we said: 'Now it's your last mouthful.' We would stick the barrel in his mouth and pull the trigger. Then we could go off with a clear conscience.

Le Poer nearly fell victim to the Black Flags, when, through illness, he began to drop out of the line. His comrades helped him, carrying his rifle and kit, so that Le Poer managed to reach comparative safety. Another man from Lorraine, similarly ill, was unable to keep up and was left behind unarmed. On a subsequent march, the legionnaires trooped past the spot where the Lorrainer was abandoned, only to find his hideously mutilated body.

Le Poer and his comrades swore revenge: 'All that day we spoke of nothing but the horrible sight we had seen in the morning. We were angry; we made resolutions to take sharp and speedy vengeance for the death of our comrade and the indignity shown his corpse.'

When they next encountered a Black Flag band the legionnaires butchered them all. 'We took a bloody vengeance on the barbarians,' wrote Le Poer, 'such a vengeance as even in the Legion was spoken of with bated breath.'

Even in less highly charged situations, captured Black Flags could expect little mercy. George Manington was assigned to a 'snatch squad' to capture a Black Flag leader and his five lieutenants. The action was a success, and while the rebel leader was held for further questioning his comrades – after basic interrogations – were condemned to death. Manington described their execution:

Behind the little procession formed by the condemned men stalked the executioner, a tall native dressed in a red embroidered vest and black silk pantaloons. Upon his shoulder he carried a heavy curved sword, about 3 feet long, and a good deal broader at the end than near the handle.

The five rebels, their hands tied behind them, walked to their death without any tremor or hesitation. Chatting together merrily, they threw curious glances at their surroundings, and expectorated from time to time, with evident unconcern, the red juice of the betal-leaf they were chewing. They were lined up, separated about four paces from the other, on the opposite side of the square occupied by the authorities facing them.

As each of the prisoners reached the place assigned to him, a native soldier unbuttoned and turned back the collar of the rebel's vest; then one after the other, they knelt upon the grass, taking every care that their position should be as comfortable as circumstances would allow.

The sentence having been read aloud to the assembled natives, the executioner, after thrusting a finger into his mouth, traced a wet line of red betel juice across the back of the neck of the first of his victims, about half an inch above the last of the big vertebra. Stepping back a pace, he swung aloft his heavy sword with both hands. It poised a second in the air; there was a glitter in the bright sunlight as it descended; then a swishing sound and a dull thud. The head of the first rebel, detached with a single blow, fell on the ground and rolled over once.

From the severed neck a rich red stream shot out quite 6 ft over the grass; the body rocked once and subsided gently. Bending over it, the executioner touched the open arteries, and smeared a little of the warm blood over his own lips as a charm against any evil influence from the spirit of the departed.

The other prisoners, who had watched the execution of their comrade with evident interest, made flattering remarks concerning the skill of the swordsman. The next to die smiled, and prepared himself calmly, stretching his neck as far forward as it was possible for him to do without losing his balance. I felt deadly sick, and could not bring myself to watch the succeeding decapitations, which were carried out with similar skill and expedition.

The bodies of the condemned were handed over to their families, but their heads, attached to the top of a tall bamboo pole, were exposed at the entrance to the fort as an example to all rebels.

By the mid-1890s the tide of the conflict began to turn against the Black Flags. Support from Chinese sources was diminishing and the relentless pressure of the French was taking its toll. According to Manington, not only was the Legion becoming increasingly proficient in counter-insurgency operations, its soldiers actually enjoyed this form of warfare:

> At this time, thanks to the experience they had acquired during the past year and a half, and also to their having been employed during the last three months in continually chasing the enemy from place to place, through the wildest country it is possible to imagine, the men of my company had become splendid jungle fighters. Each of them was now not only a hardened, almost fever-proof soldier, but also a good shot and an efficient scout, ever on the alert to notice each sign by the way, to catch each sound in the air, and understand their meaning.
>
> Conversant with the enemy's methods of fighting in the dark glades and sombre thickets of his favourite haunts, the legionnaires and their officers had learnt to trust no longer to the paths, but to advance swiftly yet silently through the undergrowth, taking advantage of every bit of cover, and making of each tree in the wood, each rise in the ground, a temporary rampart.
>
> Encouraged by their officers, the men took delight in this new sport, which seemed more like a hunt, in which the quarry was a man, than regular warfare. The fact of their not being continually in touch with their officers and NCOs, and having consequently to depend sometimes on their own resources, developed their individual initiative and self-reliance; whilst the novelty of the situation gave full scope to their courage and love of adventure. Perhaps with troops possessing less stamina and morale, even these short periods of independent action would have been dangerous, but with these well-disciplined and seasoned soldiers of the Legion this new method of attack seemed to increase the zeal and self-confidence of the men.

In Tonkin the Legion had once again demonstrated its skills in colonial warfare, consolidating the fearsome reputation gained in Africa. But in 1914 the Legion would be called upon to fight a first-rate European adversary, and the Legion's critics wondered whether it would be able to adapt to the conditions of modern warfare in Europe.

CHAPTER 10

THE FIRST WORLD WAR: DEATH IN THE TRENCHES

Although it was a colonial force whose military remit was to fight outside metropolitan France, there could be no possibility of the Legion standing on the sidelines as German forces advanced on Paris in August 1914. The large contingent of Germans within the Legion posed a potentially awkward question of divided loyalties, but it was one which caused few problems in practice. Many German and Austrian legionnaires put the time-honoured concept of '*Legio Patria Nostra*' above national considerations and fought with distinction in the trenches. Those with qualms about fighting against the Fatherland were left to garrison the turbulent frontier regions of eastern Morocco, where – safely out of harm's way – they could discreetly cheer on the Imperial German Army.

As Legion units were assembled for transportation across the Mediterranean from North Africa, the military authorities in France encountered a sudden and massive influx of foreign volunteers offering their services in the defence of France. As early as the 1 August a strident call to arms had been published in the Parisian papers, concluding: 'Foreigners, friends of France, who during their sojourn in France have learned to cherish her as a second country, feel an imperious need to offer her their arms.' Among the signatories was the Swiss-born writer Blaise Cendrars, who would have an arm amputated while fighting for the Legion in 1915.

THE FIRST WORLD WAR: DEATH IN THE TRENCHES

Idealism stimulated the volunteers into action. The young American poet Alan Seeger – author of the prophetic 'A Rendezvous with Death' – noted in his diary that he did not take up arms 'out of any hatred against Germany or the Germans, but purely out of love for France'.

Fellow American William Thaw explained his reasons for joining the Legion in a letter to his parents:

> I am going to take a part, however small, in the greatest, and probably last, war in history, which has apparently developed into a fight of civilization against barbarism. That last reason may sound a bit grand and dramatic, but you would quite agree if you could hear the tales of French, Belgian and English soldiers who have come back here from the front.

As well as altruism, a love of adventure was a powerful motivating force. Another American, Edward Morlae, summed up the prevailing mood when he wrote, 'Some of us who volunteered for the war loved fighting and some of us loved France. I was fond of both.'

For the first time in its history, young Americans flocked to the Legion's colours; many were well educated and would provide valuable testimony of their time in the trenches.

At least 40,000 foreigners volunteered for military service. The French were quite unprepared for this, and as only French nationals were eligible to serve in the French Army in 1914, the foreigners were shunted off into the Legion. Although the Legion was used to a mix of nationalities, the wide social range of the new volunteers came as a bewildering surprise. For their part, the volunteers were intrigued by the heterodoxy of their fellow recruits. Englishman J. Woodhall Marshall, who subsequently transferred to the British Army, described his comrades in a note to his mother:

> The Legion is the strangest thing ever thought up in the mind of man. In my room, which is comfortable, there is myself, an Irishman; my next neighbour is an American, and the other inhabitants include an ex-officer of [a] So. American Republic, who came specially over from South America for the war, and is my greatest friend, a Dutch solicitor, a Russian Jew, three

Cossacks, two Italians, a student from a Russian university, an Englishman who has always been resident in Paris and can hardly speak English, a Spaniard, and other mysterious individuals whose identity is absolutely hid.

Shoehorning so many different types into such a tradition-bound organisation as the Foreign Legion was almost certainly a mistake. Their integration with the hard-bitten, cynical *anciens* shipped over to France from North Africa immediately caused problems. Kosta Todorov, a newly arrived Bulgarian volunteer, was soon made aware of the distinctions between the old and new legionnaires:

Sergeant-Major Pontacier, a well educated man but a hopeless drunkard, teased us contemptuously, drunk or sober. 'Fools! So you've come to fight for freedom and civilization? Words, empty words!'

'Then why are you here?' I asked him. 'Orders, of course. We're professional soldiers. We don't give a damn what we fight for! It's our job. We've nothing else in life. No families, no ideals, no loves!'

Others, like Rouanet, who was tattooed all over with obscene pictures, considered us rank amateurs who had no right to the glorious name of Legionnaire. To earn that, one had to live through the gruelling African school of desert outposts, hunger, and thirst.

They all drank heavily, talked their own colonial slang, knew the field-service regulations by heart, were crack marksmen, bore up easily under prolonged marches, and had as much contempt for other regiments as for civilians. On their pre-Legion past they kept silent, but their military records could be read from their medals – China, Indo-China, Madagascar, Morocco . . .

Alan Seeger remained a fervent supporter of both the French cause and the Legion right up until his death on the Somme in 1916. Yet he criticised the treatment of his fellow 1914 volunteers: 'A majority of men who engaged voluntarily were thrown in a regiment made up almost entirely of the dregs of society, refugees from justice and roughs, commanded by *sous-officiers* who treated us all without distinction in the same manner that they habituated to treat their unruly brood in Africa.'

Tensions between American volunteers and the African veterans exploded into violence in March 1915, and led to the death of René Phélizot, a Chicago-born big-game hunter. The incident was described by American volunteer, Paul Rockwell:

> Phélizot and some of the Americans sat in a courtyard drinking coffee, when there appeared two veteran legionnaires belonging to the machine-gun company, old soldiers so bronzed by years of hot African sunshine and cold desert winds that race and nationality could only be guessed at. The men began to make scathing comments on the volunteers and about the Americans in particular. Each proclaimed that he could beat single-handed and in fair fight any seven of the Americans.
>
> Phélizot immediately offered to fight both men; his offer was quickly accepted, and the scrap began. It started off well for the American, who was a good boxer; he knocked down one adversary, and was severely punishing the other, when a third Legionnaire, a chum of the first two, arrived. Seeing that things were going badly for his comrades, he swung his large *bidon* (water bottle), heavy with two litres of wine, and struck Phélizot a crashing blow on the head. The latter fell unconscious; the other Americans and more veterans of the machine-gun section joined the fray, and only the arrival of a captain and several non-coms prevented blood from flowing freely.

Provided with only the most cursory medical treatment, Phélizot was sent back into line by an unsympathetic doctor. Three days later he was dead: a fractured skull had become infected with tetanus. Rockwell described the American response:

> When news of Phélizot's death reached the front, there was a pitched battle between the Americans and the veterans of the machine-gun section. Chakoff knocked down the man who struck the fatal blow, and was literally kicking him to death, when a military guard appeared, separated all the combatants, and placed both sections under arrest. Phélizot's slayer disappeared from the

Legion: it was said that he had been sentenced to the penitentiary regiment in Africa.

Before going to the front, the new recruits were given rudimentary training, and, for the most part, assigned to a quiet sector of the line (although a battalion of Italian legionnaires had been flung into combat in December 1914 and been badly mauled). Seeger believed that the Legion's assignment to quiet sectors exacerbated friction between the veterans and new volunteers. He wrote that as the Legion had not fought a major battle 'it consequently never established the bond of common dangers shared, common sufferings borne, common glories achieved, which knits men together in real comradeship'.

For the many free spirits who had joined the Legion for glory in a great pitched battle, the wretched monotony of trench warfare was hard to bear. In November 1914, Yale graduate William Thaw complained:

> War is wretched and quite uninteresting. Wish I were back dodging street cars on Broadway for excitement. Am that tired of being shot at! Got hit in the cap and bayonet – Do you mind? Have been in the trenches now nearly six weeks. Haven't washed for twenty days. Expect to get a ten days' rest after another two weeks.

Thaw, and a small but growing band of other dare-devil Americans, managed to transfer out of the Legion and join French aviation units, the most famous being the *Lafayette Escadrille*. The remainder had to endure life in the trenches.

The trench system that replaced the open fighting of the initial phase of the war was not long in coming, as David W. King observed: 'It was only November 1914, but we realised that trench warfare had come to stay. In two months the rifle pits of the Marne had spread into a complicated system of trenches, dug-outs, machine-gun emplacements. Finally a vast web of barbed wire was spun along the whole front.'

Conditions for the legionnaires in the line were poor, especially as winter set in. Before leaving for the aviation service, Thaw had written:

Early in November the very cold weather began with five inches of snow. This added a new hardship, for some of the boys got frozen feet and suffered very much. We did not have any medicines, only opium pills and iodine. No matter what your ailment was, you got one or the other. We were pretty short on food in these days, too. I do not know the reason for this, but during November I can tell you we did not overeat.

Alan Seeger also remembered the unpleasant situation current in November in a diary entry for 10 November:

Fifth Day of our second period in the trenches. Five days and nights of pure misery. It is a miserable life to be condemned to, shivering in these wretched holes, in the cold and the dirt and the semi-darkness. It is impossible to cross the open spaces in daylight, so that we can only get food by going to the kitchens before dawn and after sun-down. The increasing cold will make this kind of existence almost insupportable, with its accompaniments of vermin and dysentery.

But less than a month later, Seeger was relieved to find that front-line conditions had changed for the better:

Back in the same trenches. Matters have improved here. A well-to-do *fermier* [farmer] sends a *fourgon* [luggage van] in to Fismes every few days, which brings back abundant provisions that the soldiers can buy at moderate prices. In this way we were able to fill our sacks with chocolate and canned stuff in sufficient quantity to tide us over the six days. The trenches have been much improved by the last section. The roof has been made water-tight, more barbed wire has been strung in front, and the earth out of the deepened ditches has been piled around the walls, making the dugout much warmer. By stuffing straw into the *créneaux* [loopholes] we are now allowed to make fires at night, so we can heat our *gamelles* [mess tins] and lie down to sleep in a warm atmosphere.

In a world reduced to the essentials, shelter and food were crucial to the maintenance of morale. Seeger described the arrival of the day's provisions during the first winter in the trenches:

Before daylight it arrives and distribution takes place. Great loaves of bread are handed down the line; each man takes his ration of half a loaf. There is one box of sardines for each two men. A cup of coffee, a small piece of cheese, a bar of chocolate must last all day, until darkness permits another squad to leave the trench to go down for the evening soup. After food comes mail. Too much praise cannot be given the government for handling the soldiers' mail so well. There are daily distributions on the firing line.

The Germans on the other side of no man's land were rarely seen, although their presence was felt in the form of artillery, machine-gun and rifle fire. The men even became used to it, as Victor Chapman observed in a letter home:

The 'tap, tap' of the Bosches' bullets on the face of my *abri* [shelter] in the evening affect me as much as the lap, lap of little waves against the side of my sail boat. The rumble of distant artillery passes unnoticed, and but mild curiosity is aroused by the chug-chug-chug of a machine gun as of a steam-motor boat rounding a bend. The bursting of shells nearby, of course, attracts comment – more because it varies the monotony than anything else. The shells that fall on top of us do, to be sure, cause almost a sensation, not of danger so much as the fact that something is happening.

Chapman's deliberately insouciant style disguised the fact that accurate German shellfire could be deadly. David King described one such instance:

We found ourselves in a sort of quarry with well-made dug-outs built into the chalk above it. The machine-gun section was, naturally, installed in the strongest dug-out – machine guns cost money. We saw what an H. E. [High Explosive] 105 mm could do when a lucky shot passed through the loophole and burst clean inside. Our squad rushed in to help the survivors – there were none – so we set to work to clear up the mess. I was struck by the practical coolness of an old legionnaire who was transferring a mess of blood and brains from the floor into a kepi with the late owner's spoon.

THE FIRST WORLD WAR: DEATH IN THE TRENCHES

When trenches were close the danger from bullets and grenades could be as great as that from artillery. During the desperate fighting around Verdun in early 1916, King wrote:

> One of our listening-posts was only eight yards from a German outpost. The parapet was made up of German and French dead, and the shallow communications trench leading to it was strewn with Germans. The ground above it was swept by machine-gun fire day and night, so that the relieving guard scuttled along it bent almost double – no time to throw the corpses over the side. A huge Prussian grenadier half way along it we dubbed 'Croaking Conrad', for if one stepped on his middle he still uttered a guttural frog-like croak.

Night patrols in no-man's-land and raids into the enemy front line were a feature of trench warfare. Dreaded by many, they gave the adventurous a chance to make a name for themselves. Bulgarian volunteer Kosta Todorov certainly believed that the 'only way to distinguish one's self was through night patrol raids'. He described one such raid to capture a prisoner near Craonnelle, a village below the German lines running along the Chemin des Dames ridge:

> Our positions were north-east of the village, near an apple orchard. The Germans occupied the heights about a half-mile away. Between the two lines stood haystacks, like pyramids. The seeds had fallen and rotted but the hay made good beds for the dug-outs. At night, groups of soldiers of both sides would creep out to the stacks and drag sheaves back to their lines. At first this was done cautiously, then both sides became careless. I went to Captain Tortel. 'Sir,' I said, 'do you consider it right for the Germans to enjoy French property with impunity?'
>
> 'Of course not. What's up?'
>
> 'I'd like to set a trap near our haystacks.' He smiled. 'Not a bad idea. You might try it.'
>
> That evening I chose three men, Dufour and those mighty sleepers, Sapozhkov and Todoskov. A cold, penetrating fog had settled over the countryside, and searchlights and rockets failed to pierce its thick, white wall. Such nights were best for raids,

but it was also easy to get lost and stumble into the hands of the enemy. We should have to go very near his lines, for the Germans naturally took their sheaves from the ricks nearest them.

Our plan was, if there were many Germans, to shoot and dash back to our lines. If there were only a few, we would try to kill or capture them. One of them would have to climb onto the top of the rick. Dufour was to pick him off. One had to be below to catch the sheaves, and a third to stand guard. Todoskov and Sapozhkov were to seize the Boche who caught the sheaves. I was to take care of the sentry.

That night and the next we saw no one, although we lay in wait for hours on the damp ground. On the third, we saw three figures through the fog and heard the sound of German voices. We lay motionless, exerting every ounce of willpower not to shoot. Everything happened as we had foreseen. One German climbed aloft; a second stood below to catch the sheaves, with a heavy rope to bind them. These two dropped their guns. Only the sentry remained armed, but he smoked carelessly.

Dufour had not boasted in vain that he never missed his man. He fired twice. The figure atop the haystack vanished. I aimed at the sentry, but apparently missed him, for he dropped his gun and disappeared into the fog. Meanwhile Todoskov and Sapozhkov pinioned the third German so firmly to the ground that he could hardly breathe. They bound him with his own rope and dragged him off as if he were a sack. From the German lines came a volley, but in a few minutes we were back in our trenches with our prisoner and three rifles.

Captain Tortel and Lieutenant Leseur awaited us in the flour mill which served as the captain's headquarters, Tortel's eyes gleamed merrily through his spectacles as he poured wine. Leseur hugged us. We untied the prisoner, a Bavarian trembling with fright. When Tortel handed him a cup of wine he quickly calmed down and told Leseur, who spoke German, everything he knew about his detachment, the advance posts, the disposition of troops, and the mood of the soldiers.

The more aggressive German units were also enthusiastic trench raiders, and in January 1915 the Legion became a victim of an enemy foray. After spending Christmas and New Year in reserve, Kiffin Rockwell and his contingent of Americans returned to the front line on 4 January 1916. The Legion's defensive position included a brick wall. One part of this wall had been smashed down by a German shell and been hastily repaired with a wooden door, against which was a ladder for observation purposes. While on night guard duty, Rockwell and his fellow sentry, Alan Seeger, came under attack: a grenade fell at their feet, which Rockwell adroitly picked up and cast aside. Seeger then went to summon the section leader, Corporal Weidemann. Rockwell described the ensuing disaster:

> Just as he and the corporal came running up, the corporal called, '*Garde a vous* [Watch-out], *Rockwell*,' and another grenade fell at my feet. I jumped over the ladder towards the corporal and as I reached his side the bomb exploded. We both called out '*Aux armes!* [To arms!]' We had no more than done this, when the door gave in and a raiding party entered the side of the opening. The corporal and I were both in an open position at their mercy, so we turned and jumped towards cover. I was about ten feet when rifles flashed and I dropped to the ground. When I dropped, the corporal fell beside me and I knew by his fall that he was dead. I crouched and ran, the bullets whizzing by me, but I made it to the woods.

Rockwell and the other legionnaires at the post were pinned down by the Germans' rifle fire:

> While they had us in this position, some kept firing while others ran down to the corporal, dragged his body up towards the door, cut off his equipment and coat and took them and his gun, broke his body up with the butts of their rifles and then got away without a shot being fired on our side.
>
> Corporal Weidemann was a full-blooded German, but he had been in the Legion for fifteen years. He was ignorant but honest, impartial and afraid of nothing. In my mind he was the best of all the old legionnaires.
>
> The whole thing impressed us more like a murder than warfare. The Germans had no military point to gain by doing what they

did. It was done as an act of individualism with a desire to kill. The top of poor Weidemann's head was knocked off, after he was killed, by the butt of a rifle.

About two hours after all this happened, there came from the German trenches the most diabolical yell of derision I ever heard. It was mocking Weidemann's last words, his call '*Aux armes!*', and it almost froze the blood to hear it. Up until that moment I had never felt a real desire to kill a German. Since then I have had nothing but murder in my heart.

Alan Seeger also heard the German taunting:

> Only about midnight, from far up on the hillside, a diabolical cry came down, more like an animal's than a man's, a blood-curdling yell of mockery and exultation.
>
> In that cry all the evolution of centuries was levelled. I seemed to hear the yell of warriors from the Stone Age over his fallen enemy. It was one of those antidotes to civilization of which this war can offer so many to the searcher after extraordinary sensations.

While raids were part and parcel of trench warfare, the main function of the Legion was to act as a corps of shock troops in the succession of offensives launched by the French against the German lines. As part of the famed Moroccan Division, all four battalions of the 1st Foreign Legion Regiment were involved in the bloody battle for Vimy Ridge in May 1915. Kiffin Rockwell recounted the initial phase of the battle in a letter home:

> In a few minutes it began to sound as if all hell had broken loose, when our artillery all along the line opened up on the Germans. The damnedest bombardment imaginable was kept up until ten o'clock. Along the whole German line, you could see nothing but smoke and debris. At ten o'clock, I saw the finest sight I have ever seen. It was the men from the *Premier Étranger* crawling out of our trenches, with their bayonets glittering against the sun, and advancing on the Bosches. There was not a sign of hesitation. They were falling fast, but as fast as men fell, it seemed as if new men sprang up out of the ground to take their places. One second it

looked as if an entire section had fallen by one sweep of a machine gun. In a few moments a second line of men crawled out of our trenches; and at seven minutes past ten, our captain called '*En avant!* [Forward!]' and we went dashing down the trenches with the German artillery giving us hell as we went.

Rockwell was shortly afterwards hit by a bullet in the thigh, ending his role in the battle. Blaise Cendrars was leader of a small commando unit that had gained the crest of the ridge. He described how the battle continued:

My detachment made a half about-turn, for we were designated as 'moppers-up' in the trenches, and, while the rest of the 6th Company busied themselves with the help of small groups of men who came to lend a hand with spades, pickaxes and rifles, we went out to clean up the fourth German line, wipe out any pockets of resistance and blow up the blockhouses, around which the fighting was ferocious.

I was marching at the head carrying, in special kitbags, two melanite bombs weighing ten pounds each. I was also armed with a parabellum [automatic pistol] and a saw-edged knife. The best shots, Garnero (with a hare still dangling from his belt) and Segouana, both ready to fire and with a sack of grenades at their waists, escorted me on right and left. Farther off, other men, armed like myself and also escorted by first-rate marksmen, deployed themselves fanwise. We advanced cautiously, rifles at the ready, cutting through the barbed wire, tossing grenades into every foxhole, plunging into shell craters, crawling on all fours to approach and blow up a blockhouse, snuffing out a machine-gun nest, gaining one yard of ground, then another, filing through a collapsing trench or advancing fifty yards in the open, jumping feet first into the end of a trench, killing, re-killing the Krauts, driving prisoners ahead of us, going down to the bottom of saps to clear out the mines, climbing out into the daylight once more, losing our way, calling each other, rediscovering each other, drunk with joy and fury. It was a jolly massacre.

We were black, filthy, torn, dishevelled, most of us bare-headed and every one with scars and scratches, and arms that were almost too tired to hold their weapons. We laughed. The Jerries were also crazy with excitement, but, when we sent our prisoners behind the lines, they did not need to be told twice, preferring to run all the hazards of crossing the open battlefield with their hands in the air rather than remain another minute in the hands of the dreaded Foreign Legion. '*Die Fremdenlegion!*' We put the fear of God into them. And, in truth, we were not a pretty sight.

The advance of the Moroccan Division had exceeded the expectations of the French, and there were insufficient reserves to support them in the face of determined German counter-attacks. Paul Rockwell noted: 'With rage in their hearts, the sadly decimated battalions of Legionnaires, Zouaves and *tirailleurs* were forced to fall back, and retained only four kilometres of their dearly bought terrain.'

The Legion had little respite from battle during 1915. Units were involved in heavy fighting during the Artois offensive in May and June, while the 1st and 2nd Regiments were thrown into the maelstrom of the Champagne offensive in September 1915. General Joffre and the French High Command hoped that the attack in Champagne – supported by an Anglo-French assault further north in Artois – would achieve the decisive breakthrough. Alan Seeger confidently wrote how the 'chances for success are good. It will be a battle without precedent in history.'

The legionnaires marching up to the front in early September could see the massive military build-up. In a letter home, Edward Genet described the planning:

> The routes were jammed to overflowing with huge auto-trucks, wagons and automobiles carrying food and other supplies to the troops and tearing back to reload. Day and night they ran practically without light, as much as possible, for security against hostile aero scouts and distant batteries. It was thrilling to see those huge, powerful trucks rushing along the roads at almost breakneck speed – dark terrible symbols of the serious business before us. It seemed uncanny, weird, unnatural. The large bodies of troops were always moved at night and kept well under cover

as much as possible in the daytime. Invisibility at all times of modern warfare is of the utmost necessity – in concentrating for the actual attack as much as in the actual fighting.

David King was also impressed by the preparations for the coming offensive:

Every day officers went up the line to learn the trenches, and returning explained with plans scratched on the ground. 'A' was our first line, 'B', 'C' and 'D' evacuation trenches, and God help the man who was caught in one without a wound. Specialists were trained. Grenadiers with the new contact grenades, whose business it was to put the machine guns out; *Nettoyeurs des Tranchées* with wicked-looking trench daggers, to mop up after the first wave had swept over – there was to be no repetition of Arras. And still more troops and guns rolled up.

Our preparatory bombardment began. God! What a prelude! It crashed out on a split second, and for three days thundered relentlessly on. In the face of this, how childish our new gas masks and steel helmets . . .

The bombardment increased in intensity during the hours preceding the offensive on the morning of 25 September. On the Legion's sector, the first wave of attack would be made by the Colonial Division with the Moroccan Division – containing the Legion – following closely behind. Genet described the final stages of the artillery barrage:

The bombardment of the German trenches before the charge was terrific. The German line looked like a wall of fire and hellish flames from the bursting shells. The batteries of both sides made the world sound like Hades let loose. From the sharp crack of the famous 75's to the deep roar of the aerial torpedoes it was an incessant Bedlam. About nine o'clock a French aeroplane flew right over our first line, circled around and back. It was the signal for the French batteries to cease shelling the German front line and the Colonials to charge.

Edward Morlae prepared to go over the top, after a breakfast of hot coffee, sardines, cheese and bread. He wrote:

> At 9 the command passed down the line, 'Every man ready!' Up went the knapsack on every man's back, and, rifle in hand, we filed along the trench. Waiting seemed an eternity. As we stood there a shell burst close to our left. A moment later it was whispered along the line that an *adjutant* and five men had gone down.
>
> What were we waiting for? I glanced at my watch. It was 9.15 exactly. The Germans evidently had the range. Two more shells burst close to the same place. We inquired curiously who was hit this time. Our response was two whistles. That was our signal. I felt my jaws clenching, and the man next to me looked white. It was only for a second. Then every one of us rushed at the trench wall, each and every man struggling to be the first out of the trench. In a moment we had clambered up and out. We slid over the parapet, wormed our way through gaps in the wire, formed in line, and at the command, moved forward at march-step straight towards the German line.
>
> The world became a roaring hell. Shell after shell burst near us, sometime right among us; and as we moved forward at the double-quick men fell right and left. We could hear the subdued rattling of the *mitrailleuses* [machine guns] and the roar of volley fire, but above it all, I could hear with almost startling directness the words of the captain, shouting in his clear high voice, '*En avant! Vive la France!*'

Infantry-artillery cooperation was still in its infancy in 1915, but the slowly advancing curtain barrage seemed to work well, protecting the legionnaires as they crossed no-man's-land. Morlae continued his account of the battle:

> As we marched forward to our goal, huge geysers of dust spouted into the air, rising behind our backs from the rows of '75's' supporting us. In front the fire-curtain outlined the whole length of the enemy's line with a neatness and accuracy that struck me with wonder, as the flames burst through the pall

of smoke and dust around us. Above, all was blackness, but at its lower edge the curtain was fringed with red and green flames, marking the explosion of the shells directly over the ditch and parapet in front of us. The low-flying clouds mingled with the smoke-curtain, so that the whole brightness of the day was obscured. Out of the blackness fell a trickling rain of pieces of metal, lumps of earth, knapsacks, rifles, cartridges and fragments of human flesh. The effect was terrific. I almost braced myself against the rocking of the earth, like a sailor's instinctive gait in stormy weather.

Across the wall of our own fire poured shell after shell from the enemy, tearing through our ranks. From overhead the shrapnel seemed to come down in sheets, and from the stinking, blinding curtain came volleys of steel-jacketed bullets, their whine unheard and their effect almost unnoticed.

All of a sudden our own fire-curtain lifted. In a moment it had ceased to bar our way and jumped like a living thing to the next line of the enemy. We could see the trenches in front of us now, quite clear of fire, but flattened almost beyond recognition. The defenders were either killed or demoralized. Calmly, almost stupidly, we parried or thrust at those who barred our way.

Many accounts of the battle spoke of the demoralised Germans in the front-line trenches, only too happy to surrender to the Legion. Alan Seeger provided this description: 'Opposite us, all was over, and the herds of prisoners were being already led down as we went up. We cheered more in triumph than in hate, but the poor devils, terror-stricken, held up their hands, begged for their lives, cried "*Kamerad; Bon Français*," even "*Vive la France*".

The Germans were right to be scared. Men who surrendered as they were overrun were often despatched with a bayonet and the comment, 'Too late, chum.' Former legionnaire and German trench-fighter Ernst Jünger explained: 'The defending force, after driving their bullets into the attacking one at five paces' distance must take the consequences. A man cannot change his feelings again during the last rush of blood before his eyes. He does not want to take prisoners but to kill.'

It is likely that the German defenders did not put up much

resistance, but, according to Kosta Todorov, the legionnaires were still surprisingly restrained:

> Pale, frightened German soldiers begin to emerge, arms upraised. Many of them, fair-haired young recruits, fall on their knees and clasp our legs. 'Kamerad' they cry, 'Kamerad!'
>
> No one hurts them. Corporal Fournier, a native of German-occupied Tournai, has learned through the Red Cross in Geneva that one of his children died of hunger. He has sworn that at the first opportunity he will kill ten Germans. Now they are before him, and I watch to see that he doesn't carry out his threat. Instead, he takes out bread and gives it to the prisoners. He looks at me guiltily. 'They're swine, of course, but hungry,' he mumbles.
>
> Many soldiers follow his example. Even Dufour sacrifices a cup of his precious wine. Realizing that they are out of danger, the young Germans weep – a reaction natural enough after three days of incessant bombardment.

The extensive German trench system had to be methodically cleared and the remaining pockets of resistance eliminated. The legionnaires were impressed at the size and scale of the German underground defences, among them Edward Morlae:

> As we swept on, the trench-clearers entered the trench behind and began setting things to rights. Far down, six to eight metres below the surface, they found an underground city. Long tunnels with chambers opening to right and left, bedrooms furnished with bedsteads, washstands, tables and chairs, elaborate mess-rooms, some fitted with pianos and phonographs. There were kitchens, too, and even bathrooms. So complex was this labyrinth that three days after the attack Germans were found stowed away in the lateral galleries. The passages were choked with dead. Hundreds of Germans who had survived the bombardment were torn to pieces deep beneath the ground by French hand-grenades, and buried where they lay.

The onset of rain made life even more miserable for the legionnaires as they consolidated their positions in readiness for the assault on the second objective around the heavily fortified Navarin Farm position. All the while, they were subjected to heavy and increasingly accurate German artillery fire. While the French had been successful in capturing the German first line, the stronger and better concealed second line held firm. David King recalled the devastating German barrage as they advanced towards their jumping-off point on 28 September:

> The Germans spotted us and turned everything loose, but the columns pushed on. Shells burst full in the middle of sections, annihilating the centre. The remaining men picked themselves up and joined sections to the left and right; the march continued.
>
> Horrible apparitions crawled out of shell holes and looked at us as we went by. A thing with no face – only four caverns in a red mask, where eyes, nose and mouth had been – mooed and gibbered at us as it heard the clink of accoutrements passing. Some strong-minded humanitarian put a bullet into it as we filed by.
>
> We reached a wood. It was like a scene from the underworld – ghostly columns picking their way through shell-torn trees in the smoke and fog of high explosives. A shell burst in the section on the right – it looked like a football scrimmage writhing in agony – a swirl of men and smoke. Shells cracked over our heads – shells tore up the ground in front of us. We took the last gap at the run.
>
> All that was left of us joined the remnants of three previous attacks. We crouched at the edge of the Bois de Sabots and peered through the underbrush. Oh Christ! . . . Two battalions of the Legion and one of *Chasseurs Alpins* were stretched out in skirmish order in front of the German barbed wire. The alignment was perfect – the men were dead.
>
> We felt pretty sober till Ole Neilson began to sing 'Ragtime Cowboy Joe'. The section took it up with a roar, convulsed with mirth at the line, 'No one but a lunatic would start a war.' The other legionnaires grinned, but the *Chasseurs Alpins* looked at each other in horror, convinced we had gone mad.

The battalion commander, *Commandant* [Major] Rosé, crept forward to assess the situation prior to following his order to assault the position. King continued the story:

The place was stiff with machine guns and the barbed wire was not touched. A brief report to the general, demanding guns to blow away the wire – then we waited. Rosé had nerve. Just given command of the regiment, and his first act of initiative was to refuse to order a hopeless attack. He could have covered himself with glory while directing it in safety, from the rear. God, what a soldier he was!

Other legionnaires, including Alan Seeger, praised Rosé for his moral courage. Although Navarin Farm was taken a couple of days later in an outflanking manoeuvre, the momentum had gone out of the French advance, and the legionnaires spent the remainder of their time in the line strengthening their positions.

Given the great hopes invested in the offensive, disappointment was understandable. This was especially the case with the new volunteers who had taken to heart the inspiring call to arms of General Joffre. Alan Seeger was one such: 'It was a satisfaction at last to get out of the trenches to meet the enemy face to face, and to see German arrogance turned to suppliance. We knew many splendid moments, worth having endured many trials for. But in our larger aim, of piercing their line, of breaking the long deadlock, of course we had failed.'

For the old sweats of Kosta Todorov's section, food was a more pressing problem. The churned-up ground, continuing German artillery fire and the general post-battle confusion made re-supply extremely difficult. Todorov described the basic but indomitable spirit of the African legionnaires:

Lemercier observed sadly, 'I've searched all the dead Germans. Found some hardtack but couldn't swallow it. A dog wouldn't eat it!'

Later in the evening, news spread through the trenches that food was coming up at last. We ate ravenously, swallowed cold meat without chewing it, devoured the bread, and washed it down with wine and sugarless coffee.

Through the misty rain the yellowish rays of a searchlight crawled over the dead bodies in front of us, as if searching them as Lemercier had done. Rocket flares would soar up with a hiss and fall in sparks and sprays. The stench of putrefying flesh was growing stronger. But we were no longer hungry. Life once more became tolerable.

Even here, in barren Champagne, in puddles churned up by the shells, my old legionnaires, Clots, Dufour and Lemercier, were enjoying themselves, especially because rations had come for the whole platoon and nearly half the men were gone. Two extra gallons of wine!

They drank slowly, smacking their lips and chatting as if they sat in a comfortable inn. Their pipes glowed occasionally and lit up their faces. 'There's no army without wine,' said Clots. 'Napoleon lost his way in Russia because the wine gave out. In 1912 we took Taza, in Morocco, because the wine came in time – just before the attack.' The Moroccan war seemed to awaken pleasant memories 'That was a real war – movement all the time – bugles, drums, fifes,' Dufour sighed.

After every offensive was the requirement to dispose of the dead; the French had suffered nearly 150,000 casualties in the Champagne battle. David King was assigned to a burial party:

We would dig a hole beside the man and roll him in. As time was short, the holes were shallow. Men take strange attitudes in death. They did not always fit the grave, and someone would stand on the arms and legs, to keep them down while the others shovelled furiously. But when they have been dead a day or so they are like enormous dolls with limbs worked by elastics. In some cases the burial party miscalculated the amount of earth needed to hold them down, and as the man standing on the corpse stepped aside, an arm or leg would slowly rise through the loose sand and earth, in mute protest.

One unusual story that came from the battle was the case of a former British officer, John Elkington, who as a lieutenant-colonel of a battalion of the Warwickshire Regiment had been cashiered for cowardice during the retreat from Mons in 1914 – although it would seem that his misdemeanour of surrendering a position without a fight was one of confusion and incompetence.

A citation for bravery, published in the French *Journal Officiel*, read:

> The *Médaille Militaire* and the *Croix de Guerre* are conferred upon John Ford Elkington, Legionnaire in Company B3 of the First Foreign Regiment: Although fifty years old, he has given proof during the campaign of a remarkable courage and ardor, giving to everyone the best example. He was gravely wounded September 28, 1915, rushing forward to the assault of the enemy trenches. He has lost the use of his right leg.

Within two weeks of being cashiered from the British Army, Elkington had signed up for the Foreign Legion, determined to atone for his sins. The French citation came to the notice of the British military authorities, who reconsidered his case. A notice in the *London Gazette* recorded their decision:

> The King has been graciously pleased to approve of the reinstatement of John Ford Elkington in the rank of Lieutenant-Colonel of the Royal Warwickshire Regiment with his previous seniority, in consequence of his gallant conduct while serving of the ranks of the Foreign Legion of the French Army.

Elkington may have the lost the use of a leg but had regained his honour.

During 1915, many of the new volunteers left the Legion. Some – such as the Italians – transferred en masse to their own national armies when their countries came into the war on the Allied side. The French also changed their policy, allowing non-Frenchmen to join the regular Army, so that, for example, a number of Americans transferred to the 170th Infantry Regiment – although as an assault unit it was as dangerous an assignment as the Legion itself.

Others chose to stay. Alan Seeger had originally decided to transfer to the regular Army, but changed his mind after his experiences of combat in Champagne, which had bonded him with the old legionnaires. On 30 November 1915 he wrote: 'I cannot congratulate myself enough on my foresight in choosing

to stay with the Legion instead of going into the 170me with the   .
other Americans.'

From time to time, leave was granted to the front-line troops, and
eagerly seized upon. Edward Genet was given six days' leave in
November 1914. He subsequently wrote:

> They passed all too quickly, you may be sure. It was so good
> to get into Paris again after all the horror and ghastliness at the
> front. The few friends I have there did everything possible to give
> me a fine time and, believe me, they succeeded beyond measure.
> Dinners, the theatre, sight-seeing, movies and everything – all were
> a part of those six days. Then came the 12th and I had to take a
> sad and tearful farewell of such joys.

Wounded several times while in the Legion, David King was
eventually sent to a reserve artillery unit based at Vincennes near
Paris. Discipline was relaxed and he was able to slip away and
enjoy the delights of the capital. He described one riotous occasion
while on 'unofficial' leave:

> It started at the 'Hole in the Wall'. Billy Dugan, some 16th Canadian
> Highlanders and myself adjourned to Weber's – more drinks, and
> decided to hold Grand Fleet manoeuvres on the Champs Elysées.
> Seven *fiacres* [small horse-drawn carriages] were commandeered.
> The flag-ship was stocked with ammunition – rum, whisky and
> H. E. brandy. Being in blue, I was admiral. I named my captains
> and off we went: line ahead formation.
>
> The next evolution, line abreast across the whole avenue,
> brought down an attacking flotilla of police and *gendarmes*. They
> caught sight of me in French uniform, and the fight was on.
> Dugan was in blue too, but having eaten a tube of tooth paste,
> he was foaming at the mouth. Not even the *gendarmes* cared to
> tackle that apparition. A brawny Highlander saved the day. Kilts
> flying, heedless of traffic, he tore down the line, bellowing: 'Change
> carriages! Race around the fleet and back!'

> Instantly every one piled out, giving the imitation of a subway rush going to Jerusalem. The police fell back, and we steamed at full speed ahead for a restaurant in the Bois and scuttled our ships . . .

During the early summer of 1916 the Legion prepared for the great Anglo-French offensive on the Somme. Despite the carnage he had witnessed in Champagne, Seeger was as enthusiastic as ever for continuing the fight. In his last letter on 28 June he wrote to a friend:

> We go up to the attack tomorrow. This will probably be the biggest thing yet. I am glad to be going in the first wave. If you are in this thing at all it is best to be in it to the limit. And this is the supreme experience.

On 4 July the Legion was ordered to take and hold the German stronghold of Belloy-en-Santerre. The Germans defended the position with their usual tenacity and casualties were heavy. Jack Moyet described the attack on the village:

> I was a grenade-thrower for my squad, and so was in the first wave of the attack. I was much impressed by the conduct of the priest in my battalion, a tall, full-bearded man, who has been with the Legion for several years. He ran right along behind the grenade throwers, holding aloft his crucifix and crying: 'Long live the Legion! Forward for France!'
>
> A number of Germans tried to get out of a dugout to set up a machine-gun. We drove them back inside their shelter, hastily blocked the entrance except for a small hole, and hurled grenades in on the Bosches. We afterwards learned that we had killed over sixty Germans in that one dugout.

It was at Belloy-en-Santerre that Seeger kept his 'Rendezvous with Death'. Corporal John Barrett, an Irish legionnaire, described his last moments:

Seeger was wounded horribly by six explosive bullets from machine guns whose fire met the first wave of attack and caused heavy losses at Belloy-en-Santerre. Eye-witnesses belonging to his squad gave me information which makes it appear that he was not killed instantly, as he had taken off his equipment, his overcoat and his shirt, to dress his wounds. He stuck his rifle, with bayonet fixed, in the ground to show stretcher-bearers a wounded man was near, according to a general custom which aids the hospital corps at night.

Five out of forty-five in his section survived the attack, and they say he was utterly indifferent to the hail of lead and steel. He died as he lived, indifferent to danger, a real soldier and a hero. Often I think of his cheery smile as he advanced against the German guns, which he simply despised.

Although the Legion had lost much of its manpower through transfers of men to other units and, of course, to heavy casualties it remained an effective fighting force to the end. Paul Rockwell summed up the changes brought about by prolonged and intense combat:

Months of hardships and common danger had drawn the men close together, and what one had he shared with his comrades. The entire Legion – veterans and volunteers for the duration of the war – was imbued with a wonderful *esprit de corps*, and there were no more clashes between national groups or veterans and neophytes [rookies]. The awkward volunteers of 1914 had become good, campaign-hardened soldiers, well versed in the art of modern warfare, and in such company the newcomer soon became proficient as a fighter.

The Legion's part in the push against the Moronvilliers heights in April 1917 demonstrated an improved tactical awareness. Christopher Charles, a machine-gunner, described the attack:

At fifteen minutes to five o'clock on the morning of the 17th, with rain pouring down in bucketfuls, the boys 'went over the top' and across the fields. The Germans offered no resistance until their third line was reached. Then our boys started falling. It did not stop us any, and by noon we had gained something like four kilometres in depth along a wide front.

Something that is new to us is the way we now have of pushing forward. It is nothing like the battles I have been in before. Formerly we just started forward against the Bosches with a rush after our artillery had done its work. But in this battle it was different.

First our batteries smashed the German trenches for a few kilometres deep, and when we started forward it was not with a whirlwind dash. Instead, a few score men went out armed with hand grenades. Naturally the Germans started shooting like the mischief when they saw our fellows, but our men were picked and were known to have a lot of nerve. They kept on advancing from shell-hole to shell-hole until they were within a few feet of the German positions, when they let fly with the grenades and cleaned out the trenches and shelters. Then the reserves and machine-gun crews came and took possession. The same thing went on from trench to trench.

The fighting was some of the fiercest of the war, with two Legion battalions almost continuously engaged in fighting until they were relieved on 22 April. One of the heroes of the day was Sergeant-Major Mader, a German NCO who led repeated attacks against the lines of his fellow countrymen:

Collecting a group of ten legionnaires, he leaped out of the trench, defying the hail of machine-gun fire, and attacked the pillbox from the rear, killing its defenders. This success, however, did not satisfy him. With a fresh bag of grenades he charged the other pillboxes, whose Saxon defenders, shattered by this unexpected attack, fled in disorder; Mader and his ten legionnaires being left in possession of a heavy battery of six guns.

Throughout 1917 and into the final year of the war, the Legion held fast, before helping drive the Germans back towards their borders. When the armistice came into force on 11 November 1918, the Legion had added new laurels to its reputation, refuting any suggestion that it was only good for colonial operations. As part of General Daugan's Moroccan Division, the Legion marched proudly into the newly freed French department of Lorraine. Paul Rockwell, invalided out of the Legion because of his wounds, was there to witness the triumph of his old comrades: 'The Moroccan Division, which won more honours upon hard-fought battlefields than any other corps engaged in the World War so triumphantly ended, had the signal distinction of being the first Allied division to march across the late frontier and enter liberated Lorraine.'

General Daugan took the Division's salute in the town square of Chateau-Salins, complete with wildly cheering townspeople. After the *tirailleurs* and the Zouaves came the Legion:

> Colonel Rollet, his breast covered with medals and his sword drawn, rode at the head of his legionnaires. Behind him came the Legion's band and the Legion's battle-flag, which was decorated with the Cross of the Legion of Honour and the War Cross with nine palms and three stars, representing twelve citations in the Order of the Day – more citations than had ever been won before by any fighting corps. The spectators crowded near as the volunteer fighters of every race, creed, and social condition, representing five-score countries, and whose exploits are renowned throughout the world, went by.

CHAPTER 11

THE INTER-WAR YEARS

The Legion had suffered devastating casualties in the trenches of 1914–18, but these losses were swiftly made up from the large pool of men displaced in the war's aftermath. Many recruits came from Germany and Austria, so that by 1921 roughly half the Legion was of Germanic origin. And yet such was the Legion's confidence in its ability to transcend national affiliations that there were few anxieties about this influx of recruits from France's former enemies. The Germans were joined by a large Russian contingent, drawn predominantly from White Russians escaping the newly installed Bolshevik regime.

The whole force was divided into five three-battalion infantry regiments, plus a cavalry regiment that was three-quarters full of White Russians. The Legion grew steadily, reaching a peak of 20,000 men by the early 1930s. This enlarged Legion was needed to meet the demands of subduing the Berber tribes in the Atlas mountains, repulsing the Rif invasion from Spanish Morocco and despatching an expeditionary force to Syria to fight the Druse.

Abd el-Krim, the charismatic Rif leader who had repeatedly defeated the Spanish army in Spanish Morocco, advanced across the border into French Morocco in 1925. The Rif were as hardy and courageous as the best of the Atlas Berbers, but they also possessed superior discipline and a level of tactical expertise in the handling of modern weapons – including machine guns and even artillery – that came as an unwelcome surprise to the French.

Krim actively encouraged desertion from the Legion, using those who fled to his side to man the machine guns and artillery pieces in his armoury.

Captain Aage – the Danish royal prince serving as an officer in the Legion – admitted that 'even the Foreign Legion met its match in the Rif. I can extend to them no higher praise.' The 70 French outposts dotted along the southern foothills of the Rif mountains were vulnerable to attack. Marshal Hubert Lyautey, the French commander-in-chief in Morocco, was stubbornly determined not to let the larger forts fall, although he accepted that the smaller outposts should be abandoned. Short of men, and surprised by the ferocity of the Rif assault, Lyautey deployed the Legion as a fire brigade to defend the outpost line.

In May 1925 the Legion's 6th Battalion was ordered to rescue the garrisons at Ain-Dejane and Sidi-Ahmed, blow up the outposts and then retreat back across the Ouerrha River that now marked a dividing line between Rif and French positions. Captain Zinovi Pechkoff, then commanding the Battalion's 22nd Company, covered the withdrawal to the Ouerrha in the face of intense Rif pressure. Pechkoff described the ensuing action:

We reached the last ridge. We had only to go down to the river and cross it to be almost safe. Our men, carrying the wounded on their backs, began the descent, and at once firing started. We were assaulted from the rear and both flanks. The first soldiers were already in the water, when we saw that together with us, on the right and the left, as far as we could see, the Rif were crossing, too. There we were in the river! All of us! It flowed rapidly and its cold waters reached the armpits of the men. The Rif would reach the other bank first, for we had on our shoes and all our equipment while they were almost naked. Nothing remained for us to do but to stop and fight, standing there deep in the water.

'Fire!' was ordered. The men raised their rifles and groups on the left and the right began aiming at the Rif. They were amazed. They thought we would try to get away as quickly as possible, each one for himself, regardless of the wounded that had to be carried. Some of them started to go back. Many fell. Only a few replied to our fire. Their bullets whistled around our ears. I saw bubbles skipping along the surface of the water. Thanks to the courage and discipline of the men, we succeeded in getting across.

The 21st Company was deployed just a little further along the river from the 22nd when it was attacked, and it included Legionnaire A. R. Cooper, whose story made an interesting counterpoint to Pechkoff's account. While the Legion prided itself on its refusal to panic in tight situations, on rare occasions discipline did not hold, as Cooper revealed:

> Its mission accomplished, the battalion reformed to return to camp at Bou-Adel, across the river. Legionnaires snatched oranges from trees that clothed a hill overlooking the Ouergha, and we ate the fruit as we rested a little more than a mile from the tents of the mobile group. But while we relaxed, hordes of silent tribesmen crept up and surrounded us, except for a narrow corridor directly ahead leading to Bou-Adel. Ordinarily there would have been a steady retreat in echelon formation, companies taking it in turn to hold their ground while the others fell back. But we had been taken unawares. Masses of Rifs were already upon us and a wave of panic swept through the soldiers who, moments before, had been happily sucking oranges.
>
> '*Sauve-qui-peut!* [Save Yourselves!]' a voice screamed. Men rolled helter-skelter down the steep hill into the river, where they wallowed helplessly as an enfilade attack spat bullets into our ranks from end to end. It was a desperate struggle to get across the waist-high torrent before we were mown down by the hidden tribesmen. A hundred Rifs emerged from a ravine to pounce upon twenty legionnaires who were urging mules through the water. It was a terrible sight. The tribesmen were lashing out with long knives, cutting off the legionnaires' heads before hacking the bodies to pieces.
>
> We reached Bou-Adel in twos and threes, supporting the wounded on our shoulders. The dead had been left where they had fallen. A roll-call confirmed that the 21st Company had borne the brunt of the attack.

While it would seem that the 21st Company faced a more determined Rif attack, a salient point was the way in which the 22nd Company – acting as the rearguard – had withdrawn towards the river in good tactical order. By contrast, the complacent and relaxed 21st Company had been as ripe for the taking as the oranges they had been eating prior to the Rif onslaught.

Throughout May and June the situation in the battle of the outposts remained critical. Some were overrun, their garrisons slaughtered. Unable to break through Rif lines to help the beleaguered outposts, the French were often forced to stand impotently aside. All the while, despairing messages for help were flashed in Morse code from the garrisons.

An attempt to supply the outpost at Bibane revealed the difficulties faced by the French. A force of around 2,000 legionnaires doggedly fought its way to the outpost, suffering an untenable 500 casualties in the process. Lyautey had made the decision not to abandon Bibane, and although re-stocked with food, water and ammunition the 54-strong garrison under Sergeant Bernis was effectively left to its fate. Aage, then on the staff of General Colombat, recorded the last, agonising days of the outpost, from a position just a few kilometres away:

We knew that Bibane was doomed. Later that evening the signal blinker flashed a message that Bibane was suffering a heavy attack and requesting artillery support. The firing continued unabated through the night and we realised that the life of the post could be measured almost in hours. When the morning sun had risen sufficiently to make use of the heliograph, the signalmen again requested relief. We flashed back, 'Hold on for a few days longer,' and cursed ourselves for the false encouragement.

On the third [of June], Sergeant Bernis again requested relief, stating that he had lost eight more men. The wounded, he said, were suffering horribly, and the garrison had not slept for forty-eight hours. We fully realised their awful plight, but signalled, nevertheless, that relief was coming soon. We lied, and we knew it. And so, I imagine, did the Sergeant.

On the fourth, the Rif began closing in around the post, but our artillery was busy elsewhere and could not assist the gallant defenders materially. On the fifth, we saw shrapnel bursting directly over Bibane and realised that Krim had brought up his German artillerymen. This was at 9 a.m.

At ten, I accompanied General Colombat to our artillery observation post, where we remained throughout the day. From there we could watch the enemy drawing closer, ever closer, to the outer walls, while our guns pounded for all their worth. At four in the afternoon, the Rif rushed the walls. The heliograph flashed despairingly, '*Poste fichu!* [Post finished!].' Then came the final signal, never to be completed. We stood breathless, repeating every letter as it flashed – S-E-R-G-E-A-N-T, Sergeant B – and they scaled the walls, hundreds of them!

The General clenched his teeth. His face livid, he swung round to the artillery commander and said, 'Now! Let them have it.' In a trice every gun switched to the post and, though some of the brave men probably remained alive, pounded it to bits. The General wept.

The sacrifice at Bibane and other outposts was not in vain, however. They had blunted the momentum of the Rif assault, forcing a lull in hostilities that gave time for the French to bring up reinforcements. Marshal Pétain, the hero of Verdun, was transferred from France to oversee a massive offensive against the Rif, which, in combination with a Spanish attack, overwhelmed Abd el-Krim's forces. In May 1926 Krim surrendered to the French, the Rif campaign over.

The fighting in the Rif, as in the rest of North Africa and Syria, was brutally savage. Atrocities were routinely carried out by both sides. Aage wrote: 'It is the Berber practice first to torture and then to kill all prisoners or wounded who fall into their hands, although now and again a man has been let off with castration.'

Accordingly, surrenders were rare, and the legionnaire's adage of keeping the last bullet for himself was sometimes a necessary reality. In the battle of the outposts it was not unknown for garrisons without hope of relief to blow themselves up with sticks of dynamite, along with the outpost, rather than face capture.

As part of a punitive expedition into the Atlas mountains, Ernst Löhndorff described the fate of some unfortunate sentries abducted at night while on guard duty: 'At the change of sentry they are found naked and horribly disfigured. And in the grey light of dawn their severed heads and sexual organs come flying over our rifle stacks.'

The French, for their part, usually killed their prisoners. Löhndorff recalled an operation that was typical of this type of warfare, when his unit of legionnaires and some Moroccan auxiliaries surprised a group of enemy tribesmen:

> We took ten prisoners, all wounded, powerful young men, who wrapped themselves in defiant dumbness. The court-martial sat for a quarter of an hour, and sentenced them to death. They were proud and defiant right up to the last. They were shot. Our half company of Moroccans would have preferred to torture them to death. It is remarkable how men of the same tribe can hate one another! The whole night long the camp resounds with the devilish din of our victory-besotted natives. In accordance with the custom of their country they have cut off the heads of the dead enemies, and stuck them on poles round about the camp.

Following the dismemberment of the Turkish Empire after the First World War, France acquired responsibility for the administration of Syria and Lebanon. Tensions between the French occupiers and the mountainous Druse people broke out into open warfare in 1925. French reinforcements – including elements of the Legion – were rushed to Beirut, and then marched up into the mountains.

In September 1925 Bennett J. Doty, a young American adventurer, and the 800 men of his battalion advanced into Druse territory to occupy the village of Musseifré. The defence of the village would become one of the Legion's epic engagements. Having arrived in the village, the battalion sent out a reconnaissance patrol that was badly mauled by the Druse. Doty described the subsequent action:

> This action electrified the camp; we knew we were in for a real row. That night guards were tripled, the machine-gun men slept beside their pieces, and, as did all the legionnaires, I slept along

the wall, right beneath my *créneau* [loophole], my rifle strapped to my arm, a little heap of grenades at my feet.

Just then I saw a flash in the darkness, and a bullet went buzzing over my head. A Very light went up; in the glare we saw the slope above us, the level between, the ground on all sides, filled with silent charging forms, and let go with all we had. Simultaneously, as the light betrayed their secrecy, they broke out into a chorus of wildest yells.

It was terribly confusing fighting at first. Few Very lights were yet going up, and the night was black. It was punctured by the stabbing flashes of their rifles, and at those flashes we shot. But a lot of them managed to rush by between the walled camps, and enter the village. The camp there, and the fortified *état-major*, held staunchly, but they penetrated the cavalry quarters. Twenty-nine Cossacks guarding them were butchered, and the horses of the squadron captured.

It was one thing, however, to capture horses and another to get them out. When these wild tribesmen, on captured horses, began to gallop out of the village, a slight greenness of dawn was in the air. We could see better. Also, a horse is bigger than a man, easier to see and easier to shoot at. We turned our fire upon the horses, just visible in the growing light. They were our own horses, but we did not think of that. We would bring down a horse, and then get the rider, dismounted and helpless between our enfilading fires. Few of these got out alive, though meanwhile their brothers on the slope above poured their fire down on us.

In a few minutes, just as the day was definitely breaking, again came the cry '*Aux armes!*' and we all sprang to our loopholes. The sight that now met us was an extraordinary one, and one that might have been terrifying had we not been by this time mad with the lust of the fight. Down the slope at the bottom of the hill, the Druses were pouring down upon us as if it were the very earth itself moving in landslide – five thousand of them on horse and foot.

Pitiful things were happening too. One of the men, shot in the chest, lay dying all day in the sand. He had been sent over from another section just before the attack, and we did not know who he was. Time and time again, when we thought him dead, one or the other of us would notice that he seemed to be murmuring. Someone would crawl to him across the zone of fire to see what he wanted. It was always water. '*De l'eau, de l'eau* [water, water],' he murmured. We had very little water; we were in fact dying with thirst. But always someone would give a little out of his canteen, prop him up maybe a bit, then crawl back across the zone of fire. This kept up all day. He was slowly bleeding to death internally. It took him twelve hours to die.

Thus, the hours passed, wearily, in constant fighting, heat, clamour, death and blood, and our ammunition ebbed. We began to ask each other the time. Finally it was four o'clock, the hour we had fixed in our minds as that of the relief. But there came no relief.

The situation had become so desperate that Doty's lieutenant prepared his men for the worst. Bayonets were fixed in the ground and the few remaining cartridges were handed out, with the injunction to 'keep the last one for yourself'. Doty continued his account:

Behind us, on the side opposite the slope down which had come the attacks, the ground rose in another long slope to a crest. And then from behind that crest, far off, there came to our ears a tiny brassy sound, a tiny brassy music, as if from the insides of a closed victrola [gramophone player]. Brass bugles, far over there. And they were sounding tinily the precipitated, alert, stirring call of the charge, '*En avant!*'

And suddenly over the crest came pouring in extended line the Sixteenth Regiment of Algerian *tirailleurs*, which had come by forced marches from Ghazalé to our rescue. Down the slope the *tirailleurs* swept, and filled the plain. Those in line with the village poured into it and began a house-to-house slaughter; the others swept on to the right and the left of it, up the slopes down which the Druse had charged and up which they were now fleeing.

First letting go the last of our preciously husbanded ammunition in a general wild discharge after the disappearing fugitives, we opened the gates of our redoubt and strolled out with hands in our pockets.

Once the dust of battle had settled, Doty was forced to reconsider his formerly less-than-favourable attitude towards the *anciens* of his company:

> I found that these rascally nuisances of peace days, always drunk, always quarrelling, always late at *appel* and in continuous hot water, were transformed when real work began. Watching them, I could hardly believe the change. It was not only that they were brave, fighting with utmost heroism. But they were patient and enduring, full of devotion and self-sacrifice, helpful to everyone, and obeying every order not only without a murmur but with a sort of self-immolating alacrity. They were lions to the enemy, lambs to their officers and comrades. I never cared much what they did after that.

The French maintained a relentless pressure on the Druse, systematically forcing their villages into submission. Those that resisted or failed to pay their taxes were destroyed. An example was made of the recalcitrant Druse village of Tel-y-Ded. It was surrounded by Legion cavalrymen and then bombed by French aircraft; those trying to flee were cut down by the encircling legionnaires. John Harvey, an orderly in the cavalry regiment, recounted the attack on the village:

> With a thunder of galloping hoofs we swept forward, our sabres glinting in the first rays of dawn. The Arabs fired at us with their long muskets from among the ruins of their homes and fought us with sword and knife. Even as they fell under the hoofs of our horses they stabbed at us with the valour of despair. Their women faced the charge as unflinchingly as the men, wielding swords and knives and even farm implements. Many had children clinging to them.
>
> They had not a chance for they were hopelessly outnumbered. Within a few minutes not one was left alive. Young and old, men, women, and children, had all been massacred. We looted the smouldering ruins and stripped the dead of their trinkets. Five hundred sheep, two hundred goats, and a dozen horses were sent off to Damascus in lieu of the unpaid taxes.

The action subsequently filled Harvey with remorse, and writing after his release from the Legion he was bitterly critical of the French action:

> They were not our enemies. They were peaceful folk, supposed to be living under the protection of France, and their sole crime was the refusal to pay the taxes demanded of them. During all the time I was in the Legion I saw nothing more brutal or more nauseating than the slaughter of the women and children of Tel-y-Ded.

Towards the end of 1925 the Druse revolt began to fail, and in the following year the Legion was retained in Syria primarily for policing and construction duties. Back in Morocco, the last Berber strongholds in the Middle Atlas surrendered to the French in 1933. The Legion could take satisfaction in having achieved its military objectives, but it would soon face a greater test, where its formerly unshakeable sense of loyalty would be painfully questioned.

CHAPTER 12

THE SECOND WORLD WAR: A HOUSE DIVIDED

The rise of Nazism during the 1930s produced a flow of political refugees into France, notably Jews, Czechs and other opponents of Hitler from Central Europe. Substantial numbers offered their service to France, many of whom were sent to the Legion. Another source of manpower came from the thousands of Spanish Republicans who had fled Franco's Spain during 1939; rather than languish in vast and wretched French internment camps they accepted an offer to join the Legion. Once France declared war on 3 September 1939, the stream became a torrent. By May 1940 the total of those volunteering had risen to more than 80,000 – double the number who had flocked to support France in 1914.

Two new Legion regiments were raised in France (11th and 12th) to begin absorbing the new recruits. And in an attempt to minimise the problems that had occurred in 1914 – when many volunteers had objected to serving in the Legion – three regiments were raised for foreign volunteers that were nominally not part of the Legion: the 21st, 22nd and 23rd RMVE (*Regiments de Marche des Volontaires Étrangers*). In actual practice, however, these regiments were commanded by Legion officers and NCOs, and were considered by many of those serving in them to be Legion units. The regular Legion regiments remained in North Africa and the other French colonial outposts, although individual officers and NCOs crossed over to France to organise the volunteer units.

As had been the case in 1914, the old African hands were less than enthusiastic about their new comrades in arms. John Lodwick, an English volunteer, described the *anciens*: 'The common language of these men was pidgin French or German. Their affection for the country they served was minimal but their pride in the Legion ferocious, and it cannot be said that they looked with any pleasure upon the floods of newcomers who invaded the recruiting offices in September 1939.'

Jo Czapka, a Czech pilot who had escaped to France from his homeland after the German takeover in March 1939, was obliged to join the Legion prior to a transfer into the French Air Force. He was sent to Sidi-bel-Abbès for basic training, and wrote of his experiences:

> I confess now to being frightened by the types I met there. I have never met men so crude and rough. I was only pleased about one thing: if a fight was coming, thank heaven I was on their side.
>
> I regarded many of these old veterans as mental cases. Some of them had served fifteen years which qualified them for French citizenship and had taken the civilian jobs offered to them after this long service. In France these jobs were in the grade of postman, and it seemed that after a year of this many men returned to the Legion. I was told that they would say that they missed the life.
>
> It was extremely difficult to know if this were true for all these veterans had an icy shell around them. They were bitter and hard as well as battered and they looked right back at us with complete contempt in their eyes. It was impossible to get through to them.

From the other perspective of that of the Legion authorities, the new volunteers posed many problems. The Spaniards were considered the most difficult. Alfred Perrott-White, recently promoted to *caporal-chef*, was a machine-gun instructor stationed at Géryville in North Africa in early 1939. He remembered the arrival of 200 Spanish refugees:

We had plenty of trouble in store handling those men. For the most part, sullen and ill disciplined, very sick about joining the Legion in the first place, and with only one thought in mind – that being to desert across the Franco-Spanish border in Morocco. In fact, at one time conditions became so bad that practically the whole garrison at Géryville was used as a police force to keep the Spanish company in order. There were many fights with knives and guns, and wholesale desertions, but not one was successful. I believe more than ten men were killed in the attempt, but, as always happens in the Legion, the officers and NCOs held the upper hand. Discipline began to show, and before these men finished their training, they had more or less – outwardly at least – settled down to facing the inevitable.

Although the Spaniards would have been tricky material for any trainer of troops it is clear that Perrott-White failed to understand their special problems and qualities. Charles Favrel provided a more insightful portrait of these recruits:

For them, the Legion had not been a choice but a requirement accepted with a heavy heart, a bad moment to get over by making common cause with their companions. Resolved to remain men, they refused therefore to allow themselves to be poured into the mould of unconditional obedience. In addition to this, their combat experience caused them to reject the traditional conceptions of the Prussian system implanted at Sidi-bel-Abbès for a century. Tenacious and courageous, reluctant to accept sacrificial missions, their idea was to kill and not be killed stupidly! They were not traditional Legion timber, the docile and blind executors of the order given by a superior.

Although some of the new recruits had reluctantly come forward to avoid internment, many others were out-and-out idealists. One of these was Constantin Joffé – of Russian extraction – who was sent to the 22nd RMVE:

Every man of us enlisted in order to fight a new scourge of humanity; we were Russians, Belgians, Romanians, Egyptians,

Latin Americans, a few Chinamen, Spaniards, a very Tower of Babel, yet we spoke a common language which was our hatred of Hitler. These were men who, the moment war was declared, took to ships or to trains or to the road in order to meet here.

We were called the Legion, our regimental colours were red and green, our motto 'Honour and Discipline'. But we did not actually belong to the Foreign Legion; we had all volunteered for the duration of the war and we would not have been accepted if we had criminal records. I have rarely seen so many intellectuals, physicians, engineers and lawyers in one regiment. Many among us had never lived in France before the declaration of war but had enrolled in French consulates abroad in order to join this legion of men who loved France.

Among these middle-class professionals were large numbers of Jews, whose decidedly unmilitary appearance, cosmopolitan outlook and (often) left-wing sympathies were anathema to Legion traditionalists. The writer Arthur Koestler, a Hungarian Jew, had attempted to join the French armed forces on the outbreak of war, but instead was held in an internment camp. He wrote wryly, 'Anti-fascists were obviously a great nuisance in a war against Fascism. We were not wanted.'

He was eventually accepted into the Legion as the Germans advanced deep into France on 17 June – far too late to play any meaningful part in the fighting. Koestler was shipped over to North Africa, and there slipped away to Casablanca, and, with British help, travelled to Britain via Lisbon.

Jean-Pierre Hallo, a newly promoted regular-army lieutenant in 1939, described his Jewish recruits as being from 'comfortable backgrounds and most often cultivated. Their average age approached 30 years. Not very athletic in general, their sedentary life style had already caused some to grow a little thick around the waist.'

And the anti-semitic attitudes prevalent in the French military made life unpleasant for Jewish recruits, although it would also seem that the rough ways of the Legion came as a greater shock to the Jews than to other groups. Zosa Szajkowski, who had volunteered the day before France's declaration of war, complained:

The attitude towards Jews was not exactly friendly. Several times anti-Semitic remarks by a corporal or sergeant would lead to unpleasant incidents. The officers did nothing to remedy the situation.

The officers and non-commissioned officers were almost all brought over from the Foreign Legion in North Africa. They constantly insulted us, the volunteers. One sergeant of my unit called all [Jewish] legionnaires 'Solomon' and always yelled, 'This is the Legion, not a synagogue!' Some of the non-commissioned officers gladly accepted bribes. Among other insults, it was sneeringly remarked to the Jews that they had joined for the food.

But attitudes towards the Jews – and Spaniards – changed when they were sent to the front line and engaged in combat, as Szajkowski admitted:

The discipline was very strict, but we noticed that the attitude of the officers and non-commissioned officers towards [the] men became more humane. At the front the officers treated the Jewish volunteers as men. Perhaps the common danger of death weakened any anti-Jewish sentiments they may have had. Besides, the Jewish volunteers fought valiantly, a fact the officers frankly admitted.

The first Legion unit to see serious action was the 13th DBLE (*Demi-Brigade de Légion Étrangère*), a two-battalion half-brigade raised from volunteers in both North Africa and France that was swiftly trained in mountain warfare. Originally intended to support the Finns in their war against the Soviet Union, the armistice between the two countries in March 1940 left the DBLE without a function. The German invasion of Norway in April provided a new role, however, and the DBLE became part of an Anglo-French-Polish force shipped off to northern Norway in an attempt to expel the Germans.

Equipped with skis and cold-weather gear, the legionnaires looked forward to combat, despite the unusual nature of their geographic circumstances. British legionnaire John Yeowell recalled his arrival in Norwegian waters in the *Monarch of Bermuda*:

Our ship travelled alone and unescorted in an area infested with U-boats. When we reached the fjords north of the Arctic Circle, my section under Lieutenant Vardot was transferred to a Royal Navy minesweeper. It was an exhilarating experience to sail silently up these great inland seas at one o'clock in the morning. It was twenty-four-hour daylight and we were able to see in the distance these wonderful vistas of white mountains and tiny nestling villages with their timber houses and pastel-coloured roofs and walls. It looked idyllic.

The port of Narvik was the main Allied objective but the initial landing on 6 May 1940 was made near the small town of Bjerkvik, a few miles from Narvik. Yeowell described the naval bombardment that preceded the amphibious assault:

The town's inhabitants had already gathered on a hill at the side of the fjord so that they could be seen, and there they stood watching their homes being shelled and burned to the ground. It must have been desperate for them. A little armoured car, German, was going down by the front of the shore firing a little machine gun at the fleet until it was blasted into kingdom come.

The bombardment of Bjerkvik went on for a quarter of an hour, then we went ashore in what I suppose were ship's boats. Some had motors, others simply had to be rowed by men of the Royal Navy.

Legionnaire H., a French volunteer, was in the first wave to hit the beach: 'We came ashore; there was firing everywhere. I think it was one of the worst experiences anyone can have. My first time in battle. Your heart beats so hard. We landed and had a fight on the beach. We lost a lot of friends there.' Yeowell was also one of the first ashore:

We crossed the narrow beach and went over the road and headed through the blazing town. The place had been shot to pieces. Every garden gate and every fallen telegraph pole I suspected of being booby-trapped, and by God it was hot! We were quickly out in open countryside which was covered in snow. It was so deep in places you would sink right up to your thigh. Then we had our first meeting with the enemy. I had reached a slight rise in the ground and as I lay there looking around, I heard voices and these were very close indeed. Less than three yards in front of me was a man walking right across my field of vision. He was carrying something, but not a weapon. All the enemy were scattered about like this in isolated pockets. It was probably the only means of defence in such a complicated landscape. They did not appear to know we had landed and seemed to be taking it easy for a bit. My grenade killed all three of them, poor buggers.

Once the area around Bjerkvik was secure the Allies pressed on towards Narvik. Captain Pierre Lapie – attached to the Legion – described the rugged terrain over which the troops had to advance, and the impression given by the Spanish legionnaires:

Everywhere we came up against these problems of uneven ground. A lieutenant of the 1st Battalion stranded all night with his section at a bend in a pass was able by his tenacity to ensure a resumption of the battle next day. The Spaniards recognised in these steep slopes something of the difficulties of their own *sierras* [mountains]. They leapt from point to point like tigers, and never seemed to tire. Those officers who had had misgivings about welcoming Spanish Republicans into the Legion (they dubbed them all communists) were gratified to recognise their fighting prowess. One may instance the case of the young Spaniards who attacked a German machine-gun post behind Elvegard. One of them was literally mown down by fire at only a few yards' distance. The other sprang forward, smashed the head of the gunner with his rifle butt, and swung the muzzle of the gun into space.

The War Diary of the DBLE described the assault on Narvik itself:

The slopes which had to be climbed were precipitous, and the supporting Norwegian battalion was slow in getting under way. Hardly had we reached the crest than the enemy launched a vicious counter-attack. Captain de Guittaut, the [2nd] company commander, was killed, and Lieutenant Garoux severely wounded. Led by Lieutenant Vadot, the company managed to halt the German counter-attack and the Germans fell back, abandoning their dead and wounded . . . It was about five o'clock in the afternoon [of 28 May] when the 2nd battalion entered Narvik, Sergeant Szabo being the first man to set foot in the town. German officers disguised as civilians fled by road to Beusfjord, and the men, furious at being left in the lurch, surrendered without further resistance.

Although the Allies had comprehensively defeated the Germans in Narvik, it was to prove a hollow victory as Hitler had already instigated his great offensive against France and the Low Countries. The Allies abandoned Narvik and withdrew their forces to Britain and France. Before leaving Norway, the Legion buried its dead. John Yeowell was assigned to a burial party:

Our duty was one that haunts me to this day – to put the bodies of the legionnaires into coffins for burial. The state of the bodies was such that we were able to put two, sometimes three into a coffin. It was a horrible job, but it had to be done. It was almost dawn by the time we had finished, with brief services by the local Lutheran minister and a legionnaire who now wore the stole of the priest. There were no chaplains in the Legion in those days and the only time we saw a priest was when we had to bury someone.

While the legionnaires of 13th DBLE were securing Narvik, the Legion in France faced the onslaught of the main German offensive, launched on 10 May 1940. The Legion battalions had been deployed along the *Maginot Line*, but as the Germans advanced through Belgium so the legionnaires were rushed northward in an attempt to stem the tide. Constantin Joffé of the 22nd Regiment described how his unit repulsed a German attack:

How happy we were on the evening of 28 May, to see Germans rushing at our line after a heavy softening-up by their artillery. Rage and hatred were still very fierce among us; we had not forgotten the 26th and Villères Carbonel, where the second battalion had left four hundred and fifty dead on the field. The Germans advanced creditably; they were only two hundred yards from us when our machine guns opened up on them with due ceremony. Our mortars blazed squarely away into the advancing mass; our seventy-fives penned them in perfectly; they were caught in a trap and could move neither forward or back.

How savage man becomes! A howl of joy rose when our mortars hit their mark. We had completely forgotten that these men too had wives and children at home; revenge for the day before yesterday banished all other feelings from our hearts, and we certainly tasted revenge fully that evening. It was wonderful to see these conquerors, these supermen, react with normal reflexes, scampering away, forsaking their wounded and dead on the field, running like greased lightning just to save their precious hides. There was nothing of the bully about them now, nor were they in any way inclined to cry 'Heil Hitler!'

But, to Joffé's consternation, the legionnaires found themselves desperately short of munitions and other supplies: 'Day by day, we realised that the rhythm of our replies to the German onset was growing steadily slower; day by day we understood more glaringly that no one was going to relieve or reinforce us.'

Conditions for the men of the 22nd Regiment got steadily worse, as the Germans pressed forward on their flanks. While acting as a runner, Joffé witnessed the despair of his battalion commander:

The Major sat in the cellar of a completely destroyed house, the survivors of his staff about him. There were a few maps on the wall, a radio and a telephone set. The Major's face was bandaged, a token of the attack on 26 May. I delivered my message. He shook his head and stared at the map before him. Another messenger entered; he was from Company 5, which lay to our left. He reported that our position could be held no longer; we had practically no ammunition left and suffered exceedingly high casualties. A third messenger turned up, this time from the First Battalion which linked us to the Forty-First Infantry; he asked for immediate reinforcements. Meanwhile, here in the cellar, we could hear the shells whizzing and exploding above us. The Major asked the man at the telephone to get him regimental headquarters.

'No answer, sir. The wire's cut off again.'

'Broadcast a message, then.'

'The batteries are too weak, Major.'

'Where is my despatch rider?'

'They got him too, sir.'

'Very well. Send a cyclist at once!'

'No bicycles, Major; they were all hit.'

The Major turned towards us, three harbingers of evil. 'Tell your units to hold on at any cost. Tell them everything is going well here; in fact, tell them everything is going splendidly. Those are my orders!'

He could say no more. (I recalled how, a few days ago, he had himself stopped the German advance at a highly critical point in the line by replacing a gunner who had been killed.) The old warrior buried his head in his hands.

Of the many national and ethnic groups within the Volunteer Legion, Joffé was particularly impressed by the Jews he fought alongside, not in this case the middle-class professionals – disparagingly nicknamed the 'intellectuals' in the DBLE – but men from more modest backgrounds:

We had a fairly large number of Jews; many of them were small tailors or peddlers from Belleville, the workman's quarter of Paris, or from the ghetto of the *Rue de Temple*. No one would have anything to do with them at [the training camp of] Barcarès, especially as machine gunners or in posts of active service. They spoke only Yiddish. They looked as if they were afraid of a machine gun, they seemed to be in perpetual fear. Yet under fire, if volunteers were needed to fetch back munitions under a heavy shelling or if lines of barbed wire entanglements had to be up at night fairly in front of the enemy guns, these little men were the first to offer their services. They did it quietly without swagger, perhaps without enthusiasm; but they *did* do it. It was always they who, up to the very last moment, brought back our arms from an abandoned post.

The three RMVE regiments were virtually destroyed in the fighting, but they impressed their German counterparts and their fellow soldiers in the French Army. The two other volunteer regiments, the 11th and 12th, suffered a similar fate. The 11th Regiment was defending the Bois d'Inor, between the rivers Meuse and Chiers, when it was subjected to a mass aerial and artillery bombardment. Georges Manue described the defence:

> We held the Bois d'Inor for over a fortnight. Daily attacks and artillery bombardments made no impression on our sector. And when the order to retreat was given, although our commander knew why – we were almost surrounded – the men left their positions, bitter anger in their hearts. They hadn't been beaten! They had hoped to be given the order to attack. For them the order to retreat was entirely unjustified . . . We were still firing when the 'Cease Fire' sounded, and there wasn't a man who was not prepared to go on fighting with his bayonet alone, if need be, should ammunition run out. The regiment, which counted 3,000 men at the being of the campaign, was reduced to 800.

The remnants of the Legion in France were shipped over to North Africa. The new pro-German Vichy French regime was allowed to exercise control over its colonial possessions, although subject to pressure from the German Armistice Commission to hand over its German-born legionnaires.

The 13th DBLE had returned from Norway to France, only to witness the capitulation of the French government. The legionnaires then sailed from Brittany to England, where the new Free French leader, General Charles de Gaulle, asked them to continue the fight. Roughly three-quarters answered de Gaulle's call to arms, the remainder were shipped to French North Africa. The DBLE would continue to fight alongside the British and then the Americans until final victory in 1945.

The DBLE left Britain at the end of 1940 as part of a Free French force that sailed around Africa, via the Cameroons and Gabon, to Port Sudan on the Red Sea. At Port Sudan they joined the British in securing Italian-held Eritrea.

THE SECOND WORLD WAR: A HOUSE DIVIDED

The Free French used a number of young French-speaking British women as medical support staff and drivers. One of these was Susan Travers, who became an informal member of the Legion (after the war she was formally enrolled into the Legion as an *adjutant-chef*). The DBLE operated alongside the British, and Travers became aware that relations between the two sides were not always of the best:

It was in Sudan that I first realised that the Legion had an unsavoury reputation among the Allied military commanders. The welcome we received from our British counterparts in Port Sudan was at best unenthusiastic and at worst openly hostile. Legionnaires seemed to have an almost mythical status as a mercenary force peopled by foreign men with false names, who had joined up for the minimum five years to flee troubled pasts. I remember the legionnaires being described as a collection of hot-tempered Cossack horsemen, German officers, ill-educated Turks, Russian counts and Hungarian lotharios.

Not that the British suspicions about the Legion were altogether unfounded. Legionnaires were undoubtedly expert thieves and specialists in 'appropriating' vehicles, ammunition and military equipment from those about them. Looting and pilfering were commonplace – survival had often depended upon it. The British jealously guarded their own supplies and frowned heavily on the black sheep in their midst.

In June 1941 an Anglo–Free French force invaded Syria, then held by the pro-German Vichy French. It was an unfortunate if necessary campaign, with Frenchmen fighting Frenchmen and legionnaire fighting legionnaire. The Vichy French put up a stronger fight than the Allies had expected, and the DBLE encountered the Vichy 6th Foreign Legion Regiment. A DBLE legionnaire wrote:

We faced each other there in the hills for what seemed to be hours. Neither side wanted to make the first move. We were brothers. Yet we were strangers. We were enemies too? We had been told that the Vichy forces would not put up more than a token resistance. But what is a 'token' in war?

The superior firepower of the Allies told in the end and the Vichy French were forced to surrender. The 6th Regiment was broken up, with nearly one thousand men (but only two officers) crossing over to the DBLE. The remainder of the 6th Regiment was repatriated to North Africa, holding bitter memories of the debacle in Syria. With these reinforcements the DBLE could now field three battalions. It was deployed in the Western Desert, where it gained renown fighting Rommel's Africa Corps.

Susan Travers – who was now acting as a driver for the Free French commander, General Marie-Pierre Koenig – described conditions in the new theatre of operations:

> The Western Desert was a severe shock to our systems. Not only were the conditions physically draining but the vast empty landscape that stretched to the horizon imposed its own psychological strain. Just finding one's way around was exhausting. We had to navigate using a sun compass, and often got lost. The few linen maps we had of the area had so few bearings marked that they looked more like naval charts.

As part of the British Eighth Army, the DBLE was engaged in building a defensive line stretching from Gazala on the Mediterranean coast southward to the outpost of Bir Hakeim. The Legion was assigned to hold Bir Hakeim just prior to the Axis assault launched at the end of May 1942. The capture of Bir Hakeim was vital to the Africa Corps' great outflanking manoeuvre around the British line. Accordingly, the position was subject to ferocious attacks from Stukas, artillery and tanks. The first assault was fairly easily repulsed, and the fighting ceased when the area was enveloped in a sandstorm. Susan Travers was part of the garrison, and she described the battle:

> The following day, 1 June, the enemy resumed in earnest, with Stuka dive bombers, and Rommel's Panzer Mark IVs bearing down on Bir Hakeim from the north-west. We gave as good as we got, firing back with our 75mm guns and our anti-aircraft weapons. Even the mighty 40mm Bofors guns were put to good use, despite the fact that their poor English operators were still waiting for official instructions on how to use them.

The German and Italian losses were great in those early days, with legionnaires and colonials attacking their tanks with grenades and *Molotov* cocktails. Men would stumble from their burning vehicles in flames, desperately rolling in the sand. The suffering was appalling, and as all of us had the most tremendous respect for those we were fighting, we found it difficult to watch helplessly. There was never any sense of satisfaction in watching others die; just sadness at the lunacy which had brought us all to this oven of a place.

Whenever a position was taken or a crippled vehicle saved, the legionnaires would triumphantly being home their spoils – weapons, ammunition, even entire vehicles sometimes, although the Italian Lancia trucks with their solid tyres were not much favoured. On the corrugated lunar landscape, the tyres shook the trucks to pieces. But what was inside them was coveted – hams, wines, sweetmeats, preserves and cheese. As in Eritrea, the Italians seemed extremely well stocked with provisions.

The defenders of Bir Hakeim continued to fight on, despite a personal plea from Rommel to surrender the position. But by 10 June the situation had become impossible, with both water and ammunition running out. Aware of the hopelessness of the position, the British high command ordered Koenig to fight his way out on the night of 10–11 June. This was no easy matter, however, as the French were surrounded by the bulk of Rommel's mechanised forces. The breakout from Bir Hakeim was almost as much an epic as its defence. Using the cover of darkness a corridor was smashed through the Axis lines, through which all mobile units of the Free French were to pass. One incident from the breakout was described in the Legion's *Livre d'Or*:

The sky was lighted up by flares revealing troops and lorries herded together in the narrow passage. The legionnaires redoubled their assaults on the encircling lines. Hand-to-hand combat, slaughter with the bayonet, grenades! Lieutenant Deve in his Bren carrier overran a couple of machine guns and was charging headlong at an anti-tank gun when he was killed. His sacrifice was not in vain. The men of his company, following close on his heels, broke through the first, second and third enemy lines, while the lorries carrying the wounded and salvaged material were able to pull through, lurching and skidding across the sand.

News of the Legion's defence and breakout from Bir Hakeim was broadcast to the world, signalling the arrival of a new, resurgent anti-German France.

Conditions for the Legion in Vichy North Africa were bad, however: it had been left to rot, starved of weapons and equipment with no military role to fulfil. The volunteer legionnaires, who had crossed over from France to North Africa, received a hostile reception from the old regulars. Ted Harris was bitterly dismayed at the attitudes of the German NCOs he encountered on his arrival in Oran:

> The first concern of all these gentlemen was to stop all our passes into town. Why? The jealously of the well-fed, pot-bellied, red and immoral NCOs. 'Ach, you dirty swine, so you're back from the war? I don't care two pence, anyway! Now that you're here, you'll do as you're told, and nothing else! Besides, you've lost your war, so you had better shut up and get out of my sight!'
>
> All these fat subalterns [sic], who had never thought of anything but their billy-can and their pint, who exploited without qualm all those returning from France and Norway, gloated over their German origin and took pleasure in mortifying us.

Alfred Perrott-White, now a sergeant, lamented the state of affairs that affected even the better-off NCOs:

> Christmas of 1940 was not a very lively affair. We all felt the weight of defeat, and food was beginning to run short, and clothes, too. Gone were the days when one could go to the supply sergeant and get a new shirt or a new pair of socks for the asking. All that one got now was a needle and thread to repair tears and gashes. The possibility of getting clothes new or second-hand was out of the question. The wine ration was cut in half. Sugar, butter, milk, and coffee completely disappeared from our menu.

THE SECOND WORLD WAR: A HOUSE DIVIDED

A. D. Printer, a volunteer who left the Legion for the United States in December 1941, explained the baleful influence of the Nazis over the North African Vichy administration, and the desperate conditions faced by many legionnaires:

> When the German Armistice Commission came to North Africa, the French were forced to reduce the effectives of their garrisons. Thousands of legionnaires were ostensibly discharged but were in reality formed into new military units and sent to the southern part of Algeria and Morocco to work on roads and on the trans-Saharan railway. The men had all the disadvantages of being soldiers and none of the advantages. They wore soldiers' uniforms, but they were treated as if they were men condemned to hard labour. They were worked from eight to ten hours a day in heat that at noon would rise to 140 degrees. They slept in tattered tents that offered little protection against sand storms or rain. Seventeen men shared a tent built for ten. Their clothes swarmed with lice, and boils spread from one to another as they lay crowded together in their rags. In most of the camps water was scarce – hardly enough for drinking and cooking. The men didn't wash for weeks. There was not enough food.

Even worse conditions were experienced by those sent to the *compagnie de discipline des travailleurs*, not only for disciplinary offences but, as Printer commented, 'for being opposed to the spirit of Vichy'. Printer continued:

> Anyone who passed through this company came out a broken man. Even in the regular working companies nearly everyone became affected after a time – nearly everybody except the Spanish. They built up a very intelligent collective self-defence. Like everybody else, they grabbed and stole whatever they could outside the camps, but they shared their booty with all. They fought anybody who attacked their rights, superiors or fellow soldiers, but they never quarrelled among themselves. They were the only ones in the camps who found the strength to sing and joke, and if once in a while they found enough wine, they showed the rest of the men the noble art of getting drunk in a decent and quiet way.

The sense of frustration felt by all legionnaires was revealed in comments made by British legionnaire Anthony Delmayne:

> Few of us had any wish to fight undernourished natives unable to pay their taxes, when there were so many Nazis waiting to be killed. Many of us had a considerable stake in the war. There were Jews and other refugees from Germany, Czechs and Poles, Italians and many Spanish Republicans who were naive enough to think that if fascism was destroyed in Germany, democracy would be restored in their own country too. Rumours that Vichy was going to sell us down the river filled these men with dread.

The situation of the North African legionnaires was transformed by *Operation Torch* – the Anglo-American landings of 8 November 1942. A series of coordinated amphibious assaults along the coast of Morocco and Algeria caught the Vichy French and Germans by surprise. The Vichy French put up only nominal resistance before wisely changing sides to support the Allies.

Alfred Perrott-White was a senior NCO in a battery of vintage 75mm guns stationed in Casablanca when the landings began. Woken from his sleep by the crash of large-calibre high-explosive shells, Perrott-White dashed towards his guns:

> My observation point was on the crest of a hill and I had a fine view of the flames which issued from the warship's guns, but of the ships themselves I could see nothing even through my powerful night glasses. I estimated the range as about nine to eleven miles. That, of course, completely outranged our 75mm guns, so there was nothing we could do about it but wait until we could fire at something within our range.

At first Perrott-White and his comrades assumed the ships to be German, but when it dawned on them that they might be Allied vessels they fired off a few mis-aimed shots in the general direction of the amphibious landing. But this did not stop them coming under aerial attack. Unaware of the power of Allied fighter-bombers, the Legion battery was deployed in the open with no attempt made to camouflage the guns. Perrott-White described the ensuing disaster:

The planes began to fly across to us, no doubt to bomb the fort. I saw in a flash what would happen. Our two guns were right out in the open together with four ammunition trucks. My car was parked under the only tree for a mile. I snatched up the telephone. I knew it was too late to do much. The guns could not be removed in time, but the men could at least scatter and save themselves.

Alas, it was too late. Those planes simply tore through the air. As I had expected, they did not fail to see the guns sticking out like sore thumbs. In five minutes it was all over. I crept out of the ditch where I had flung myself when the first bomb fell, and counted up the damage. Out of thirty men and one officer, fifteen men and the officer were dead; ten more were wounded. The two guns were out of commission and two trucks were on fire, the ammunition they carried exploding in flames.

For a moment I felt great bitterness in my soul as I saw my comrades scattered all around. Ever since the fall of France, we had dreamed of deliverance, but we did not want it that way. As is the custom in the Legion, we buried our comrades where they fell. It did not take long to make graves in that sandy soil, and we were finished by half-past nine.

The ambivalence felt by the Legion towards the Allied invaders was expressed by Erwin Deman, a Hungarian Jew who had volunteered for the 22nd Regiment. Having survived the battles of 1940 he spent the next two years in North Africa, under the tyranny of the old German NCOs. This was a time to settle long-standing grievances:

On the day following the invasion we were rushed in buses to establish some defensive line. And we were ordered, as one always is, to dig in – and we dug fox holes the depth of mine pits, for at that stage of the game no one wished to be exposed to bullets that we all thought came from our friends.

Among the very old members of the Foreign Legion there was a paying off of old scores. When Allied spotter planes flew over us, and machine gun was opened up on them on order, I don't think anyone aimed at them. But after these raids were over there were usually a few senior NCOs found with bullets in their backs.

After North Africa was cleared of German troops, elements of the Legion joined the Allies in the invasion of Italy, and then in September 1944 took part in the liberation of southern France. The 13th DBLE and a new *Régiment de Marche* fought their way through France and into Germany. By the time of the German surrender in May 1945 advance units of the regiment had already crossed the Danube.

With some very notable exceptions, the Second World War did not see the Legion at its best, but this was essentially a reflection of France's own disastrous part in the conflict. After the Second World War, the Legion would return to the colonial wars it knew best, although, ultimately, with tragic consequences.

CHAPTER 13

TRAGEDY IN VIETNAM

Following the defeat of Japan in 1945, the British and Chinese initially took control of Indochina before handing it back to France. But when the French returned to Vietnam in early 1946 they were opposed by a well-organised, communist-inspired national liberation movement under the leadership of Ho Chi Minh and his military planner, Vo Nguyen Giap.

The Vietnamese communists (Viet Minh) instigated a guerrilla war against the French. At first this consisted of little more than a series of minor skirmishes, but all the while the Viet Minh were building up their strength in the remote mountainous region of north-east Vietnam and the Red River Delta. From 1948 onwards the fighting increased in intensity, followed by a full-scale offensive against the French in 1950.

As French conscripts were forbidden to serve outside metropolitan France, the bulk of the French forces stationed in Indochina came from colonial units and the Foreign Legion. The 2nd Foreign Legion Regiment came ashore at Haiphong Harbour in February, to be joined by three other infantry regiments: the cavalry regiment and two newly raised paratroop battalions (with a third acting as a depot battalion).

To counter the Viet Minh, the French adopted a containment strategy by building strong-points across the country, often dotted along a major highway (*Route Colonial* or RC). The Viet Minh began to attack the more remote outposts in earnest during 1948, beginning with the assault on Phu-Tong-Hoa (along RC 3) on the evening of 25 July. The post was held by 104 legionnaires commanded by Captain Cardinal, along with Lieutenant Charlotton and Second Lieutenant Bevalot. The attack began at 1930 hours with a bombardment from 75mm field guns and mortars that destroyed much of the post's defences, mortally wounding both Cardinal and Charlotton. This was followed by a series of human-wave attacks from Viet Minh infantry that breached the post's outer defences. The fort was set to be overrun. Legionnaire X described the fight for survival:

> The south-east bastion, Second Lieutenant Bevalot himself directing the defence, held. The moon came through the clouds dispersing a feeble light, but enough to enable our men to see what they were doing. The rebels were subjected to a violent fusillade. The 81mm mortar managed to land a bomb just outside the breach. In the northern angle, Sergeant Guillemand hung on with a few survivors, showering grenades into the courtyard. Near the main gate, Corporals Huegen and Polain were killed, the latter being bayoneted after a most courageous fight. It was nearly 22 hours.
>
> From this moment, however, the balance of the combat began to swing in our favour. Sergeant Andry and Sergeant Fissler, with three legionnaires, advanced, firing their automatics from the hip at point-blank range, and cleared the central buildings of the enemy. Corporal Camilleri and two legionnaires crawled through the breach and slaughtered the Viets who had occupied the north-west bastion.
>
> By 23 hours, the post was entirely in our hands and trumpets could be heard sounding the retreat. Though no further attacks were launched, the enemy kept up a sporadic bombardment.
>
> Lieutenant Charlotton asked a legionnaire to sit beside him and talk about the Legion; he died just after one o'clock. Captain Cardinal died about four, happy in the knowledge that the post was held.
>
> A bloody dawn broke on the 26th over the post of Phu-Tong-Hoa. Within the walls lay over forty Viet Minh dead. There were bodies strewn outside the walls, in the gaps in the bamboo; we counted more than 200 of them.

During the attack the post had radioed to nearby Bac-Kan for help. Major Paul Grauwin, a senior medical officer who would win fame at Dien Bien Phu, was in Bac-Kan at the time:

> A relief column set out from Bac-Kan; it ran into a terrible ambush and had to return to Bac-Kan with a great number of wounded.
>
> Another relief column set out from Cao-Bang, under Colonel Simon, who was in command of the regiment. After two days of difficult and dangerous progress, Colonel Simon and his column came within sight of Phu-Tong-Hoa, thinking to find nothing but ruins and corpses. They were received at the entrance to the shattered outpost by the forty [unwounded] legionnaires, drawn up in perfect order, wearing their superb parade uniforms.

The successful defence of Phu-Tong-Hoa did not prevent the Viet Minh from continuing their attacks on isolated outposts and the convoys that connected them. RC 4 ran parallel to the Chinese border, from Lang Son in the south to Cao Bang in the north, through the remote mountainous region of the Viet Bac that had become a Viet Minh stronghold. The battle to hold open RC 4 would become one of the toughest engagements ever fought by the Legion.

Elements of the Legion were deployed along RC 4 to act as *patrouilles d'overture* (opening patrols); these cleared mines and booby traps and defended the convoys from Viet Minh ambushes. The French journalist Lucien Bodard accompanied a convoy driving northwards up RC 4:

> In the green darkness I could not even see the soldiers who were supposed to be protecting us. I asked the radio sergeant whether the covering force had in fact been posted there. It had. At dawn men had left all the posts and they had climbed and marched for hours, taking up their positions in all the dangerous places. Perhaps during this taking up of positions all over the countryside there had been skirmishes and men killed – I did not know and I never shall know; this was merely everyday routine. And when we were gone by they would leave their positions, march for hours and hours and then shut themselves in their posts. Perhaps they

would not have fired a single shot; perhaps they would have had to fight to save their lives or to guard the convoy. They were the world's most extraordinary traffic police.

We were beginning to rise to the Luong Phai Pass. This was the most blood-drenched area in the whole of Indochina. The road climbed the sheer mountainside like a winding ladder, turning its dizzy hairpin bends: and there was not one of these corners that had not been used for an ambush and which had not seen the most savage hand-to-hand fighting.

I sensed the convoy's intense apprehension from the automatic head movements, all swinging together. Far away from here, right down in Cochinchina on the Camau road, I had seen men's eyes all turn together at the same second, staring, searching, first on the right and then on the left. But then there were only a score or two of them. Here on the RC 4 there were hundreds of us, perhaps a thousand, and we were all swinging our heads with the same automatic reflex. It was extraordinarily comic, and at the same time extraordinarily dramatic. And the weapons which bristled from every vehicle followed the heads and eyes that were searching for the signs of danger.

The convoy arrived safely, yet the strain of those travelling with it was clearly apparent, as Bodard recalled: 'That night the whole convoy got drunk. It was a tradition: the military authorities allowed it. This time it was nothing extraordinary. But if there had been men killed or wounded the survivors would have drunk until they reached oblivion – until they had lost all recollection, all awareness.'

Leslie Aparvary, a soldier in the newly formed 1st BEP (*Bataillon Étranger de Parachutiste*), had fled the post-war communist regime in Hungary to join the Legion. He recalled an attack on a convoy that he and his paratroopers were guarding near the outpost of Dong Khe on RC 4:

We climbed up the hill to secure a vantage point from which we could scan the road. The advance guard appeared around noon, and the convoy was almost past us when all hell broke loose. The Viet Minhs, hiding in the hills facing Dong Khe, had waited until most of the convoy had shifted into firing range, and then they had opened fire from all sides. We hastened to assist the others just as fast as we could. We succeeded in running perhaps one kilometre before their shots bogged us down. It was possible to make headway only by creeping and crawling, darting about, and taking cover if we could find it behind trees and bushes. By this time we could see the enemy clearly. There were so many of them!

There was not time to take aim. All we could do was shoot in their general direction. 'Douze-septs' [12.7mm (0.5ins) heavy machine guns], mortars and small cannon spread death everywhere. The vehicles in the convoy ignited one after the other. We tried to force our way through to reach the central point of the attack. The number of defenders had already diminished to half the original number and the cry for assistance was great. The rattle of firearms was deafening. Movement of any sort was treacherously difficult on the steep mountainside. We tried to carve a path upwards, while our opponents were shielded and fired at us from the comfort of their trenches. It was thanks to our 'douze-sept' and the small cannon on our tanks that we gained ground step-by-step and eventually were able to send the enemy flying.

Every now and then a man senses that the end is near. Never in my life had the wings of death loomed so close.

Less well-defended convoys could face disaster, however. A veteran legionnaire sergeant described a Viet Minh ambush on RC 4:

Technically it was far and away the best – really scientific, with everything synchronised. And you can believe me when I say so, because I was there. To begin with the Viets paralysed the convoy. Mines went off behind the armoured cars at the head of the column, cutting them off from the trucks. Immediately after that a dozen un-attackable machine guns in those limestone cliffs opened up, raking the whole line. Then came a hail of grenades. These [came from] regulars lying close-packed along the embankment over the road and they dropped them just so, tossing a dozen at each vehicle. There were flames everywhere. Anywhere you looked there were burning trucks, and they completely blocked the road. All this took only a minute.

Then there was a terrific shouting. It was the charge. Thousands of naked bodies leaped up from the sides of the road, just by us, and hurled themselves at the convoy. We were still inside. But before this tide broke over us we jumped out and forced our way through the current. Our idea was to climb the embankment and regroup into little fighting units. We shouted to one another to keep in touch, but the Viets shouted louder still. We could see mobs of Viets below us, attacking our comrades who had not been able to follow us and regroup. They went under in a few seconds.

The Viets were very methodical. Regulars went from truck to truck, gathering the weapons and the goods that had been left behind; then they set fire to the vehicles. Other regulars attacked the French who were still fighting on the embankments. Coolies with jungle knives finished off the wounded who had fallen onto the roadway or into the ditches. It was hand-to-hand fighting everywhere. There were hundreds of single combats, hundreds of pairs of men killing each other. In the middle of all this mess the political commissars very calmly supervised the work in hand, giving orders to the regulars and the coolies – orders that were carried out at once.

The middle of the convoy was wiped out. The armoured cars at the tail end began firing their guns point-blank into the trucks the Viets has taken. There were Red officers hurrying about in the midst of the fighting calling out 'Where is the colonel? Where is the colonel?' in French. They meant Colonel Simon, the CO of the 3rd *Étranger*, the man with a bullet in his head – it had been there for years; he got it long before the war in Indochina. He was in the convoy and Giap had ordered that he should be taken alive.

I was in the part of the convoy that was destroyed. I found myself on the embankment together with a few legionnaires, and we fought furiously for half an hour: then we were overwhelmed. I escaped into the forest and hid in some undergrowth about fifty yards from the road. Just next to me I heard some shots. It was the legionnaires blowing their brains out – the Viets had discovered them. As for me, I was not discovered.

I don't know how the whole nightmare ended. They say that Colonel Simon managed to gather a hundred of his men around him and form them up in squares that thrust back the waves of Viets with grenades for hours on end. Three hours later the reinforcements came up – the heavy armour. A few minutes before the sound of the tracks was heard the Viets had disengaged. At the very beginning when they attacked, they had sounded the charge on the trumpet. Now there was another trumpet call for the retreat and they vanished into the jungle in perfect order, unit by unit. Special formations of coolies carried off their killed and wounded, as well as all the loot they had taken.

We remained on the battlefield. The road was a graveyard, a charnel-house. Nothing was left of the convoy but a heap of ripped-open bodies and blackened engines. It was already beginning to stink. The survivors gathered on the roadway; we cleared it and picked up the corpses and the wounded. And what was left of the convoy set off again.

Despite the fact that the defence of RC 4 and its outposts was clearly untenable, the French refused to give it up to the Viet Minh. It was only in 1950 – when the Viet Minh had been massively reinforced by the new communist regime in China – that the French made plans to evacuate the route. By then, however, it was too late. On 18 September an overwhelming force of 16 Viet Minh battalions, supported by artillery, was unleashed against the outpost at Dong Khe – held by two companies from the 3rd Legion Regiment, just 260-men strong. The result was inevitable. Lucien Bodard described the disaster, as those on the outside anxiously awaited news of the outpost's fate:

One Saturday at noon came the first message from Dong Khe, the one that said that Giap had set things in motion, that he had begun his 'general counter-offensive'.

On the first day, however, the outcome was not clear. The messages from Dong Khe said the losses were very small, and even that the garrison's artillery had silenced two Viet guns. But the second day, a long drawn-out Sunday, the messages became progressively fewer and shorter, and they contained all the formulas of a 'deteriorating situation': by twilight on that Sunday more than half the legionnaires had been killed or wounded. There was one last but not entirely desperate message, but the coming of night brought an unbroken silence – Dong Khe no longer answered.

There was still silence on Monday morning and the sky was so low that Upper Tonkin was nothing but a grey sheet, the mountains entirely lost in the clouds. Nevertheless a Junkers [Ju-52 aircraft] was ordered to go and look at Dong Khe – an almost impossible flight through the monsoon and among the mountain tops. And the Junkers, when it had last pushed through, when it was circling over the Dong Khe basin, knew what the news was. The French flag had disappeared from the shattered mast; great blackish flames were still rising from the post; there was nothing but ruin and desolation.

The dying of the post, held by the finest troops in the Legion, had lasted sixty hours. The death throes were known only by a few radio messages; then came the great silence of the end. For that was what the war in Indochina was like – the fighting men died alone and the high command did not even know the manner of their death.

The French were finally convinced that RC 4 must be abandoned, but the loss of Dong Khe meant that the most northerly outpost, Cao Bang, was now dangerously isolated. Under the command of the tough Colonel Charton, the legionnaires stationed in Cao Bang prepared to evacuate the position. Meanwhile, a column of North African troops under Colonel Marcel Le Page was to march northward from That Khe, recapture Dong Khe and then rendezvous with Charton's force, before they both moved southward along RC 4 to Lang Son.

On leaving That Khe, Le Page's column was strengthened by the 1st BEP. On 30 September, with the paras in the lead, the French fought their way directly towards Dong Khe, but were repulsed by mass Viet Minh attacks and then pinned down in the shattered limestone jungle gorges to the west of Dong Khe. On 3 October, Charton's force – which included wounded and Vietnamese civilians – left Cao Bang. Initially all went well until Charton's progress down RC 4 was blocked by the Viet Minh; he was then instructed to march along a jungle trail skirting Dong Khe to meet up with Le Page's increasingly beleaguered force. The Viet Minh now concentrated on Charton's troops, and although the French fought their way to a rendezvous with Le Page, casualties were enormous and the situation desperate.

One of Charton's Legion officers witnessed the meeting with Le Page's North Africans: 'In a matter of seconds, when I saw what was coming from the Le Page column, I realised that we were already on the beaten side – that the Viets were stronger than we were. These broken men were afraid; they spread fear all around them among our people.'

He went on to describe the final hours of the French trapped in the jungle defiles:

A little after four we began to march towards That Khe, about twenty miles off. The column was very long; and in the rear there were still some Cao Bang civilians! Charton was wounded by a grenade thrown from a thicket and he disappeared. When the column came up close to a pass the ambush opened fire – it was all over very quickly. Tens of thousands of Viets rushed at us. It was a sudden storming operation with no precautions or manoeuvres, to get it over and done with – liquidation. An execution. For a few minutes the column fought back furiously, waving to and fro and breaking into thousands of separate personal battles in the midst of this wild tumble of rocks and greenery.

We were attacked with everything that could kill – there were still shells coming in, but now they were reaching us at point-blank range. And then it was the grenade and the knife; and above all there was this huge number of Viets rushing at us – they kept coming out of the jungle, little smooth men with green leaves on their helmets. Yet there was still time for some bitter unhappiness. Just next to me I saw a captain collapse, weeping; and a little farther off a sergeant was wandering about, careless of the bullet that would kill him, waiting for it. There were officers who got their men to shoot them. Some completely surrounded Moroccans charged, singing a battle chant until they were all killed. There were a few last words of farewell between friends; then everything stopped.

There was a silence over the destroyed column; and a smell. That silence, you know, with groaning in it; and that smell of bodies that comes with a great slaughter – they are the first realities of defeat. Then presently there was another reality, and a far more surprising one – that of Viet Minh discipline. I had expected barbarity; but within a few moments after the last shot what I saw was an extraordinary scrupulousness – the establishment of exact order. Viet officers moved all over the battlefield, not at all as conquerors – merely as though one operation had been finished and another one was beginning. I could make no vanity in them – no triumph.

The men of 1st BEP and the 3rd Legion Regiment fought to the end. After Charton had been wounded and captured by the Viet Minh, Le Page instructed the remnants of his command to break up into small groups and fight their way back to That Khe; just 23 Legion paras from an entire battalion managed to escape the Viet Minh. But even as the survivors staggered back to the relative safety of That Khe, they found that they had already been outflanked. A general panic ensued and the French shamefully evacuated the garrison of Lang Son without a fight, scrambling back to the Red River Delta and leaving vast amounts of munitions and equipment to the enemy.

Fortunately for the French, Giap and the Viet Minh overreached themselves and they suffered repeated setbacks as they tried to breach the defences surrounding the Red River Delta. This bought the French in Tonkin a much-needed, if temporary, respite.

Although Tonkin was the main theatre of war in Vietnam, Cochin China in the south of the country was also an important area of operations, as the Viet Minh fought to gain control of the low-lying paddy fields around the city of Saigon. Viet Minh activity in the south tended to be on a smaller scale than in Tonkin, their fighters infiltrating villages and conducting small-scale raids and assassinations before slipping away into jungle and marshland. Fighting this 'invisible enemy' was virtually impossible. Even when there was good intelligence, the Viet Minh were adept at avoiding contact. A young officer in the Legion's 13th DBLE (*Demi-Brigade de Légion Étrangère*) recalled an attempt to pin down the enemy:

My objective was a Viet Minh 'factory' on a little island in the Plain of Reeds [close to Saigon]. Usually I put my men into sampans and we'd go up the canals, whose banks are lined with water palms so that they can hem you in like the walls of a prison. You can't see anything, but you can be seen. This time, so as not to be picked up, we went on foot through the shit, as we call it – the stinking marsh covered with reeds and lotus that stretches out for ever.

The approach lasted for hours, and all the time we were up to our waists in the muck. We had started at midnight: by dawn we had still not been seen. We were only a few hundred yards from the factory. Then came the horn sounding the alarm. I looked through my field glasses. The little island was like an ant hill that had been stirred up. I heard explosions and saw flames. I knew what that meant. The Viets were taking their heavy equipment away in boats and they were carrying out their scorched-earth policy with the rest. It always happens that way.

It took us another half hour to get ashore, to struggle up onto firm ground. There was nothing but destruction and emptiness. Some frantic buffaloes by the remains of the burning huts. We killed them. The stocks of rice had been soaked in gasoline and now they were only smouldering heaps. We found little in the way of machinery, all smashed with hammers. But all the truly valuable equipment, the lathes for making shells and electric motors, had been carried off, in spite of its weight.

We did not see a single man, either. There were certainly hundreds of Viets still there, but so hidden there was no hope in finding them. Some would have turned into bushes. Others would be right down in the mud, breathing through hollow bamboos. Most would be in carefully prepared burrows. It was like being surrounded by a crowd of ghosts: they would stay for hours on end, waiting for us to go.

The officer went on to describe the frustration of these operations in the wetlands of the Plain of Reeds, between Saigon and the Mekong River:

It is unbelievably monotonous. There are the ambushes – the ones you set and above all the ones you fall into. Suddenly men you can't see, amphibious creatures in the water and the mud, start firing: you don't even know where the shots are coming from. Then there is the chasing. Sometimes it is we who are after the Viets and sometimes the other way about, but it is always the same business. Men sunk deep into the mud, the gluey mud, slowly forcing their legs through it to catch other men who are bogged down in the same way. You only see their heads, and the Plain of Reeds is so flat that you might think they were dots stuck to its surface. When you come to the open space of a canal or an irrigation ditch you swim under water, so as not to present a target: all that you see of a man is one hand holding up a tommy gun or the part of a mortar that must never get wet. Often some of my men are drowned.

In an attempt to provide mechanised support to the hard-pressed infantry, the French deployed two US amphibious vehicles of Second World War vintage: the armoured Alligator vehicle, equipped with heavy machine guns and a recoilless rifle, and the lighter Crab. British legionnaire Adrian Liddell Hart was assigned to a Crab, first as a machine-gunner and then a driver, and he outlined operations in and around the Mekong Delta:

Here and there we came across long strips of thick jungle forest often fringed with irrigated banana plantations and other evidences of human cultivation. Occasionally a radio aerial could be seen protruding from the foliage – a sign of military as well as human habitation. After the Crabs had nosed up like half submerged dinosaurs to provide covering power, some of us would scramble through the clearing to investigate. Sometimes there were already groups of infantry in evidence, slowly working through the forest in the hope of flushing out the rebels.

Here and there we rooted round for dumps of arms or other supplies which might be concealed, overturning heavy bowls of rice and peering under floorboards. Several times I came across little notebooks with Chinese characters neatly and methodically inscribed in then. Then once more we pressed forward against a receding vista or reeking forest.

But the enemy? He was everywhere – and nowhere. Inevitably warned by spies, by sympathetic or fearful inhabitants of our approach, possibly before we had even left the camp, he had vanished into the vast wilderness which he knew so much better than we. For hours, for days, we scanned the horizon in vain. Beyond the still grass, deep in the menacing woods, far up the muddy swollen tributaries, lay the enemy . . . We might make wide sweeps but our net had wide meshes.

Just as it was possible get used to the bizarre conditions on operations, so I became acclimatised to the daily life and atmosphere of the camp, with its characteristic confusion and suspicion and grind. Indeed, this whole existence of fighting and working had a single rhythm – slogging work in the camp, hectic days of preparation for an operation, hours of uneasy relaxation as the legionnaires drank on the landing craft, days and nights of strenuous, marauding sweeps as we heaved and dug and churned our way through swamp and jungle, songs over forest fires, and then once more, without a break, the work of cleaning and repairing the Crabs, maintaining and guarding the camp, with snatched moments, often late at night, of drinking from the upturned bottle in the foyer. '*En Avant!*'

The Legion had its successes, however, as the DBLE officer explained:

> Not long ago we got three hundred at one go. An informer guided our legionnaires to a Viet meeting that was being held on the banks of the Saigon River. The meeting was camouflaged in a field of maize. But we knew where it was a going on, and we charged right for the spot. The Viets flung themselves into the river, sinking into the water and the mud of the submerged forest and wriggling in among the mangrove roots. But the Saigon River is a tidal stream and the tide was on the ebb. We only had to wait. Two hours later the first Viets, stark naked, were in sight. They tried very hard to bury themselves deeper, digging down in the drying mud with their hands. We shot them like so many rabbits. The water ebbed further and further, and as it retreated every yard of mud had its quarry in it.

As the officer was quick to concede, however, simply killing Viet Minh was not enough – 'there's an inexhaustible supply' – and, worse still, the French were indiscriminate in their methods: 'It's not only the full-blown Viet that we kill. We only know afterwards, and not always then. Often they are just villagers, people's militia, half or even only a quarter Viet.'

The French attitude to the Vietnamese population was, at best, indifferent. Little or no attempt was made to distinguish between civilians and combatants, and atrocities were commonplace. Lacking popular support, the French used extreme methods to gain intelligence of Viet Minh activities, further alienating the ordinary Vietnamese farmers and their families. Henry Ainley – a legionnaire sent to his battalion headquarters north of Saigon while working alongside the intelligence section – was sickened by French methods in Vietnam:

> Torture and brutality were routine matters in the questioning of suspects, and frequently I was obliged to be an unwilling and disgusted witness, powerless to intervene. Unfortunately, brutality and bestiality were not exclusively reserved for official suspects. Rape, beating, burning, torturing on entirely harmless peasants and villagers were of common occurrence in the course of punitive patrols and operations by French troops, throughout the length and breadth of Indochina; the same measure evidently being applied to bona fide Viet Minh as well. Not only were these measures exclusively applied by the men; officers and NCOs assumed an active and frequently dominating role.
>
> It was not an infrequent occurrence to hear these men bragging of the number of murders or rapes they had committed or the means of torture they had applied or the cash, jewels or possessions they had stolen. If one queried the morality of their actions the immediate reflection was 'Well, hell they are only "bounyouls" [natives]. Who the devil cares, anyway?' Before such a widespread and generally accepted practice there was nothing to do but look, listen and say nothing.

The fundamental counter-insurgency principle that 'the people are the prize' was lost on the French. And this failure only hurried the French ejection from Indochina.

By 1953 the French were losing control of Tonkin outside the defensive lines of the Red River Delta. This allowed the Viet Minh to push into neighbouring Laos with little opposition. In order to inhibit these Viet Minh operations the French decided to seize and hold Dien Bien Phu, a village that lay astride the main Viet Minh route into Laos. Two French airborne battle groups (including the Legion's 1st BEP) parachuted into Dien Bien Phu in November 1953, fortifying the area and constructing two air strips.

The apparent success of this move encouraged the French to extend their plan to include the possibility of waging a set-piece battle against the Viet Minh, where, it was believed, French superiority in artillery and air power would prove decisive. Giap seemed to have taken up the challenge when the French discovered that he had sent two of his best divisions towards Dien Bien Phu. The French flew in reinforcements and hurriedly began to improve the site's defences. Dien Bien Phu lay in a bowl-shaped valley, surrounded by densely wooded hills. The French lacked the time and resources to defend the hills, but instead contented themselves in building a series of mutually supporting strong-points in the valley, each one reputedly named after the mistresses of the garrison commander, Colonel (later General) Christian de Castries. Of the 13 fighting battalions at Dien Bien Phu, seven would be supplied by the Legion.

Sergeant Bleyer was assigned to the strongpoint called *Beatrice*, where he and his platoon began to dig in:

> We immediately went to work clearing brush, cutting trees and building the most solid blockhouses possible, each platoon competing with that intensity particular to the Legion. I could only encourage my men. Having had a little experience during the Russian campaign [1941–5], I knew the damage that could be done by artillery. My legionnaires – terrific lads – were also well aware of the risks we were running.

Bleyer and his comrades, were, in fact, being dangerously complacent. Once again, the French underestimated the Viet Minh's military capabilities. An army of coolies had dragged 75mm field artillery and 120mm mortars to the hills surrounding the French positions.

Meticulously camouflaged – and well dug-in – the Viet Minh artillery would prove decisive. The French, by contrast, had not built the reinforced-concrete bunkers necessary to withstand Viet Minh shells, relying on relatively flimsy timber-and-dirt defences.

The bombardment of Dien Bien Phu opened on 31 January 1954, and after steady probing and the digging of assault trenches, Giap launched attacks on 13 March against the more exposed French positions. Among these was *Beatrice*, whose defenders included the 3rd Battalion of the DBLE. Captain Nicolas of the 10th Company described the beginning of the attack:

> On 13 March the Viet Minh artillery preparation began. The entire day had been spent trying to fill in the Viet Minh approach trenches. During this extremely violent preparation the Viet Minh reopened their trenches and pushed them up to the wire under cover of the thick dust raised by the explosions that surrounded the centre of resistance with a veritable smoke screen.

Sergeant Kubiak, of the 1st Battalion, saw the attack on *Beatrice* from the main position:

> The day began just like any other, digging fatigues, working on our defences . . . Towards 16.55 hours, I was having a drink with a friend. Then suddenly, without warning, it was what I imagine the end of the world will be like. The post Beatrice just went up in smoke, reduced to rubble . . . Blockhouse by blockhouse, trench by trench, everything collapsed, burying men and weapons under the debris.

Bleyer, meanwhile, was in the thick of the bombardment and subsequent Viet Minh attack:

> Heavy artillery fire smashed everything, and it had barely stopped when the Viets were already in our wire. I went to get my orders, but the blockhouse of Lieutenant Carriere had collapsed under direct fire from bazookas and recoilless rifles. The lieutenant himself had been killed, and the controls of the defensive charges weren't working. I tried in vain to make contact with Lieutenant

Jego. Then I found myself facing the Viets, who I welcomed with shots from my Colt. A grenade exploded between my legs.

Although wounded, Bleyer rallied other legionnaires before the whole position was taken. Only a few men got back to friendly lines. Major Paul Grauwin, one of the senior medical officers at Dien Bien Phu, treated some of the wounded survivors:

> I returned to the field hospital, where some men with minor wounds had just arrived, having managed to escape from *Beatrice*. Their eyes were round with terror as they told of their experiences. 'If you could have seen them, Major, thousands and thousands of them, jumping over each other, over the ones who were already dead, mown down by our fire. Then the thousands of shells – when they had finished falling, half our shelters had collapsed.'

Gabrielle, another outer strong-point, then came under intense pressure. The 1st BEP was ordered to launch a counter-attack in support of *Gabrielle*'s hard-pressed defenders. Almost immediately the Legion paratroopers came under intense fire from a Viet Minh blocking force along the Nam Ou River. According to Lieutenant Desmaizieres, of the battalion's 3rd Company:

> The fighting began brutally; the 4th [Company] suffered serious losses. Norbert [the company commander] was wounded by a bullet in the thigh that made him howl with rage and pain. Standing under fire, he dropped his pants to apply a dressing while his orderly provided cover. Lieutenants Boisbouvier and Bertrand had crossed the ford, but they were pinned down with their legionnaires. Manoeuvring to the left of the trail, the source of the main firing, and supported by the tanks, the 3rd Company succeeded in breaking through and proceeded towards the objective.

But to the consternation of the paras, they saw the defenders beginning to withdraw from *Gabrielle*. The legionnaires of 1st BEP then began to retire as well, their efforts in vain. Desmaizieres concluded: 'a few [Algerian] riflemen held on till dusk before being overrun. The withdrawal of what was left of the BEP's companies was carried out under fire from the Viet cannons. They seemed to be celebrating their victory.'

The fall of *Beatrice* and *Gabrielle* was followed by the loss of *Anne-Marie* on the night of 17–18 March. The main airstrip was now vulnerable to Viet Minh artillery fire, and after the loss of several aircraft on the runway it was closed; the only assistance that could be provided to the garrison would have to come from parachute drops.

Despite this blow, the French fought on stubbornly, repulsing a series of Viet Minh offensives at the end of March and beginning of April. Casualties were heavy, however, and the garrison's medical organisation began to buckle under the strain, especially now that the seriously wounded could not be evacuated by air. Major Paul Grauwin left this graphic account of the conditions he was forced to work under:

Next came paratroopers from the Eighth Assault and the First Battalion of the Foreign, North African sappers, Senegalese gunners, Vietnamese, Thaïs. A leg torn off, a wheezing thorax, an open stomach, a bloody hole in place of an eye, with the eye, smashed, hanging down on the cheek. An artery spurting up a jet of warm blood, abrupt and relentless; another leg torn off, a shoulder gaping open . . .

I had Major Martinelli put into Lieutenant Gindrey's shelter. But still they came, more and more of them, a lieutenant, a captain, a string of coolies helping one another along. Shells were whistling, ten or more at a time, exploding all at once. The shelters were full and fresh arrivals no longer even had room to lie down.

'Put them in the X-ray room – we can get four in there.' The next order was, 'Put them in the resuscitation ward – we can squeeze a few more in there.' Ten minutes later I found myself wedged between the phone and Lachamp's desk. A Vietnamese with the upper jaw broken had collapsed at my feet and was grasping my legs with his arms. Each time he breathed he spat blood and his eyes reflected his terror.

The next order was, 'Use the operating theatre.' I had to put a stop to operations. God help us. The first thing was to protect the wounded from the shells which were falling worse than ever. The operating theatre was soon full up. Howls, cries, groans and the ringing of the phone all mingled with the unholy din outside, filling my ears so that I could no longer think. From that moment I was no longer aware whether it was day or night, whether I was hungry or thirsty, whether I was a living human being or only a character in a nightmare.

I remember having heard someone say: '*Gabrielle* has fallen. *Anne-Marie* has been abandoned.' Is that important? What does strategy or the number of Viets killed in the barbed wire around *Gabrielle* matter to me? Because this little fellow from Montpelier lying on a stretcher in the X-ray room is going to die; because there is blood spurting up into my face from a hole in this thorax and I can't stop it; because this abdomen, which is as hard as stone, belongs to a legionnaire who tells me, '*Ich bin fertig, ich weiss* [I'm ready, I know]'; because this Vietnamese's dark eyes are full of reproach as he asks me why I have cut his leg off.

During April the Viet Minh steadily encroached on what remained of the French positions, digging trenches and building up supplies in preparation for the final assault. The French, meanwhile, were reinforced from the air by four paratroop battalions (two from the Legion), which provided much-needed practical support, as well as improving morale. But the defenders were even more impressed by a further parachute drop, as Grauwin explained:

Towards the middle of April, a special order of the day, signed by General de Castries, informed us that, in response to a request from the commander-in-chief, thousands of men in all branches of the service had volunteered to drop on Dien Bien Phu, without making any preliminary drops or having any previous training.

It was unbelievable, unprecedented; we could hardly believe our eyes as we read. Our hearts were filled with relief; around me I could hear the soldiers, visitors and wounded expressing their joy and enthusiasm. Now they were convinced that everything would be done for Dien Bien Phu, that the higher command had decided to hold on to the end – until victory.

There could be no doubting the heroism of these novice paratroops, especially as many knew only too well – unlike Grauwin – the real hopelessness of the situation. French aircraft were operating towards the end of their range, and were unable to supply the garrison with sufficient supplies and munitions. They had also failed to make much impression on the Viet Minh artillery that was pounding the French positions into oblivion. As the French got weaker, so Giap's forces grew stronger. Matters were made worse by the coming of the monsoon on 22 April, leaving the French defences waterlogged; the more battered simply collapsed into a sea of mud.

On 1 May the Viet Minh threw all their forces at the remaining French positions. Sergeant Kubiak recorded the final days of Dien Bien Phu in his diary:

> 5 May 1954
>
> We've been fighting for fifty days. Sheer hell!
>
> The Viets are bombarding us with their '*orgues de Staline*' – twelve-barrelled rocket launchers – and my sector is having particular attention paid to it. Again I feel it's the end of the world, and I'm not the only one who feels that way. In the dark I cross myself. It's extraordinary how intensely one believes when death is roaming around. I got a splinter in my face. It gave me a lovely pair of black eyes. Blood spurted and I was almost knocked out.
>
> But I realised that if I could still keep on my feet, things weren't too bad. I got my automatic well sited. About time. Another wave of Viets was coming at us. Independent fire. Death spitting from every corner. Men falling like flies on both sides.
>
> Today is the 6 May.
>
> The heat is killing as soon as the sun rises. The piles of fly-covered corpses are decomposing rapidly. The air we breathe is scarcely perfumed with attar of roses!

On 7 May the Viet Minh overran the main French position, but the legionnaires – including the wounded – were determined to fight on, as Kubiak explained:

Legionnaire S. was by my side. He'd been hit several times in the belly and walked doubled up. He was in agony . . . Suddenly firing broke out from a blockhouse and I saw Viets falling. I ran across, went in, and could hardly believe my eyes. It was a couple of wounded men who were firing the machine gun. They grinned when they saw me. 'I've got the odd hole in me,' said one, 'but I can still fight.' He had a huge bandage round his belly and, as he staggered to his feet, blood began to ooze through. As for the other, who had been acting as leader, he had only one arm and a shell splinter in the lung.

Suddenly I heard the battalion commander swearing like a trooper. I turned in the direction he was looking and saw a white flag fluttering over the General's HQ. It was difficult to guess his reactions.

We opened on the Viets with everything we'd got and it wasn't long before they were answering back in no mean manner, the whole mass of their artillery concentrating on us. For me the last few minutes are hazy. A shell spat under my nose and I collapsed in the mud, hit in the right leg. Suddenly a Viet jumped into the trench, saw me and I'd had it. He came slowly towards me, and I couldn't move. He cocked his sub-machine, aimed deliberately and fired. I don't know what happened, but suddenly he collapsed on top of me and I passed out.

I learnt afterwards that a legionnaire had killed him just as he fired and the shot had missed me by a millimetre. It was his corpse falling on me that protected me from the other Viets.

It was the 7 May. For me the battle was over, my life as a prisoner beginning.

Following de Castries' decision to surrender, a few determined defenders tried to fight their way out, but almost all were either killed or captured. Some 11,000 men – many of them wounded – were led away into what would become a prolonged and cruel captivity. Pierre Schoendoerffer remembers feeling 'rage and bitterness at being abandoned' and seeing the enemy at close hand:

We left the putrefaction of the battlefield, and suddenly saw grass, trees, and inhaled good odour. There was a clear sunset, and high in the sky the last [French] Dakota [supply plane] was dropping a cargo of medicine. The Viet Minh were tense and very young. Despite their heavy losses, there was no brutality. We climbed a hill, and, reaching the crest, we could see an entire valley filled with Viet Minh troops ready to attack. They watched us intently as we passed.

The defeat had destroyed the elite of the French army, and France had little alternative but to withdraw from Indochina. On 21 July 1954 the French signed a negotiated settlement: Laos and Cambodia received their independence while Vietnam was divided at the 17th parallel into a communist North and a US-sponsored South. More than 10,000 soldiers and officers of the Foreign Legion had been killed in a hopeless bid to hang on to this colonial possession thousands of miles from France.

CHAPTER 14

THE END IN ALGERIA

In 1954 Arab nationalism in Algeria exploded into violence, initiating a bloody war of liberation that rocked the French political establishment and caused sections of the French Army to mutiny. Algeria was France's first and most important colony, and as far back as 1848 it had been declared an integral part of metropolitan France. The country had been extensively settled by Europeans – known as *pied noirs* – who were determined to maintain their favoured position. Algeria was also the home of the Legion, and for many legionnaires the idea of surrendering it to the communist-backed Algerian nationalists was unthinkable.

The Algerian nationalists, or FLN (National Liberation Front), began their war by using terror tactics against the *pied noirs* that provoked revenge attacks on Muslims. These outrages, in their turn, further alienated Muslims from the French, and provided a groundswell of support for the FLN. Both sides fought the war with the utmost savagery. Muslims seen to be supporting the French in any way were slaughtered by the FLN, who instigated a campaign of vicious intimidation to force the indigenous people to provide them with assistance.

Some idea of the general brutality of the war came from this account by a regular French paratrooper, Pierre Leulliette. He and a small group of paras were pinned down by an FLN force during the hours of darkness. Two badly wounded paratroopers lay out in no-man's-land, two hundred yards from Leulliette's position.

As three separate rescue attempts had failed, only causing further casualties, the wounded men were left to await dawn and the arrival of reinforcements. One of them called out desperately for help:

> My poor friend V. lay howling on his bed of stones till morning. He suffered unimaginably, both physically and mentally, a prey to mortal terror. He only really stopped at dawn, when we could have perhaps saved him. For several hours a rebel had been slithering towards him. He could have seen him all that while. There he was. The rebel touched his body. He took away his weapons. Then he gouged out his eyes. Then he slashed his Achilles tendons, afraid, perhaps, that he might still come back and die with us. But he didn't finish him off, merely wanting him to have to lie still and suffer. His friend T., the *sergent-chef*, also died shortly afterwards, a hundred yards away, his eyes gouged and tendons slashed; a slow death, while we were waiting for the dawn.

Set against this background of savagery, neither side made much effort to take prisoners, except briefly for the purposes of extracting information.

Initially, the FLN had concentrated its energies in building up strength in the rural areas. Success was mixed, however, and in 1956 the FLN's leadership was replaced and a new strategy adopted. This was to be spearheaded by terror attacks in the main urban areas, especially in the city of Algiers, whose vast rabbit-warren of streets in the old *Casbah* provided the FLN with cover for their activities. A series of bombing and shooting incidents provoked the expected backlash from Algiers' *pied noir* population. The city seemed to be on the point of anarchy, and the governor invited the army to take total control of Algiers.

General Jacques Massu's 10th Parachute Division – including the 1st REP (*Régiment Étranger Parachutiste*) – marched into Algiers in January 1957, and immediately instigated a systematic and ruthless campaign against the FLN and its supporters. An FLN-organised general strike was broken up, with the strikers forced back to work at gunpoint. And torture became widespread as a means of gaining intelligence of the FLN groups operating within the city.

During 1957 the French para commanders began to build up a detailed picture of their FLN opponents, who were led by Saadi Yacef and a gang of gunmen who included Ali La Pointe. The FLN refused to back down in their campaign, and in June instigated bombing attacks that killed many *pied noirs* and resulted in retaliatory attacks on the Muslim population. But the net was closing on the FLN leadership, whose security had been compromised by the covert introduction of Muslims loyal to the French into FLN areas. On 24 September the villa in which Yacef was hiding was surrounded by the 1st REP under the command of Colonel Pierre Jeanpierre. Although Jeanpierre was wounded in the ensuing engagement, Yacef was captured alive and revealed details of the whereabouts of Ali La Pointe and the remaining hardcore terrorists. Two weeks later La Pointe and his comrades were blown to pieces in a French counter-insurgency operation. The Battle of Algiers was over.

The paratroopers' victory was bought at a price, however. The official use of torture and the widespread killing of FLN suspects (some 3,000 individuals died in suspicious circumstances) could not be easily hidden. Massu and his paratroopers insisted that these measures, while regrettable, were a necessary tool in the war against the FLN. The paras' methods had proved highly effective: the FLN ringleaders had been eliminated and terrorist activity had all but disappeared from the streets of Algiers. But the open knowledge that the French state, through its armed forces, was sanctioning torture and summary execution, caused unease within much of the French Army and widespread public condemnation in both France and the wider world.

At least one thoughtful legionnaire saw that the paras' tactical success had unfortunate strategic consequences. Simon Murray, a paratrooper in 2nd REP, wrote in his diary:

> The effectiveness of torturing people to make them betray their cause cannot be disputed. But with all the good results – the 'fingering' of many *fellouze* [FLN fighters], the betrayal and subsequent capture of many of the rebel leaders was a steady build-up of hatred against the French – a hatred that comes from living in fear and terror. And this antagonism drew the Arabs, so often before divided among themselves, into a common cause;

it made them feel the necessity of combining for survival and it made them finally aware of their own strength. The French became the foreign intruder and the concept of nationalism was born in the Arabs, which was never there before. By their short-sightedness the French have forced nationalism on the Arabs and despite [President] de Gaulle's avowed intention to keep Algeria part of metropolitan France, it is doubtful if he will succeed.

Away from the cities, the French campaign against the FLN continued in the Algerian *bled*, a vast expanse of wooded valleys, desert plateaux and precipitous mountain peaks. The suddenness of the outbreak of FLN violence had caught the French by surprise, and while they were successful against untrained FLN war bands, the more experienced *fellouze* (or *fell*) proved elusive opponents. Captain Pierre Sergent, a veteran officer in the 1st REP, complained of the tactics adopted by the French at the war's outset:

Like all officers who served in Indochina, everywhere I am struck by our slowness to adapt our methods to those required in a counter-guerrilla campaign. At Army Staff HQ, they do not wish to admit that tanks are useless, as useless as these jets, which are too fast to be practical in hunting down an enemy who is on foot. This type of war requires an infantry response: infantry, infantry and more infantry. It requires a sort of 'super-infantryman' who is light, fast and similar to the paratroops or the legionnaires, of whom there are too few among the troops in Algeria.

Captain Antoine Ysquierdo, another REP officer, highlighted some of the problems faced by the French:

The supposedly innocent inhabitants know everything, say nothing or tell you that they have never seen the *fellouze*, when they are sitting in an arms cache. Everyone works for the rebels. The most insignificant shepherd knows everything. But to capture the bands, that is another story! We have sent out 5,000 to 6,000 men and who knows what material to kill a dozen poor fools and recuperate a pile of rusty shotguns, some semolina and cans of sardines . . . But then, to track down the real *fellouze*, those who slit the throats of the civilians in the bus the other day, nothing, zero! Impossible to keep an operation like this secret when it has been prepared for months by 36 chaps and in which participates a bunch of good-for-nothing soldiers.

Ysquierdo was venting his frustration at the security problems that were endemic in all forms of counter-insurgency warfare. On other occasions the French and the Legion scored some notable successes. Pierre Leulliette described an operation conducted by Legion paratroopers in the Némentchas mountains:

For three days, two companies had been blockading a cliff. They were unable to dispose of a very strong rebel band, solidly entrenched in some caves. They tried everything, even flame-throwers, though they are in theory forbidden by what is called the Geneva 'convention', yet are on issue to the majority of regiments. Nothing doing. The caves were impregnable. Every legionnaire who tried to force his way in was machine-gunned at point-blank range, after a dozen steps in the dark. They decided to reduce the besieged men by smoking them out. But there was no wood. They would have needed hundreds of smoke grenades, because the caves were so vast. Then, tired of waiting – the rebels seemed to have the caves filled with provisions – they had an amazing idea, a typical legionnaire idea: they sent for quicklime and gravel by helicopter: and they calmly sealed all the caves in the cliff, one by one, hermetically, under covering fire of a battery of machine guns! After which they went away.

A few months later, they went back for a look. They carefully dismantled their untouched walls. A horrifying stench of death emerged. The stiffened corpses of rebels massed behind them fell into their arms! They had died from hunger or suffocation, probably both simultaneously, and the suffering with which they paid for their resistance can be imagined.

Even as French tactics improved, Simon Murray experienced the frustrations of the ordinary legionnaire in a fruitless counter-guerrilla operation during a cold and wet February in 1961:

Everyday we rise at dawn and then begin our wanderings. There is never any rest, there is no respite from the routine of the effort, of the bent backs and the sweat. And even at night we are restless, prowling the hills constantly prodding the invisible enemy waiting for him to make the slightest mistake.

One evening we left camp just after midnight and had a nightmare journey across twenty miles of this rugged country. The ceaseless rain and the wind had brought down many trees over which we stumbled in the darkness. We crossed rushing rivers and scrambled on hands and knees up slippery banks. Visibility was nil and the sound of heavy breathing from the man in front was the lantern through the night. Many fell and were made to continue by force and even threats of being left behind. Caulier collapsed after the first five miles, which we covered in just over an hour.

We arrived somewhere in the early dawn and took up positions as the guns. Our friends in the second company worked the daylight shift and sought to drive the birds [FLN] our way. None came by and in the late afternoon, with daylight still fortunately in the skies, we wandered home the way we had come, with empty nets, empty stomachs and empty souls, wondering just what the hell this was all about.

On another occasion, however, the legionnaires had more luck, as Murray recalled:

At last the *fellagha*! We started out this morning on what was to be a routine patrol through the mountains and began climbing the main Chélia peak, which is 7,000 feet, shortly after lunch.

The 2nd Company, which was to our right on an adjacent hill, suddenly came under fire and we were immediately ordered to the top of the peak at a run, so that we would be overlooking the other hilltop on which the enemy was entrenched. Within minutes reinforcements arrived and the sky began to hum with helicopters. The deafening never-ending chatter of machine-gun fire and hand grenades quickly stirred the scene into a full-scale scramble.

At one stage an attempt was made to drop the 1st Company by helicopter onto the hill held by the Arabs, but as the first wasp came in and made ready for a quick touchdown to drop the men, a burst of machine-gun fire practically cut it in half. The helicopter managed somehow to get off again but not before one man had jumped. As the helicopter took off, he found himself alone facing the enemy and a hail of bullets. He was carrying five grenades and, by some miracle, throwing them in every direction and at the same time running madly for cover, he made it.

Meanwhile, from our vantage point overlooking the enemy hill we were able to do some damage with the LMGs and our mortar, and to a lesser degree the rifles. The sub-machine guns were useless.

All the long hot afternoon we slogged it out with the Arabs. So well dug-in were they that without the helicopters it is doubtful whether we would have moved them before nightfall, for our mortars seemed to have little effect. Intensive machine-gun fire from fast-moving *Alouette* helicopters finally wore down the resistance. At about four o'clock the 1st and 4th Companies were ordered to '*Montez à l'assaut!*' and in one line began to move up the hill.

We could see them weaving their way upwards, darting from rock to rock, never still for a moment except for the fractional pause for breath behind cover and quickly on again. We in the 3rd continued to rain fire onto the other hill and continued to receive it back – they don't give up, those Arabs. The 2nd Company had withdrawn to lick its wounds and grab some food, having been on the hill all afternoon.

And finally, in the late afternoon, it was over. The legionnaires could be seen on the hilltop, darting from bush to bush and bunker to bunker, firing bursts from their sub-machine guns and dropping grenades into trenches. Fifty-three Arabs lay dead. There were no prisoners.

James Worden, a legionnaire in the 3rd Foreign Legion Regiment, was soon made aware of the realities of fighting in the *bled*, in an ambush that had netted several FLN prisoners. Worden accompanied his lieutenant to question them:

After being interrogated, they were searched and relieved of all their possessions. Looking somewhat dejected and miserable, they sat crouching and squatting, their hands firmly clasped on their heads about ten minutes away. No effort was made at guarding them. The section responsible for their capture was sitting drinking coffee, and I had been invited to join them.

The section sergeant approached the *fell*, and told them to 'pee off', but none showed any inclination to depart, despite his repeated shouts, and it required none too gentle kicks even to get them on their feet. They rather reluctantly, they began to edge away. None of the legionnaires sitting drinking had a weapon in his hands; all were only interested in making the most of the break offered. At a distance of thirty to forty metres, the poor bloody *fell* broke into a panic-ridden mad stampede for what they mistakenly thought would be their freedom. Without even standing up, the group of legionnaires with whom I had been sitting simply picked up the weapons lying by their sides and opened fire. None of the *fell* survived. None gained a greater distance than sixty metres away. All were reported as killed whilst trying to escape.

Although the FLN was being defeated militarily, it had the vital advantage for a guerrilla force of friendly bases in Morocco and Tunisia, countries that bordered Algeria to both the west and east. The governments in these newly independent countries were prepared to provide the FLN with bases for supply and sanctuary from the French. The French response was to construct barriers along both sides of the Algerian border – comprising minefields and electrified barbed-wire fences – that isolated the FLN guerrillas in Algeria from outside support. The system was surprisingly successful, and while the FLN could penetrate the barriers those that did were regularly caught and destroyed by French mobile groups.

One of the more notable French successes occurred at the end of April 1958, when several FLN groups broke through the wire from Tunisia in the wooded hills around Souk-Ahras. Airborne forces, including 1st REP, were soon on the scene, and in sustained and savage fighting over 600 FLN fighters were killed or captured from a force of 820, the remnants fleeing back to Tunisia or a stark future as fugitives in the Algerian mountains. The REP had tracked down the FLN on 29 April, the eve of Camerone Day. Trapped by the Legion paras, the FLN dug in to await their attack. An accompanying war correspondent described the ensuing battle:

> The companies moved up to the attack. In line, automatics at the hip, the legionnaires advanced under heavy fire from a couple of dozen light machine guns. Pushing on slowly and deliberately, the legionnaires cleaned up the first of the FLN trenches. Halting only to throw a grenade, they moved forward again to the accompaniment of shouts of 'Camerone!'
>
> Before they could get to grips, the FLN broke, trying to escape individually or else go to ground in some dense thicket or tumble of scrub-covered boulder. To winkle them out in this final stage, the legionnaires split up into pairs. It was a hunt. The leader of the two, playing the role of pointer, edged slowly towards a likely-looking hiding place. Then, when he spotted some hint of movement, some foreign body, he stopped, pointed and with a yell fell flat on his face. More often than not the ruse worked. The hiding rebel was startled into firing, whereupon the second legionnaire, following up, finger on trigger, let fly a burst. Four and a half hours of scattered combat and the last of the rebels had fallen. It was a good haul, and a triumph for Colonel Jeanpierre, the regimental commander . . . 192 rebels killed, 8 prisoners, 43 light automatics, 76 rifles . . . an excellent start to Camerone Day.

The French Army and the Legion were undoubtedly winning the military conflict, but the French people were tired of the war, and throughout the Western world the whole concept of colonialism was becoming increasingly unpopular. Politicians in France moved towards granting Algeria its independence. But to the European *pied noir* population, the concept of an *Algérie française* was sacrosanct, and any deal with the FLN was seen as treason. The paras and other Legion units closely identified with this view, and a significant number of officers began to openly associate with radical *pied noir* elements in a bid to seize power in Algeria and overthrow the government in Paris. Events came to head on 21 April 1961 when four French generals instigated a military coup in Algiers, supported by sections of the French armed forces that included 1st REP and the cavalry regiment, 1st REC (*Régiment Étranger de Cavalerie*).

VOICES OF THE FOREIGN LEGION

While the 1st REP took a highly active role in the coup, other Legion units prevaricated. To cross the line into outright mutiny against the French government was a step not to be taken lightly. The commanding officer of the 2nd REP preferred to wait on events but his subordinate officers decided on direct action, and from a temporary base at Philippeville the legionnaires of 2nd REP advanced on Algiers. Simon Murray described events in his diary entry for 23 April:

> In the middle of the night we were aroused and ordered to collect our equipment and board the trucks. In a long column the regiment drove due west towards Algiers, three hundred miles away.
>
> Dawn came slowly through, cold and slate grey – and then suddenly it was day and sun. Thousands and thousands of Europeans lined the roads madly cheering us through. Car horns hooted and hooted – three short blasts and two long (*Al-gé-rie fran-çaise*) – again and again. Teeming crowds of wild faces laughing and yelling, pushing and shoving in a great heaving morass of bodies. Our trucks were barges floating in a sea of faces and waving arms. They loved us, they raved for us. They have never shown this emotion before and I suspect its depth is not substantial, but we must seem to them to be their saviours.
>
> In all of this there is one amazing and incomprehensible fact. One question has not yet been answered at all clearly and that is, what side are we really on?
>
> We crawled through the streets of Algiers in the late evening and occupied barracks of French regulars who appear to have temporarily disappeared – still unbelievably no attempt at explanation from an officer. This credits us with nil intelligence. They assume we will just obey orders as we have always done; so we remain at the mercy of rumour based on snatches of information from transistor radios.
>
> The Following Day
>
> First thing this morning we drove to the airport and our role became immediately clear. We were to occupy the airport, which was held by French marines, and they weren't having any of it.

So we were given wooden batons, heavy, with sharp points, and in one long line we slowly eased into the marines, pushing them forward like bolshie rams. They frequently turned and attacked with aggression. This was met in many cases with savage beatings and it became a sad and shoddy business. Marine officers were pushed around by our officers – there were scenes of officers yelling at one another with questions of loyalty and accusations of traitor and so on. L'Hospitalier bust his baton on the head of one of the marines. Gradually they were herded out of the airport premises and we were in control of the base from which we will apparently make the drop on Paris.

The evening has come. A kind of stalemate appears to have been reached. De Gaulle has brought up tanks in France and threatened to shoot parachutists out of the air if a drop is made. This had dampened some of yesterday's thoughts of dancing in Paris and put prospects of dinner at Maxim's tomorrow night slightly further away.

The mutineers held Algiers for just five days. The support they had hoped for never materialised: the French Air Force, Navy and the majority of the Army remained loyal to the government, and faced by a firm display of national solidarity the 'General's Putsch' fell apart. The generals and other leading conspirators were arrested, and the 1st REP disbanded in perpetuity.

The coup's failure was a source of regret for some legionnaires. James Worden 'felt let down in not being able to join the coup – a question of feeling frustrated and disappointed. We would have wanted to have gone on.'

While not agreeing with the mutineers, Hungarian legionnaire Janos Kemencei, a senior NCO in the 2nd REP, stated: 'The soldiers in the two large and prestigious units of the Foreign Legion [1st REP, 1st REC] that joined the rebels obeyed their officers, as all Foreign Legion soldiers always obeyed their superiors. If I had been in their position, I would have followed orders to the letter in the same way, without the slightest equivocation.'

But regardless of the wishes of the Legion, its old homeland in Algeria was to be lost for ever. In July 1962 Algeria was given its independence, and although elements of the Legion would remain in Algeria for several years to come, a new future would have to be forged in France itself. James Worden was among the last legionnaires to sail from Algeria:

> We departed at midnight and arrived in France forty-eight hours later. None of us was sleeping as the ship left the port of Oran. Most crowded the ship's side, watching the coast lights of Algeria slipping away and reducing in size. Most of us saw Algeria disappear with reluctance, regret and a sense of loss at leaving this paradise of mountainous beauty. It was as if we had seen the death of a close comrade, had buried him and were now leaving the burial place for ever. No violent cheers at the thought to entering France, just a complete feeling of emptiness in a hopeless situation. It needed only one bloody legionnaire to start singing *En Algérie* and every man would have cried his eyes out.

The Legion had been created as a force to gain and secure France's colonial possessions. Now that France's once-great empire was being dismantled, was there a future for the Foreign Legion?

CHAPTER 15

POST-COLONIAL CONFLICTS

The declaration of Algerian independence in July 1962 not only robbed the Legion of its traditional home in North Africa, it confirmed the end of hostilities and opened up the dubious prospect of a long peace. Simon Murray explained the problem of peace for the Legion: 'Life comes to a halt. Suddenly there is no purpose, there is no direction. Bewilderment is quickly superseded by boredom, which is itself overtaken by a rapid decline in morale. Discontent follows and the system begins to rot.' Assigned to road-building and construction duties during the second half of 1962, morale in the once-proud 2nd REP (*Régiment Étranger Parachutiste*) wavered and desertion increased to alarming proportions.

President de Gaulle was less than enamoured of the Legion, and there were rumours that an attempt to disband it had only been thwarted by the intervention of the then French Army Minister, Pierre Messmer, formerly an officer in the Legion. And yet, in what was probably the Legion's darkest hour, there were grounds for hope. The French military authorities took the bold decision to recast the Legion into what would subsequently be called a rapid reaction force, to defend French interests around the globe at a moment's notice. The 2nd REP would act as a spearhead for the force. On 10 December 1962, the Inspector-General of the Legion, General Jacques Lefort, informed the paratroopers of their new role. A delighted Simon Murray recalled how Lefort 'gave us information that might turn out to be that which saves us from insanity'. Murray continued:

The regiment is to undergo a massive metamorphosis designed to make us the crack unit of the French army, ready to participate in combat operations that may arise in the seventies and eighties. If we do not do this, it is likely we will eventually disappear as a regiment. The French requirement for ground troops now that they have lost Indochina and North Africa is going to be considerably less, and the axe will fall on those units that are the least useful. Hence the regiment is going to set about training up specialised sections in underwater combat, demolition, guerrilla warfare, night fighting, special armaments. We will be trained to operate tanks and armoured vehicles, we will be taught to ski and mountaineer, we will become familiar with submarines, we will be sent on survival courses and we will become highly skilled and dextrous with multipurpose capability.

This is all terrific stuff. At last someone has come forward with a directive on where we are going. The message has been well received. Morale has in one stroke been given a gigantic shot in the arm. We're back in business. Somebody thinks we can do more than just build bloody roads all day. Suddenly the mountain of the next two years diminishes, there is a feeling of moving forward again. The mind moves back into gear.

Under the energetic leadership of Lieutenant-Colonel Robert Caillaud, 2nd REP began the transformation from hard-hitting airborne heavy infantry into a genuine special-forces unit capable of fulfilling almost any military mission. The regiment first saw action – albeit limited – in Chad in 1969 where it supported President Tombalbaye's administration against various rebel groups. There was further action in Djibouti in February 1976 when elements of 2nd REP operated with 13th DBLE (*Demi-Brigade de Légion Étrangère*) in rescuing a bus-load of children taken hostage by Somali terrorists. Thus, the Legion found itself part of an ironic role-reversal: instead of acting as a colonial aggressor, it was increasingly being invited by the governments of the former colonies to help restore and maintain order in their countries. Although the Legion had proved its worth in Chad and Djibouti, it gained international renown at Kolwezi in 1978.

Kolwezi was a mining town in Africa's mineral-rich province

of Shaba, a part of the newly independent state of Zaire. But sovereignty of the region was disputed by various factions, and in May 1978 a force of 4,000 rebel fighters crossed the border from bases in Angola to capture Kolwezi, which contained as many as 3,000 European engineers and their families (mostly French and Belgian). The Europeans effectively became hostages, and Zaire's President Mobutu appealed to the French and Belgian governments for military assistance. While the Belgians prevaricated, the French ordered the 2nd REP – on six hours' reaction notice – to capture Kolwezi and free the hostages.

The Legion paratroops arrived at the airport of Zaire's capital of Kinshasa – just over 24 hours from the order for action being given. From there they made plans for a parachute drop over Kolwezi, speed becoming paramount with the knowledge that the rebels had started to kill the hostages. Short of supplies and munitions, the men of 2nd REP also had to contend with unfamiliar US-supplied T-10 parachutes. Four C-130 and one C-160 transport aircraft were made available for the air drop. American Sergeant Paul Fanshaw described some of the problems encountered by the first wave as it took off on the morning of 18 May:

> We originally had 66 jumpers, but on take-off one C-160 blew a tyre and the troops were told to un-ass and get on the other planes. In the transition we picked up 14 extra men. We were packed in like sardines. The engines increased rpms and the plane lifted off. The heat was suffocating and we fought sleep.
>
> Taking off my helmet and leaning back, I closed my eyes and tried not to think of my predicament. The ride was pure torture: 80 combat-laden paratroopers were packed into a 66-jumper aircraft – with which they were not familiar – wore strange 'chutes and were expected to descend on an enemy force that outnumbered us five or six to one. Everyone looked anxious.

After an interminable three and a half hours in the air, the lumbering transport aircraft circled over Kolwezi. Fanshaw continued the story:

Looking out of the window, I saw nothing but bush for miles; then some houses came into view. The plane made a steep bank and two dozen legionnaires fell on their asses. The jumpmaster moved the weapon containers to the door. The red light came on.

Reaching into my breast pocket, I pulled out a little bottle of Johnnie Walker and took a long swig. I gave the remainder to Sgt Marques, a Portuguese, pointed to the label, and said, 'Johnnie Walker whisky, 100 years old and still going strong.' He grinned back at me and replied: 'May we live so long!'

Green light. Jumpers tumbled out the doors and, for a few seconds, I could breathe. The plane dipped and quaked and, while butterflies kicked in my stomach, I pushed Legionnaire Misse, who could hardly walk because of the weight of his machine gun and other gear. On my left entangled legionnaires fought to tear themselves away from their seats.

We fell out of the door simultaneously: feet, sky, earth, sky, shock. The big American 'chute popped open! All around me billowed green 'chutes; under me a large cluster of houses stood. My rate of descent told me my 'chute was okay, so I didn't waste time in checking it. After unhooking my reserve, I pulled the fork on my quick-release. I was going to get out of this 'chute fast.

In the distance, I heard a few rounds of .50-calibre MG fire, then everything was quiet – neither soldiers nor civilians moved on the ground. My eyes searched futilely for the underpass [Fanshaw's Drop Zone (DZ)] but, seeing some railroad tracks, I pulled on my two forward risers to change my direction of descent and land as close to them as possible. I ploughed in 400 metres from the Impala Hotel.

Although Fanshaw's section had missed the DZ, by good fortune it landed close to its objective. The paratroopers began to consolidate their position, but a shortage of heavy weapons was critical:

Armed with two machine guns [and] one grenadier with nine anti-personnel rifle grenades, we were supposed to block the road. It didn't take a genius to figure out we couldn't do it; we had no anti-tank weapons. I sent Cpl Moran to find our weapons container.

We had been on the ground for 15 minutes and hadn't heard a sound – no people, dogs or birds. To relieve the tension created by the madness of the last 24 hours, the lack of sleep and the suffocating plane ride, I had the men test-fire their weapons. This everyone did in good order. Then we started digging in.

Cpl Moran returned at a run carrying an LRAC [anti-tank rocket launcher], which was great except he didn't have any rockets. I told him to leave the LRAC in place and go find the rockets. None too soon, either, for from [Kolwezi's] New Town the sound of armoured vehicles carried up the street to our ears.

We gripped our weapons and crouched behind the embankment. Cpl Moran, clutching two rocket tubes, jumped back into position, and tore at the tape on the circular carton. I tore at the other. To our front, gears grinding, appeared the first of three Panhard armoured cars. The first one, an AML-60 with a large green flag flying, moved around the corner of the intersection about 100 metres distant, slowed to change gears, then headed straight towards us at high speed.

Slamming a rocket into LRAC and rolling to one side, I screamed, 'Fire!' I glanced over at the embankment. The first AML was only 50 metres away, its short-barrelled 60mm mortar aimed straight ahead. '*Nom de Dieu*,' I yelled. 'Fire! Fire!'

CRASH! The launcher barked and the rocket smacked into the vehicle's turret. The AML came to an immediate stop and its driver, dead, fell out of its side door. Seeing this, the second AML stopped, reversed gears, fired a 90mm round in our direction and headed back the way it came. I couldn't get another rocket off fast enough to track him, but both MGs plastered him with bullets and my grenadier fired a well-intended rifle grenade in its direction. The third AML, which had just entered the street, quickly reversed and followed the second one back to New Town.

Just then, the turret hatch of the destroyed AML flew up and the commander jumped out and ran hell-bent for the brick wall under a hail of lead. I fired three or four short bursts at him but he reached the wall and dived over. 'My God,' I mumbled, 'that man must be saying his prayers.'

Although there had been some resistance from the rebels, the paratroopers secured their initial objectives by the end of the first day's fighting. They awaited reinforcements, due to arrive the following morning. After encouraging his men to take dexedrine tablets, in an attempt to keep them awake, Fanshaw awaited dawn and the arrival of the second wave:

> At first light, four C-130s and one C-160 dropped the remainder of the regiment. They landed almost 1,000 metres in front of my position on the opposite side of New Town. About an hour later the 4th Coy moved by, on line. They passed the Impala Hotel grounds and disappeared off to our left.

Jonathan Harris, a sergeant attached to the newly arrived 4th Company, recalled his march through Kolwezi:

> There were some horrific sights there. Bodies – mostly Europeans – piled up one upon the other, quite disgusting to see, lying out in the streets and at the end of drives. Otherwise it was a very civilized looking town, when you walked through it – apart from the horrible smell of death all over the place. The paras were highly trained and didn't stop to commiserate. Legionnaires are used to hard times. We took quite a lot of prisoners that day, youngsters mostly, who didn't know what was going on – some of them out of their brains with alcohol.

On the afternoon of the 20th, the 4th Company spearheaded the attack on the last rebel stronghold, an old copper mine and village complex called Metal-Shaba. Harris recounted the ensuing battle:

> This was the largest engagement I was involved in. All-in-all, there must have been about 500–600 rebel fighters in the village. They were armed with every sort of weapon: Kalashnikovs, M16s, Lee Enfields, Belgian recoilless rifles – quite a nice, tidy bit of gear. It took us all afternoon to drive them out. We gave them the chance to get back to the main road to Angola – which a lot of them tried to take. But I don't think many of the ordinary legionnaires thought of letting them escape. After seeing what had happened,

there was more than a bit of retribution or revenge on behalf of the hostages. A final body count's never been done but I think there must have been 300–350 bodies lying around afterwards. The legionnaires did a very good bit of work there.

Although most of the surviving rebels fled back to Angola, there was sporadic fighting for several days, until the Legion was withdrawn on 28 May and replaced by Moroccan troops. While visiting the looted post office in Kolwezi, Fanshaw came across Sergeant Canova, the NCO responsible for rounding up civilian vehicles for use by the Legion. Fanshaw recalled how Canova called him over to inspect his latest acquisition:

> I rounded the corner and saw a blue Mercedes 280 with all its windows knocked out. It was full of everything: wine, whisky, food, weapons, grenades, ammo. He handed me five bottles of wine, some food and 300 rounds of 9mm ammo.
>
> I saw Canova a few days later. He was driving around to all the sections distributing food and water. He carried a dead Katangese soldier across the roof of his Mercedes, tied down like a slab of beef. If a legionnaire wanted his picture taken with a dead rebel, Canova threw the cadaver to the ground, pulled out a few FALs or AK-47s and positioned the legionnaire over the body. He charged for the props. Some people can live like a king anywhere.

Kolwezi was a resounding success for 2nd REP, a vindication for the Legion's new role. Although 190 Europeans and over 200 black civilians had been killed, a far greater massacre had been averted, while the rebels had been routed for the cost of five legionnaires killed and 25 wounded.

French Somaliland achieved partial independence in 1967 before becoming the fully independent state of Djibouti in 1977, but faced by aggressive neighbours – Ethiopia, Eritrea and Somalia – French military assistance was provided to the new country in the form of 13th DBLE, supported by elements of 2nd REP. The main task of the Legion was to deter incursions by other military forces and block the influx of foreign civilians fleeing their own war-torn countries for the relative safety of Djibouti.

While serving with the DBLE in 1973, American legionnaire Bill Brooks acted as one of the guards defending the border with Somalia. Much of his time was spent patrolling a 10-ft-high wire fence set behind a 10-metre-deep minefield, known as *La Barrage*, which protected Djibouti City:

> I performed more than 150 days of duty on *La Barrage*, each time as 'Corporal of the Relief', changing the guards, establishing ambushes or doing dawn foot patrols to see where the *Bounjouls* (French slang for Arabs) had sneaked through the wire during the night. It never ceased to amaze me how many people successfully negotiated the mines and obstacles, eluded the patrols and ambushes, and successfully entered the city undetected. No matter how much wire was strung, every night someone got through successfully.
>
> Many, however, were not so lucky. Each tour at *La Barrage* was marked by death in some form, usually by people striking *Stolperdraht* [trip wires] and sending a parachute flare through their torsos. These accidents always seemed to take place on my patrol route, so I usually had the task of extracting the fly-covered corpses from the barbed-wire apron, a job I found quite distasteful and which has since ruined my appetite for any type of burnt meat. For days after, I would wash my hands with Cologne.
>
> Service on *La Barrage* also entailed water ambushes. At night many insurgents would attempt to swim around the barrage, and we would hide in wait in the reeds near the coast or in the bottom of our rubber raft.
>
> Service on *La Barrage* was totally one-sided, since I do not know of one person attempting to enter Djibouti who ever shot back. Most of them were captured at night after trapping themselves in a minefield, being caught in a blinding searchlight and scared shitless by having the ground to their front and rear riddled with hundreds of bullets. They were mostly half-naked illiterate scarecrows, shivering in fear before these stereotypes of imperialism festooned with weapons. What I captured at *La Barrage* was only half-starved misery.

Before returning to a posting in France in April 1975, Brooks was involved in a fire-fight with Ethiopian troops. He had successfully completed an NCOs' course for promotion to sergeant, and an impromptu celebration was planned:

That night we cooked a freshly slaughtered goat and drank some *pinard*. Some got drunk. Around midnight the lieutenant entered my tent and asked who else I knew who wasn't drunk. I mentioned a few names and he said, 'Good. I'll go wake them up. You get dressed, get a PM (sub-machine gun), two full magazines, and some defensive grenades. Take your canteen and blacken your face; meet me in 10 minutes outside my tent.'

'*Oui, mon lieutenant*,' I said sleepily. Another ambush, I thought. Why me this time, though? I was tired. What the hell, I thought: maybe we'll see some armed *Bounjouls*.

I waited outside the lieutenant's tent. Six of us showed up. We were told to occupy the ground 4 km from Ali-Sabieh next to Fort Daovenie. We were to watch the trail and the railroad, report anything that looked suspicious and stop anyone who was armed. 'And stay awake!' the lieutenant concluded.

There was no tenseness – it looked routine; after all, I'd been doing it two and a half years. We advanced to the base of the hill and placed ourselves in position to fire upwards. I was on the extreme right, about five metres from the railroad. I could see the lights in Daovenie and the road running up from Ethiopia ending at a pig pen. I opened my canteen and began to drink. Everybody was just as relaxed. The *Belge* and the Greek [armed with a light machine gun] were smoking and clanking the ammo belts and machine-gun bipod against the rocks.

Suddenly I heard a truck engine. My throat froze. I felt like vomiting. It was an Ethiopian squad, jumping off the trail and moving down the railroad. Five, six, seven, eight, I counted. One was coming up the tracks towards me, a banana clip plainly silhouetted in his weapon. I dropped my canteen and picked up my PM and screamed.

I was squeezing the trigger. The 20-round magazine almost emptied in one long burst. Immediately the machine gun opened up. I slammed my face down on the ground and tried to reload but my second magazine had fallen into the rocks. Suddenly everyone was shooting. I looked up over my rock and fired another short burst, emptying my weapon, then, once again hid my face in the sand.

Then it all stopped. The truck was no longer in sight but I could hear its engine whining in low gear. Lights were on all over Daovenie and trucks were racing to our rescue from Ali-Sabieh, headlights on full beam! There was much nervous chatter when the lieutenant arrived. We were all called in, and he made out a report which we all signed. By this time it was 4 a.m., so we all walked to the mess hall and had some coffee.

While operations in Djibouti seldom exceeded a local skirmish of the type related above, the war against Saddam Hussein's Iraqi Army in 1990–1 opened up the possibility of a large-scale military operation. As part of the Allied coalition preparing to attack Iraq, France provided the 6th Light Armoured Division, which included elements of the Legion, notably armoured units from the cavalry regiment, the 1st REC (*Régiment Étranger de Cavalerie*). Operating on the left flank of the Allied line, the French advanced into Iraq on 24 February 1991. Mark Morris, a legionnaire in the REC's 4th Squadron, was surprised by the lack of opposition as they crossed the border:

I expected the shit to hit the fan as we went in, to hit minefields and be bombarded by the Iraqi Army. We were told that the 45th Iraqi Infantry Division was in the vicinity. But the only people we came across were an Iraqi patrol in a Toyota Land Cruiser having tea in the desert. They soon decided to retreat and quickly disappeared.

We pushed up to Masouba as fast as we could and camped there for the night, before going on to capture the airfield and town. We took quite a few prisoners and fired on a tank – a T-55 – that was knocking about. As we went on we captured more and more prisoners. Many people just gave themselves up. We handed the prisoners over to the regimental HQ, who dealt with them. Of all the Iraqis we captured not one showed any form of resistance whatsoever. They were completely dehydrated, hadn't eaten for a long time – demoralised.

> We were catching up with the main Iraqi Army when suddenly
> the fighting stopped – the 100-hour war – very unfortunately.

Sergeant Dave Cunliffe, of the 2nd REI (*Régiment Étranger d'Infanterie*), was similarly disappointed that the fighting was over so quickly, but he relished the scale of operations: 'I was lucky enough to be sent out to the Gulf: taking part in a divisional attack with air power and an artillery barrage, with engineers and the cavalry. It was the most exciting thing I'd ever done. For most of us, it was a once-in-a-lifetime experience that we'd never get again.'

The vicious war between Serbs, Croats and Bosnians – as the former Yugoslavia broke apart – was the next posting for the Legion. Pádraig O'Keeffe, a legionnaire in the combat engineers, the 6th REG (*Régiment Étranger Genie*), arrived at the airport of Sarajevo in January 1995 before driving out to the nearby UN base at Scandarija. He described conditions in Sarajevo:

> The trip from the airport to Scandarija left us in no doubt as to what we faced. The landscape reminded me of pictures of Stalingrad, Berlin or Warsaw after World War II. What had obviously been a beautiful city was now little more than rubble and the shells of scarred buildings. There was evidence of heavy artillery and mortar fire everywhere. Some buildings were so heavily hit by bullets that they looked like concrete sieves. Every person we saw was hunched over and hurrying for safety. No one seemed happy about being in the open. And on every major intersection there was the tell-tale sign of heavily armed militia groups.

Having to operate under the restrictive rules of the United Nations mandate was a cause of deep frustration to the Legion. Matt Rake, a legionnaire in 2nd REP, recalled the irritation of having to modify their uniforms: 'This was the first UN mission the Legion had ever done. We had to change our berets to the blue UN ones. This didn't go down well – we'd signed up for the Legion, and not the UN. And we were made to wear the French flag on our arm, which we'd never done before, and that didn't go down well either.'

But the Legion's main grievance was the operational restriction imposed on them, as O'Keeffe explained:

> Our mission in Bosnia was a joke – as far as I was concerned we were helping no one. We knew it, and so did the Serbs, the Bosnians and the Croats. We were glorified aid workers. We had been trained to take military action, we knew the action that was required, and yet we were told to sit on our hands. And while we stood by, innocent people died. I was sick of all the bullshit – the constant walking on eggshells when it came to dealing with the militias, many of whom were little more than street thugs and common criminals.

The legionnaires were themselves victims of the militias, regularly coming under sniper fire, as well as having to endure the humiliation of their convoys being searched and fleeced at militia checkpoints. O'Keeffe recalled an example of the tribulations he and his fellow legionnaires often encountered:

> In Sarajevo our every move was scrutinised and judged; at least in the countryside you would have a small amount of unit discretion, but in Sarajevo we often felt that we were alive only because the militia groups didn't want the hassle of killing us.
>
> But there were exceptions. Once, I was assigned to a mine-laying detail on a roadway running parallel to 'Sniper Alley', where we had an observation post called 'Sierra November'. The UN had strict rules about such missions. The location of our mines had to be recorded and the direction of the trip-wires carefully noted. The Serbs, for their part, warned that any offensive action by the UN would be met by force. We regarded the mines as defensive, but no one knew what the Serbs would think about that.
>
> I was working on my hands and knees in an open area with Master-Sergeant Leurs beside me when I heard the tell-tale whizz of two 7.62mm Kalashnikov rounds passing within inches of us. The dust from one bullet as it impacted on the ground actually hit my face. Instantly, we both broke for cover and tried to shield ourselves from the wrecked multi-storey building where

we judged the fire had come from. This building was between us and Sniper Alley. Less than two minutes later, we heard two fresh rounds being fired, but they seemed to have been fired in a different direction. Slowly and carefully we made our way back to safety of our vehicle and reported back to base.

The Legion did fight back when suitable opportunities arose, away from prying eyes, as Rake recalled:

We weren't supposed to reply to enemy fire but we did – but not through the UN. If someone was going to shoot at you, you'd shoot back. When on patrol, you were supposed to go out with 50 rounds and come back with 50 rounds, but 'miraculously' there were always spare rounds about to make up any shortfall. It was simply a question of the Legion looking after its own.

Much of O'Keeffe's work was based around mine-clearing. Here, he described a particularly hair-raising incident:

We were working on another minefield in the countryside outside Sarajevo, using special inflatable gear called 'M-Ms' [Matra-Mines or Mine-Mats], which were designed to disperse the weight of our footsteps and thereby avoid the triggering mechanism for anti-personnel mines. The equipment was apparently state-of-the-art, but I felt a little like a guinea pig. I knew they had been used in the Gulf War just five years before but I also knew that in Kuwait and Iraq they were used on flat, desert surfaces. Here in Bosnia, the minefields were laid in rutted, uneven and stone-pocked fields, substantially different from desert plains. It was very awkward moving in the gear which, because of its function, was filled with eight air pockets. It was like trying to walk around in a pair of giant inflatable slippers.

In either hand I held two special testing poles designed to probe the ground for any indication of mines and to erect special warning signs afterwards. Each had a sharp spike at their end and, trust my luck, didn't I actually puncture one of my inflatable 'slippers' with a spike. So I was now standing in the middle of a minefield with one leg boasting a weight-dispersing device and my other leg

resting, like normal, on my boot. All I could do was raise my eyes
to heaven and silently curse myself. My partner kept working and
I had no option but to walk on with him. A few strides later my
blood froze with the distinctive grating sound of the probe of an
anti-personnel mine scraping along the bottom of my boot.

The mine had been planted in a small hollow which I hadn't
spotted. The detonator had scraped off the underside of my boot
and I was now mincemeat. I stood there motionless, waiting for
the percussion of the exploding mine to blow my feet off. But there
was nothing but silence – the only sound the manic beating of my
own heart. It felt as if my heart was caught in my Adam's apple,
but I forced myself to remain calm. I slowly raised my hand to
indicate a mine contact, and the rest of the team froze in position.
I can't remember how long I stayed motionless but it seemed like
for ever. Then, slowly, and in agonising suspense, I lifted my leg
away from the contact. And still nothing happened. By now the
sweat was pouring from my forehead in a torrent. As I stepped
away from the anti-personnel mine I felt wasted.

Fortunately for O'Keeffe, the firing pin on the mine had rusted
and blocked the detonating mechanism. But as he got back to
base O'Keeffe couldn't help believing he had enjoyed 'divine
intervention'.

Despite the many frustrations it had to endure, the Legion did
good work in Bosnia. As part of the team that guarded Sarajevo
airport, Matt Rake drew some positives:

When we went to Bosnia, the Legion worked particularly well. For a
start, we had so many people who spoke different languages, and they
were put forward to do the translations. In contrast, the Canadians, and
other troops who were there, had a much harder time communicating
with the local people. And I thought the French regulars barricaded
themselves in, whereas we went out into the community. We were sent
to guard the airport at Sarajevo, which we kept running during a very
difficult situation. From the time we were sent there to the time we
left, the airport became a totally different place.

After Bosnia, the next major Legion operation was another classic

African rescue mission, this time in the Republic of the Congo, formerly the French Congo. Factional fighting between rival political groups led to a collapse of law and order and, in June 1997, the outbreak of civil war. The large French expatriate community in the Congo was directly threatened, and French forces, including the Legion, were sent to organise an evacuation.

The capital of Brazzaville was overrun by rival militias, who preyed upon civilians, both black and white. Simon Low, by now, a sergeant in the 2nd REI, explained the background to his unit's intervention in the Congo:

> Though the names of these militia groups bordered on the comic
> – the 'Ninjas', the 'Zulus' and the 'Cobras' – their fighting, true
> to most African struggles, was fierce, brutal and uncompromising.
> They even had the audacity to ambush the two Foreign Legion
> companies in the city streets of Brazzaville, killing two legionnaires.
> This was a big mistake, in retaliation for which 20-odd rebels
> met their deaths.
>
> As a result of this incident, reinforcements were deployed in the
> country, me among them. My company, the 4th, was then serving
> in Chad, just a few hours' flight on a Transall C-160 away. Within
> a day of the ambush, we were on Congolese soil and swiftly
> established a defensive perimeter at the then abandoned Aero Club
> adjacent to the main airport, ready to evacuate the refugees and
> expats from both Kinshasa and Brazzaville. Our mission was not
> only to secure the airstrip but to send sorties into Brazzaville to
> round up the expats, most of them stranded in their villas and
> hiding from the murderous rebels.

Based around Brazzaville's airport, Low was made aware of the real dangers faced by the expats:

> I can't remember which of us noticed it first, but a lot of the
> European women we saw had cut their hair, and that of their
> daughters, short. They told us it was to make them look like men
> so they wouldn't be raped. Some had already suffered this fate
> at the hands of the marauding, heavily armed gangs, who were
> frequently stoned on drugs. As we escorted the expat refugees on

foot across the 500 metres from the Aero Club to the main runway to embark on the Transall C-160, its propellers already turning so as to spend as little time on the ground as possible, some of the women could be heard inconsolably sobbing. It was pretty obvious why. We later learned that at least one of these women, unable to come to terms with her ordeal, had committed suicide.

Gareth Carins, a paratrooper in 2nd REP, was among those legionnaires responsible for organising the convoys that were to bring the expats to the airport. He described an attack on one of these convoys:

> With the evacuations starting at first light, our team took its turn as the rapid reaction force. This entailed having two men on a roving guard, whilst the rest waited, fully kitted and ready to go at a moment's notice. With nightfall I'd fitted the night scope to my sniper rifle, and was busy checking everything was working when we received news of an ambush. A team had been on a late run from the airport and had been ambushed on the way back. It was difficult to get a clear picture of events but there were definitely casualties and they needed help. 'You three . . . get on the truck . . . you're escorting the ambulance.'
>
> Ducs grabbed extra rounds for the Minimi [light machine gun] and we sprinted towards the waiting trucks that were already filled with most of the platoon. Valera helped me up and we sped off into the night. There was one truck in front of the ambulance and ours at the rear. I could hear a fire-fight raging in the distance and wondered if it was our guys.
>
> We didn't know much of what we were we were heading into but all down the truck people were checking their weapons. Ducs had dispensed with the M16 magazines and had slapped a 200-round belt on instead. My night scope was working well and further down the truck Jim, the platoon medic, was checking his kit. The tension was intense as we headed towards the noise of the fire-fight, which seemed like it was in full flow. My heart was pounding as the reality of the situation began to dawn. Whatever we were heading into, I just wanted to get it over with and pushed forward the bolt on my rifle, putting a round into the chamber.

'. . . WATCH OUT . . . ENEMY LEFT . . .' A second later there was a sound like heavy hail landing on a steel roof and bees buzzing past your ears as enemy bullets sprayed the truck, bringing it to an instant halt. Not waiting for the command, we leapfrogged over the side, landing in a heap before sprinting to a ditch on the opposite side of the road. Chaos reigned as people fell over each other trying to sort themselves into firing positions. Corporals were screaming above the noise of incoming automatic fire to make themselves heard and to regain command.

It looked like we'd arrived at the scene of the initial ambush and had driven headlong into the middle of a gun battle. Our small convoy, including the ambulance, had been attacked but by sheer good fortune it looked like we'd escaped without injury.

The amount of incoming rounds was intense and it was obvious we were outnumbered. With the adrenaline pumping, and without taking any real aim, I quickly squeezed off a couple of rounds in the general direction of the enemy, whilst at the same time trying to expose as little of my body as possible above the protection of the ditch. With the street lamps lit up, the night-sight became next to useless, returning the rifle to an outdated single-shot bolt action, surrounded by modern automatic weapons. I heard Ducs open up with the Minimi at the enemy, who were located on the far side of the main road, and were protected by a small wall and a few buildings. Its high rate of fire seemed reassuring and after the initial few seconds of confusion, our response started to seem more organised.

'. . . APC . . . DEAD AHEAD . . .' Valera slapped a rocket onto the end of his FAMAS [assault rifle] and, without taking any real aim, fired it in the direction of the enemy. It slammed into the front of the APC as it tried to exit from a gated entrance. The APC was a South African model, originally designed for riot control, and was more of an armoured truck than an Armoured Personnel Carrier. The small rocket hit the engine and exploded with a huge bang and a small cloud of smoke, bringing the truck to a standstill. Another slammed into its side at almost point-blank range and left it smoking and stationary.

Whilst some of the platoon pushed through the enemy's position, Fino and I were allocated to sorting out what vehicles could still be used. We started with the ambulance and apart from suffering two flat tyres and a few bullet holes, it seemed okay. The rest of the trucks were also still capable of running and so we set about loading our dead and wounded. As for the enemy, they were either dead or had retreated, but not wanting to hang about any longer than necessary, we started back towards our base.

Within the space of a week the expats had been safely evacuated; the Legion soon followed – a job successfully accomplished.

Even though legionnaires have reservations about acting as peace-keeping troops – preferring a more full-on military role – they have had to accept that this is a reality of modern warfare for France's armed forces. As the Legion advances into the twenty-first century, its deployments in Kosovo, Côte d'Ivoire and Afghanistan see a continuation of this trend.

Potentially more worrying for the Legion's future has been the change in the French Army's structure. Throughout the Legion's history the French Army had relied on conscription for the vast bulk of its manpower, but with the end of National Service in the early years of the new millennium France is now looking towards a smaller, high-quality, professional army. As a consequence, the exclusive status of the Legion – and a few other elite army units – has come under threat. The Legion has always had traditional rights to serve overseas – the most interesting posting to any real soldier – but the new professional army will want to share, if not take over, these more challenging theatres of operation.

But the legionnaires this author has spoken to have few such doubts about the Legion's future. They point to the continuing excellence of its combat record, one that would be hard if not impossible, to match. They also point to the special non-military qualities the Legion possesses, not least its inherent multi-lingual capability and the wide occupational experience of its recruits, so that, for example, in a recent peace-keeping operation in Rwanda that involved Russian, French and British troops, the Legion was called upon for both its translation and organisational skills. Perhaps, more to the point, the ambivalent yet hard-forged link the French have with their foreign troops is unlikely to be severed and will ensure the Legion's survival in an uncertain world.

POSTSCRIPT

As a legionnaire's five-year contract comes to an end, he must make the decision to either stay in the Legion or go back to civilian life. If he decides to remain, there is a well-mapped career structure and a pension after 15 years of service. If the legionnaire chooses to call it a day after completing his contract, he will be returned to Aubagne for the processing of his departure. This concludes with a few words of farewell from the Legion Commandant and the issue of the Certificate of Military Service that confirms he has served the Legion with '*honneur et fidélité*'.

Whatever a man's length of service, the Legion will have made an indelible impression on him. This book concludes with some final thoughts from a few legionnaires on their experiences of being a member of the French Foreign Legion:

> The Legion gave me back a bit of my self-respect, because with my marriage breaking up I was starting to go downhill. When I went to the Legion I got on with the job and started to feel a bit like a man again. I had achieved something not many people can do. There's nothing romantic about the Legion, I can assure you. It's physical, hard, and it's an experience that once you've done it, you either regret it or don't regret it. And I don't regret it. I thoroughly enjoyed it.
>
> In all the 12 years I was in the British Army the only outside countries I saw were Germany, plus a six-week tour in Canada, an

exercise in Denmark and five and a half years' service in Northern Ireland. In my five and a half years in the Legion I was based in Corsica, I went to French Guyane, Djibouti, the Republic of Central Africa, Rwanda, Chad, and served on the frontiers of Ethiopia and Somalia. So I did a lot more with the Legion than I ever experienced in the British Army. The Legion goes anywhere and everywhere when needed.

Sometimes I thought, maybe I came out too early, maybe I should have stayed on with some of my mates for 20 years or so and come out with a bloody good pension. I must admit I do miss the Legion but I would never, never, never, ever do the first two years again.

Carl Jackson

Because I'd messed up in 'Civvy Street', joining up for five years was probably the best thing I could have done. I was with a good group of lads, and from there I never looked back. I feel I paid my penance for a lot of things. We were all in the same boat and got on with the job. I've learned a lot of skills – military skills, life skills, whatever. I've got nothing but praise for the Legion. But you've got to go in with the right attitude. The problems start if you don't. If you accept the Legion as it is, it's a great five years. If you want to join the military to be a soldier, and be prepared to go to war, the Legion is definitely there for that. Really, it's a soldier's dream.

Matt Rake

The only regret I had about the Legion was leaving after five years. I should have stayed in and done my 15 – after all, I'd done the hard part. But being in the Legion is something that never leaves you. It's life-changing, whether you like or not, whether it's for the better or the worse. And I am convinced it was for the better. The Legion gave me something I couldn't have learned anywhere else. In fact, my own outlook on life changed in the space of my first 10 or 12 weeks.

David Taylor

I loved being in the Legion, but I decided I didn't want to stay on any further and become old and disillusioned. And I didn't want promotion to a cushy job. To my very last day, I wanted to be running round with a rifle in my hand and a helmet on my head. After 15 years I was able to say I'd done everything I'd wanted to do, and stayed faithful to what I wanted to do. Also, I realised that the lads were getting younger and fitter, and that I couldn't go on doing this for ever. I don't miss it, even though I loved every minute of it. I lived the dream.

Dave Cunliffe

APPENDIX

LEGION STRENGTHS AND DEPLOYMENT

DEPLOYMENT IN 1933

In 1933 the strength of the Foreign Legion stood at approximately 20,000 men, with 17,500 stationed in North Africa and Syria and the remainder in Indochina and Madagascar. The Legion's deployment – with the bulk of its forces in Morocco – reflected its recent campaign against the Moroccan Berber tribes who had only recently been defeated.

1st Foreign Regiment	Sidi-bel-Abbès, Algeria
2nd Foreign Regiment	Meknes, Morocco
3rd Foreign Regiment	Fez, Morocco
4th Foreign Regiment	Marrakesh, Morocco
5th Foreign Regiment (one detached battalion in Syria)	Tonkin, Indochina
Foreign Cavalry Regiment	Taroudent, Morocco

DEPLOYMENT IN 2009

The modern Legion comprises 7,669 officers, NCOs and legionnaires, divided into 11 regimental formations deployed across the globe.

1st Foreign Regiment   Aubagne, France
1 RE (*1er Régiment Étranger*)
(administrative regiment)

4th Foreign Regiment   Castelnaudary, France
4 RE (*4ème Régiment Étranger*)
(training regiment)

GRLE (*Groupement de Recrutement*   Fort de Nogent, Paris
de la Légion Étrangère)
(recruitment group)

1st Foreign Cavalry Regiment   Orange, France
1 REC (*1er Régiment Étranger de*
Cavalerie)

1st Foreign Engineering Regiment   Laudun, France
1 REG (*1er Régiment Étranger*
de Génie)

2nd Foreign Engineering Regiment   Saint Christol, France
2 REG (*2ème Régiment Étranger*
de Génie)

2nd Foreign Infantry Regiment   Nîmes, France
2 REI (*2ème Régiment Étranger*
d'Infanterie)

2nd Foreign Parachute Regiment   Calvi, Corsica
2 REP (*2ème Régiment Étranger*
Parachutiste)

3rd Foreign Infantry Regiment   Kourou, French Guiana
3 REI (*3ème Régiment Étranger*
d'Infanterie)

VOICES OF THE FOREIGN LEGION

13th Foreign Legion Half-Brigade 13 DBLE (*13ème Demi-Brigade de Légion Étrangère*)	Djibouti, Republic of Djibouti
Foreign Legion Detachment DLEM (*Détachement de Légion Étrangère de Mayotte*)	Mayotte, Indian Ocean

SOURCE NOTES

The many direct quotations used in this book are reproduced verbatim whenever possible, but obvious errors have been corrected and minor confusions clarified. It has not been thought necessary to indicate where quotations have been abridged.

CHAPTER ONE

pp. 13–14   Never has a . . . Simon Low, *The Boys from Baghdad*, p. 118.

p. 14   It was very . . . David Taylor, author interview.

p. 14   There are many . . . Frederic Martyn, *Life in the Legion*, p. 6. See also George Manington, *A Soldier of the Legion*, p. 9.

p. 15   There was a . . . Simon Murray, *Legionnaire*, p. 14.

pp. 15–16   The pen trembled . . . Jaime Salazar, *Legion of the Lost*, pp. 14–15.

p. 16   In some ways . . . Carl Jackson, author interview.

p. 16   *La Legion c'est* . . . quoted in Simon Jameson, *The French Foreign Legion*, p. 57.

p. 17   The atmosphere of . . . Erwin Rosen, *In the Foreign Legion*, pp. 5–6.

pp. 17–18   There are a . . . Adrian Liddell Hart, *Strange Company*, p. 203.

p. 18   I can't understand . . . Sadlowski, in Salazar, p. 26.

p. 19   We reflect the . . . Robert Devouges, in Brian Moynahan, 'Faithful Unto Death' in *Soldier of Fortune*, December 1981 (Vol. 6, No. 12), p. 46.

p. 19   I found that . . . A. R. Cooper, *Born to Fight*, p. 146.

pp. 20–1   Driving up to . . . Christian Jennings, *Mouthful of Rocks*, p. 25.

p. 21   I spent three . . . Pádraig O'Keeffe, *Hidden Soldier*, p. 37.

p. 21   There is a . . . Major Karli, in Richard Lucas, 'Viva La Compagnie' in *Soldier of Fortune*, December 1996 (Vol. 21, No. 12), p. 41.

p. 22   This was a . . . O'Keeffe, pp. 38–9.

pp. 22–3   In the dawn . . . Liddell Hart, pp. 4–5, 5–6.

p. 23   We leave for . . . Murray, p. 20.

CHAPTER TWO

p. 25   We now began . . . John Yeowell, in John Parker, *Inside the Foreign Legion*, p. 99.

p. 26   We visited the . . . Christian Jennings, *Mouthful of Rocks*, pp. 33–4.

pp. 27–8   The French army . . . Reproduced from Erwan Bergot, *The French Foreign Legion*, p. 266.

p. 29   The appeal of . . . *Sergent-Chef* LaBella, in Geoffrey Bocca, *La Légion!*, p. 6.

p. 29   It is at . . . James Worden, *Wayward Legionnaire*, p. 91.

p. 30   On Bastille Day . . . Dave Cunliffe, author interview.

p. 30   From the highest . . . Raymond L. Bruckberger, *One Sky to Share*, p. 100.

pp. 30–1   In 1945, an . . . ibid., pp. 100–1.

p. 31   Some time or . . . Colin John, *Nothing to Lose*, p. 139.

p. 31   The story is . . . Bergot, p. 159.

p. 32   Once, when we . . . Zinovi Pechkoff, *The Bugle Sounds*, pp. 243–4.

p. 33   All civilisations have . . . André Maurois, in Pechkoff, p. v. For a down-to-earth American reaction to Maurois's text, see Bennett J. Doty, *Legion of the Damned*, p. 17.

pp. 33–4   The Legion is . . . Adrian Liddell Hart, *Strange Company*, pp. 202, 207.

p. 34   Many legionnaires took . . . A. R. Cooper, *Born to Fight*, p. 74.

pp. 34–5   Over the decades . . . Jennings, pp. 27–8.

CHAPTER THREE

p. 36   Everything had to . . . Tony Sloane, *The Naked Soldier*, p. 21.

p. 36   On the day . . . Dave Cunliffe, author interview.

pp. 36–7   Here indeed I . . . Bennett J. Doty, *The Legion of the Damned*, pp. 18–19.
p. 37   This is quite . . . ibid., p. 21.
p. 38   He rummaged in . . . Erwin Rosen, *In the Foreign Legion*, p. 54.
p. 38   We had ironed . . . Sloane, pp. 32–3.
p. 39   We were given . . . Gareth Carins, *Diary of a Legionnaire*, p. 25.
pp. 39–40   One morning, a . . . Pádraig O'Keeffe, *Hidden Soldier*, pp. 51–2.
p. 40   take you down . . . Cunliffe, author interview.
pp. 40–1   Recruits come from . . . Carl Jackson, author interview.
p. 41   Learning French was . . . Matt Rake, author interview.
p. 41   The sergeants had . . . Jaime Salazar, *Legion of the Lost*, p. 44.
pp. 41–2   A Chilean recruit . . . Erwin James, 'Legion of Honour' in *Guardian*, 13 January 2006.
p. 42   [Corporal] Vigno had . . . Christian Jennings, *Mouthful of Rocks*, p. 58.
p. 42   What struck me . . . Frederic Martyn, *Life in the Legion*, p. 88.
p. 42   Until you start . . . Cunliffe, author interview.
pp. 42–3   This is a . . . Colin John, *Nothing to Lose*, p. 66.
p. 43   The Legion has . . . ibid., p. 124.
p. 43   Tremendous emphasis is . . . Simon Murray, *Legionnaire*, p. 35.
p. 44   I didn't really . . . Sloane, p. 26.
pp. 44–5   The legionnaire can . . . Rosen, pp. 87–9.
pp. 45–6   We marched fast . . . Jennings, pp. 59–61.
pp. 46–7   We dumped our . . . Carins, p. 56.
p. 47   After just four . . . Jackson, author interview.
pp. 47–8   A lot of . . . David Taylor, author interview.
p. 48   It may not . . . Simon Jameson, *The French Foreign Legion*, p. 26.

CHAPTER FOUR

p. 49   the type of . . . Pádraig O'Keeffe, *Hidden Soldier*, p. 56.
pp. 49–50   I quickly learned . . . ibid., pp. 57–8.
p. 50   our new teachers . . . Erwin James, 'Legion of Honour' in *Guardian*, 13 January 2006.
p. 50   We spent hours . . . Christian Jennings, *Mouthful of Rocks*, p. 84.
p. 51   This was the . . . Simon Low, *The Boys from Baghdad*, p. 130.

pp. 51–2   The Transall accelerated . . . ibid., pp. 136–7.

pp. 52–3   Mont Louis, located . . . O'Keeffe, pp. 56–7.

p. 53   We learnt how . . . Tony Sloane, *The Naked Soldier*,
            pp. 67–8.

pp. 53–4   We went as . . . Carl Jackson, author interview.

pp. 54–5   In some ways . . . Matt Rake, author interview.

p. 55   We learnt all . . . Sloane, p. 155.

pp. 55–6   Objective one of . . . Simon Murray, *Legionnaire*,
            pp. 236–7.

pp. 56–7   On one occasion . . . ibid., p. 239.

p. 57   At *appel* [Sergeant] . . . ibid., p. 243.

pp. 57–8   The system is . . . Frederic Martyn, *Life in the Legion*,
            p. 22.

p. 58   Their prestige, their . . . Bennett J. Doty, *The Legion of the
            Damned*, p. 22.

p. 58   A regiment of . . . George Manington, *A Soldier of the
            Legion*, p. 29.

pp. 58–9   The Legion mentality . . . Rake, author interview.

p. 59   When I was . . . David Taylor, author interview.

pp. 59–60   You pushed them . . . ibid.

p. 60   You're trying to . . . Dave Cunliffe, author interview.

pp. 60–1   Some of our . . . Jackson, author interview.

p. 61   The *silo* consisted . . . Erwin Rosen, *In the Foreign Legion*,
            pp. 228–30.

p. 62   On this night . . . Martyn, pp. 186–7.

pp. 62–3   In solitary, they . . . Taylor, author interview.

p. 63   They are promptly . . . Rosen, pp. 64–5.

p. 64   I ended up . . . Taylor, author interview.

p. 64   Hard the Legion . . . Doty, p. 36.

CHAPTER FIVE

p. 67   you must fight . . . Legionnaire H., IWMSA 14192.

pp. 67–8   Leborgne charged. The . . . Antoine Sylvère, *Le Légionnaire
            Flutsch*, p. 206, in Douglas Porch, *The French Foreign Legion*,
            p. 199.

p. 68   A Spaniard and . . . Christian Jennings, *Mouthful of Rocks*,
            p. 26.

p. 69   Because the Legion . . . Jean Martin, *Je suis un légionnaire*,
            p. 114, in Porch, p. 199.

p. 69   '*les fuckings*' . . . Jennings, p. 55.

p. 69   thought themselves above . . . Kevin Foster, IWMSA 15438.

p. 69   The French wasted . . . Jaime Salazar, *Legion of the Lost*,
            p. 121.

p. 70   We Brits liked . . . Dave Cunliffe, author interview.

pp. 70–1   By now every . . . Jacques Weygand, *Légionnaire*, pp. 126–7.

p. 71   Theft is rampant . . . Evan McGorman, *Life in the French
            Foreign Legion*, p. 116.

pp. 71–2   *Voleur*! [Thief!] cried . . . Erwin Rosen, *In the Foreign Legion*,
            pp. 113–14.

p. 72   After Garcia had . . . Jennings, pp. 191–2.

p. 72   When they found . . . ibid., pp. 191–2.

p. 73   For the legionnaire . . . Walther Kanitz, *The White Kepi*,
            p. 343.

p. 73   There are certain . . . David W. King, *L. M. 8046*, p. 20. In the
            original – to protect his readers' sensibilities – King or his
            publishers wrote: '*Debrouillez-vous*' – 'to get out of a fix'.

p. 74   The able men . . . George Manington, *A Soldier of the Legion*,
            p. 237.

p. 74   Having money in . . . William Stamer, *Recollections of a Life
            of Adventure*, p. 84.

p. 74   Then there is . . . Rosen, pp. 108–9.

p. 75   Klaus lent money . . . Adrian Liddell Hart, *Strange Company*,
            p. 68.

p. 75   A parcel from . . . Simon Murray, *Legionnaire*, p. 175.

pp. 75–6   The mail was . . . Jennings, p. 76.

p. 76   The cribs were . . . ibid., p. 66.

pp. 76–7   We went to . . . Salazar, p. 169.

pp. 77–8   We were not . . . James Worden, *Wayward Legionnaire*,
            pp. 43–4.

pp. 78–9   It was a . . . Henry Ainley, *In Order to Die*, pp. 59–60.

p. 79   The Legion goes . . . Murray, p. 40.

p. 79   We had a . . . ibid., pp. 183–4.

pp. 80–1   It became almost . . . Worden, p. 96.

p. 81   But the legionnaire . . . quoted in Charles Mercer, *The Foreign
            Legion*, p. 205.

pp. 81–2   The regimental canteen . . . Rosen, pp. 62, 64–5.

p. 82   Every man has . . . King, L. pp. 28–9.

p. 82   Wine is cheap . . . Fritz Klose, *The Legion Marches*,
            pp. 121–2.

p. 83   the magical Kronenbourg . . . Worden, p. 187.

p. 83   The town was . . . Tony Sloane, *The Naked Soldier*, p. 97.

pp. 83–4   When the ship . . . Bennett J. Doty, *The Legion of the Damned*, pp. 52–3.

p. 84   There are no . . . Zinovi Pechkoff, *The Bugle Sounds*, pp. 78–9.

p. 84   in our post . . . Ernst Jünger, *Jeux africains*, p. 128, in Porch, p. 222.

p. 85   She threw a . . . Manington, pp. 167–8.

p. 85   The oasis-dwellers . . . Ernst Löhndorff, *Hell in the Foreign Legion*, p. 257.

p. 86   There are girls . . . ibid., p. 145.

pp. 86–7   I went into . . . Murray, pp. 46, 47.

p. 87   When the worst . . . Ernst Jünger, *African Diversions*, p. 92.

pp. 87–8   The *congaï* formed . . . Ainley, pp. 58–9.

p. 88   The girls were . . . ibid., p. 59.

pp. 88–9   We had a . . . Foster, IWMSA 15438.

p. 89   The mixture of . . . Jennings, p. 126.

CHAPTER SIX

p. 90   When we came . . . Frederic Martyn, *Life in the Legion*, p. 220.

pp. 90–1   Our men in . . . Zinovi Pechkoff, *The Bugle Sounds*, pp. 46–7.

p. 91   This seems to . . . Simon Murray, *Legionnaire*, pp. 85–6.

p. 91   We covered many . . . ibid., p. 95.

p. 92   Besides what is . . . Clemens Lamping, *The French in Algiers*, pp. 45–6.

p. 92   Besides his provisions . . . ibid., p. 46.

pp. 92–3   The most marked . . . G. Ward Price, *In Morocco with the Legion*, p. 132.

p. 93   I have already . . . Ernst Löhndorff, *Hell in the Foreign Legion*, pp. 287–8

pp. 93–4   A wind had . . . Alfred Perrott-White, *French Legionnaire*, p. 98.

p. 94   We had been . . . Pechkoff, p. 141.

pp. 94–5   The country through . . . Prince Aage, *My Life in the Foreign Legion*, p. 34.

p. 95   What silence envelops . . . Pechkoff, p. 140.

p. 95   I discovered that . . . James Worden, *Wayward Legionnaire*, p. 89.

p. 96   In July the . . . George Manington, *A Soldier of the Legion*, p. 157.

p. 96   The road passed . . . ibid., pp. 225–6.

p. 97 The coolies, on . . . ibid., pp. 226–7.
pp. 97–8 Working parties chopped . . . Martyn, p. 152.
p. 98 The [Tonkinese] *tirailleurs* . . . Manington, p. 132.
pp. 98–9 The fort was . . . Ward Price, pp. 201–2.
pp. 99–100 The commander of . . . Pechkoff, pp. 72–3.
pp. 100–1 *Reveille* at dawn . . . Ward Price, pp. 203–4.
p. 101 What most recruits . . . German NCO, in Ward Price, p. 249.
pp. 101–2 What surprised [the . . . Jacques Weygand, *Légionnaire*, p. 102.
p. 102 Twenty days without . . . ibid., pp. 154–5.
pp. 102–3 For the next . . . Pádraig O'Keeffe, *Hidden Soldier*, pp. 65–7.
p. 103 The work goes . . . Murray, pp. 210–11.

CHAPTER SEVEN

pp. 105–6 I myself lived . . . Erwin Rosen, *In the Foreign Legion*, pp. 183–4.
pp. 106–7 The oasis of . . . Ernst Löhndorff, *Hell in the Foreign Legion*, pp. 229–30.
p. 107 A great deal . . . Frederic Martyn, *Life in the Legion*, pp. 223, 224.
p. 108 Many times I . . . Gareth Carins, *Diary of a Legionnaire*, pp. 62–3.
p. 109 There was nothing . . . Christian Jennings, *Mouthful of Rocks*, pp. 112–13.
pp. 109–10 These are the . . . John Patrick Le Poer, *A Modern Legionary*, p. 89.
p. 110 The first was . . . Jacques Weygand, *Légionnaire*, pp. 181–2.
pp. 110–11 Schmitt looked like . . . Tony Sloane, *The Naked Soldier*, p. 46.
p. 111 The company was . . . ibid.
pp. 111–12 The 'cuckoo' is . . . Weygand, p. 183.
p. 112 Almost all legionnaires . . . Adrian Liddell Hart, *Strange Company*, pp. 77, 78.
p. 113 Although there may . . . Weygand, p. 182.
pp. 113–14 When most people . . . Jennings, pp. 179–80.
p. 114 I always said . . . Carl Jackson, author interview.
pp. 114–15 The little pointless . . . Sloane, pp. 43–4.
p. 115 Lefevre and Aboine . . . Simon Murray, *Legionnaire*, pp. 56–7.
p. 116 When they were . . . ibid., pp. 57–8.
p. 116 His wrists had . . . Carins, p. 41.
pp. 116–17 Later that morning . . . ibid., p. 42.

CHAPTER EIGHT

p. 122   We had just . . . Achille de Saint-Arnaud, *Lettres du maréchal de Saint Arnaud*, in Patrick Turnbull, *The Foreign Legion*, pp. 33–5.

p. 123   Advancing towards the . . . ibid.

p. 123   My first action . . . ibid.

p. 124   I was attacked . . . ibid.

pp. 124–5   The battalion is . . . Clemens Lamping, *The French in Algiers*, p. 23.

p. 125   They attacked with . . . ibid., pp. 24–5.

p. 126   A hundred and . . . E. Perret, *Récits Algériens*, in Turnbull, p. 43.

pp. 127–8   As I gazed . . . John Patrick le Poer, *A Modern Legionary*, pp. 56–8.

pp. 128–9   The company was . . . Frederic Martyn, *Life in the Legion*, p. 220.

p. 129   The fifty men . . . War Diary of 12th Mounted Company, in Turnbull, pp. 105–6.

p. 129   difficult lot to . . . Reginald Rankin, *In Morocco with General D'Amade*, p. 29.

p. 130   At the second . . . ibid., pp. 30–1.

p. 130   These young women . . . Martyn, p. 178.

p. 131   We rushed to . . . ibid., pp. 169–70.

p. 131   Our first salvoes . . . Legionnaire's diary, in Turnbull, p. 96.

p. 131   We were on . . . Martyn, p. 170

p. 132   In spite of . . . ibid., p. 98.

p. 132   When we at . . . Martyn, p. 192.

p. 133   Kana is made . . . Legionnaire's diary, in Turnbull, p. 100.

p. 133   It was no . . . Martyn, p. 212.

p. 134   The legionnaires got . . . Legionnaire 'X', in Turnbull, p. 102.

p. 134   The flying column . . . E. F. Knight, *Madagascar in War Time*, pp. 303–4.

CHAPTER NINE

pp. 135–7   Notwithstanding the fact . . . George Manington, *A Soldier of the Legion*, pp. 52–5.

p. 137   An unbelievable spectacle . . . Bôn-Mat, *Souvenirs*, pp. 188–9, in Douglas Porch, *The French Foreign Legion*, pp. 233–4.

p.137   In the town . . . ibid., pp. 233–4.

p. 138   Now let me . . . John Patrick le Poer, *A Modern Legionary*, pp. 143–4.

p. 139   It was now . . . Frederic Martyn, *Life in the Legion,* pp. 140–1.

p. 140   As we lifted . . . ibid., p. 141–3

pp. 140–1   I think that . . . ibid., p. 154.

p. 141   The legionaries were . . . Pastor Boissot, in Patrick Turnbull, *The Foreign Legion*, p. 90.

p. 141   At the sound . . . ibid.

p. 142   While I was . . . Le Poer, p. 194.

p. 143   Despite our marches . . . Jean Pfirmann, *Le sergent Pfirmann* (unpub. ms, ALE), p. 69, quoted in Porch, pp. 239–40.

p. 143   When we were . . . Martyn, p. 137

p. 144   The worst thing . . . Antoine Sylvère, *Flutsch*, p. 64, quoted in Porch, p. 241.

p. 144   All that day . . . Le Poer, pp. 128–9.

p. 144   We took a . . . ibid., pp. 128–9.

pp. 145–6   Behind the little . . . Manington, pp. 201–3.

p. 146   At this time . . . ibid., pp. 312–13.

CHAPTER TEN

p. 148   Foreigners, friends of . . . Paul Ayres Rockwell, *American Fighters in the Foreign Legion 1914–1918*, p. 3.

p. 149   out of any . . . Alan Seeger, *Letters and Diary of Alan Seeger*, p. 141.

p. 149   I am going . . . William Thaw, in Edwin W. Morse, *The Vanguard of American Volunteers*, p. 15.

p. 149   Some of us . . . Edward Morlae, *A Soldier of the Legion*, p. 8.

pp. 149–50   The Legion is . . . Lt J. Woodhall Marshall, in Laurence Houseman (ed.), *War Letters of Fallen Englishmen*, pp. 189–90.

p. 150   Sergeant-Major Pontacier . . . Kosta Todorov, *Balkan Firebrand*, p. 50.

pp. 150–1   A majority of . . . Seeger, p. 153.

p. 151   Phélizot and some . . . Rockwell, p. 55.

pp. 151–2   When news of . . . ibid., p 57.

p. 152   it consequently never . . . Seeger, p. 153.

p. 152   War is wretched . . . Thaw, in Morse, p. 18.

p. 152   It was only . . . David W. King, *L. M. 8046*, p. 48.

p. 153   Early in November . . . Thaw, in Morse, pp. 18–20.

p. 153   Fifth Day of . . . Seeger, p. 18.

p. 153   Back in the . . . ibid., pp. 22–3.

p. 154   Before daylight it . . . ibid., p. 47.

p. 154   The 'tap, tap' . . . Victor Chapman, *Victor Chapman's Letters from France*, p. 84.

p. 154   We found ourselves . . . King, pp. 48–9.

p. 155   One of our . . . ibid., p. 112.

p. 155   only way to . . . Todorov, p. 57.

pp. 155–6   Our positions were . . . ibid., pp. 57–8.

p. 157   Just as he . . . Rockwell, pp. 47–8.

pp. 157–8   While they had . . . ibid., pp. 48–9.

p. 158   Only about midnight . . . Seeger, p. 69.

pp. 158–9   In a few minutes . . . Rockwell, p. 73.

pp. 159–60 My detachment made . . . Blaise Cendrars, *Lice*, pp. 59–60.

p. 160   With rage in . . . Rockwell, p. 78.

p. 160   chances for success . . . Seeger, p. 160.

pp. 160–1   The routes were . . . Edmund Genet, *War Letters of Edmund Genet*, pp. 129–30.

p. 161   Every day officers . . . King, p. 91.

p. 161   The bombardment of . . . Genet, pp. 131–2.

p. 162   At 9 the . . . Morlae, pp. 28–9.

pp. 162–3   As we marched . . . ibid., pp. 32–4.

p. 163   Opposite us, all . . . Seeger, p. 166.

p. 163   The defending force . . . Ernst Jünger, *Storm of Steel*, in Richard Holmes, *Firing Line*, p. 381.

p. 164   Pale, frightened German . . . Todorov, p. 65.

p. 164   As we swept . . . Morlae, pp. 37–8.

p. 165   The Germans spotted . . . King, pp. 105–6.

p. 166   The place was . . . ibid., pp. 106–7.

p. 166   It was a . . . Seeger, p. 170.

pp. 166–7   Lemercier observed sadly . . . Todorov, pp. 68–9.

p. 167   We would dig . . . King, pp. 108–9.

p. 168   The *Médaille Militaire* . . . in Rockwell, p. 123.

p. 168   The King has . . . ibid., p. 124.

p. 169   I cannot congratulate . . . Seeger, pp. 176–7.

p. 169   They passed all . . . Genet, p. 111.

pp. 169–70 It started at . . . King, pp. 177–8.

p. 170   We go up . . . Seeger, p. 211.

p. 170   I was a . . . Jack Moyet, in Rockwell, pp. 176–7.

p. 171   Seeger was wounded . . . Corporal Barrett, ibid., p. 180.

p. 171   Months of hardships . . . Rockwell, pp. 219–20.

pp. 171–2   At fifteen minutes . . . Christopher Charles, in Rockwell, pp. 224–5.

p. 172   Collecting a group . . . Jean des Valliéres, *Et Voici La Légion*

Etrangère, quoted in Patrick Turnbull, *The Foreign Legion*, p. 119.

p. 173   The Moroccan Division . . . Rockwell, p. 343.

p. 173   Colonel Rollet, his . . . ibid., pp. 343–4.

CHAPTER ELEVEN

p. 175   even the Foreign . . . Prince Aage, *My Life in the Foreign Legion*, p. 155.

pp. 175–6   We reached the . . . Zinovi Pechkoff, *The Bugle Sounds*, pp. 229–31.

p. 176   Its mission accomplished . . . A. R. Cooper, *Born to Fight*, pp. 165–6.

pp. 177–8   We knew that . . . Aage, pp. 179–82.

p. 178   It is the Berber . . . ibid., p. 86.

p. 179   At the change . . . Ernst Löhndorff, *Hell in the Foreign Legion*, p. 294.

p. 179   We took ten . . . ibid., pp. 295–6.

pp. 179–80 This action electrified . . . Bennett J. Doty, *The Legion of the Damned*, pp. 84–111.

p. 181   Behind us . . . ibid., pp. 113–15.

p. 182   I found that . . . ibid., pp. 101–2.

p. 182   With a thunder . . . John Harvey, *With the Legion in Syria*, pp. 161–2

p. 183   They were not . . . ibid., p. 162.

CHAPTER TWELVE

p. 185   The common language . . . John Lodwick, *Bid the Soldiers Shoot*, p. 14

p. 185   I confess now . . . Jo Czapka, *Red Sky at Night*, pp. 29–30.

p. 186   We had plenty . . . Alfred Perrott-White, *French Legionnaire*, p. 128

p. 186   For them, the . . . Charles Favrel, *Ci-devant legionnaire*, pp. 53, 222–3, in Douglas Porch, *The French Foreign Legion*, p. 450.

pp. 186–7   Every man of . . . Constantin Joffé, *We Were Free*, p. 19.

p. 187   Anti-fascists were . . . Arthur Koestler, *Scum of the Earth*, p. 168.

p. 187   comfortable backgrounds and . . . Jean-Pierre Hallo, *Képi blanc*, no. 490, p. 47, in Porch, p. 452.

p. 188   The attitude towards . . . Zosa Szajkowski, *Jews and the French Foreign Legion*, p. 61.

p. 188   The discipline was . . . ibid., p. 72.

p. 189   Our ship travelled . . . John Yeowell, in John Parker, *Inside the Foreign Legion*, p. 106.

p. 189   The town's inhabitants . . . ibid., p. 108.

p. 189   We came ashore . . . Legionnaire H., IWMSA 14192.

pp. 189–90   We crossed the . . . Yeowell, p. 108.

p. 190   Everywhere we came . . . Pierre O. Lapie, *With the Foreign Legion at Narvik*, pp. 38–9.

pp. 190–1   The slopes which . . . 13th DBLE War Diary, in Patrick Turnbull, *The Foreign Legion*, p. 158.

p. 191   Our duty was . . . Yeowell, p. 113.

pp. 191–2   How happy we . . . Joffé, pp. 42.

p. 192   Day by day . . . ibid., p. 43.

pp. 192–3   The Major sat . . . ibid., pp. 32–3.

p. 193   We had a . . . ibid., pp. 27–8.

p. 194   We held the . . . Georges R. Manue, *Vu du Rang*, in Turnbull, p. 155.

p. 195   It was in Sudan . . . Susan Travers, *Tomorrow be Brave*, p. 66.

p. 195   We faced each . . . Quoted in Charles Mercer, *The Foreign Legion*, p. 227.

p. 196   The Western Desert . . . Travers, p. 136.

pp. 196–7   The following day . . . ibid., p. 160.

pp. 197–8   The sky was . . . *Livre d'Or* (1955), quoted in Turnbull, p. 160.

p. 198   The first concern . . . Ted Harris, *Escape from the Legion*, p. 9.

p. 198   Christmas of 1940 . . . Perrott-White, p. 166.

p. 199   When the German . . . A. D. Printer, in Szajkowski, p. 103.

p. 199   Anyone who passed . . . ibid., pp. 102–3.

p. 200   Few of us . . . Anthony Delmayne, *Sahara Desert Escape*, p. 19.

p. 200   My observation point . . . Perrott-White, p. 184.

p. 201   The planes began . . . ibid., p. 187.

p. 201   On the day . . . Erwin Deman, IMWSA 9412; from 1945, Peter Deman.

CHAPTER THIRTEEN

p. 204   The south-east . . . Legionnaire 'X', in Patrick Turnbull, *The Foreign Legion*, p. 175.

p. 205   A relief column . . . Paul Grauwin, *Doctor at Dien Bien Phu*, p. 235.

pp. 205–6   In the green . . . Lucian Bodard, *The Quicksand War: Prelude to Vietnam*, pp. 54–5.

p. 206   That night the . . . ibid., p. 55.

pp. 206–7   We climbed up . . . Leslie Aparvary, *A Legionnaire's Journey*, p. 123.

pp. 207–9   Technically it was . . . Legion sergeant, in Bodard, pp. 57–8.

pp. 209–10   One Saturday at . . . Bodard, pp. 264–5.

p. 211   In a matter . . . Legion officer, in Bodard, p. 306.

pp. 211–12   A little after . . . ibid., pp. 306–7.

p. 213   My objective was . . . ibid., p. 39.

pp. 213–14   It is unbelievably . . . ibid., pp. 39–40.

pp. 214–15   Here and there . . . Adrian Liddell Hart, *Strange Company*, pp. 138–9, 160–1.

p. 215   Not long ago . . . Legion officer, in Bodard, p. 40.

pp. 215–16   there's an inexhaustible . . . ibid., p. 40.

p. 216   Torture and brutality . . . Henry Ainley, *In Order to Die*, p. 30.

p. 217   We immediately went . . . Sergeant Bleyer, in Howard R. Simpson, *Dien Bien Phu: the Epic Battle America Forgot*, p. 37

p. 218   On 13 March . . . Captain Nicolas, in Simpson, pp. 67–8.

p. 218   The day began . . . Sergeant Kubiak, in Turnbull, p. 194.

pp. 218–19   Heavy artillery fire . . . Bleyer, in Simpson, p. 69.

p. 219   I returned to . . . Grauwin, pp. 98–9.

p. 219   The fighting began . . . Lieutenant Desmaizieres, in Simpson, p. 78.

pp. 219–20   a few [Algerian] . . . ibid.

pp. 220–1   Next came paratroopers . . . Grauwin, pp. 102–3.

p. 221   Towards the middle . . . ibid., p. 205.

p. 222   5 May 1954 . . . Kubiak, in Turnbull, p. 197.

p. 223   Legionnaire S. was . . . ibid., p. 198.

pp. 223–4   We left the . . . Pierre Schoendoerffer, in Simpson, p. 168.

CHAPTER FOURTEEN

p. 226   My poor friend . . . Pierre Leulliette, *St Michael and the Dragon*, p. 176. See also Alistair Horne, *A Savage War of Peace*, p. 171.

pp. 227–8   The effectiveness of . . . Simon Murray, *Legionnaire*, pp. 67–8.

p. 228   Like all officers . . . Pierre Sergent, *Ma Peau au bout demes idées*, p. 158, quoted in Ekard Michels, 'From One Crisis to Another: the Morale of the French Foreign Legion during the Algerian War', in Martin S. Alexander, Martin Evans, J. F. V. Keiger (eds), *The Algerian War and the French Army, 1954–62*, p. 92.

pp. 228–9   The supposedly innocent . . . Antoine Ysquierdo, *Une guerre pour rien*, pp. 53–4, quoted in Douglas Porch, *The French Foreign Legion*, p. 575.

p. 229   For three days . . . Leulliette, p. 78.

p. 230   Every day we . . . Murray, pp. 119–20.

pp. 230–1   At last the . . . ibid., pp. 96–8.

pp. 231–2   After being interrogated . . . James Worden, *Wayward Legionnaire*, pp. 104–5.

p. 233   The companies moved . . . War correspondent, quoted in Patrick Turnbull, *The Foreign Legion*, p. 207.

pp. 234–5   In the middle . . . Murray, pp. 136–8.

p. 235   felt let down . . . Jim Worden, IWM SA14288.

p. 235   The soldiers in . . . Janos Kemencei, *Légionnaires avant!*, quoted in Michels, p. 98.

p. 236   We departed at . . . Worden, p. 153.

CHAPTER FIFTEEN

p. 237   Life comes to . . . Simon Murray, *Legionnaire*, p. 190.

p. 237   gave us information . . . ibid., p. 191.

p. 238   The regiment is . . . ibid., p. 211.

p. 239   We originally had . . . Paul Fanshaw, 'Target Kolwezi' in *Soldier of Fortune* (Special), December 1983, p. 51.

p. 240   Looking out of . . . ibid., p. 52.

pp. 240–1   Armed with two . . . ibid., pp. 52–3.

p. 242   At first light . . . ibid., p. 55.

p. 242   There were some . . . Jonathan Harris, IWMSA interview, 15102/9.

pp. 242–3   This was the . . . ibid. (An official French Army report, 'Lessons Learned from Kolwezi – May 1978' gives figures for rebel forces in Metal-Shaba at around 200 men – see www.cdef.terre.defense.gouv/fr/publications – *Supplément á Objective Doctine 31, Les Cahiers de Retex No. 12*).

p. 243   I rounded the . . . Fanshaw, p. 108.

p. 244   I performed more . . . William Brooks, 'The French Foreign Legion Today, Part 2', in *Soldier of Fortune*, September 1978, Vol. 3, No. 5, p. 40.

pp. 245–6   That night we . . . Brooks, 'The French Foreign Legion Today, Part 3', in *Soldier of Fortune*, November 1978, Vol. 3, No. 6.

pp. 246–7   I expected the . . . Mark Morris, IWMSA 14578.

p. 247   I was lucky . . . Dave Cunliffe, author interview.

p. 247   The trip from . . . Pádraig O'Keeffe, *Hidden Soldier*, pp. 88–9.

p. 247   This was the . . . Matt Rake, author interview.

p. 248   Our mission in . . . O'Keeffe, p. 109.

pp. 248–9   In Sarajevo our . . . ibid., pp. 91–2.

p. 249   We weren't supposed . . . Rake, author interview.

pp. 249–50 We were working . . . O'Keeffe, pp. 121–2.

p. 250   When we went . . . Rake, author interview.

p. 251   Though the names . . . Simon Low, *The Boys from Baghdad*, p. 89.

pp. 251–2   I can't remember . . . ibid., p. 90.

pp. 252–4   With the evacuations . . . Gareth Carins, *Diary of a Legionnaire*, pp. 146–7, 149, 150.

SELECT BIBLIOGRAPHY

BOOKS

Aage, Prince, *My Life in the Foreign Legion* (London: Eveleigh, Nash and Grayson, 1928)

Ainley, Henry, *In Order to Die* (London: Burke, 1955)

Alexander, Michael, *The Reluctant Legionnaire* (New York: E. P. Dutton, 1956)

Anderson, Roy C., *Devils, Not Men: The History of the French Foreign Legion* (Newton Abbot: David & Charles, 1988)

Aparvary, Leslie, *A Legionnaire's Journey* (Calgary: Detselig Enterprises, 1989)

Ashby, John, *Seek Glory, Now Keep Glory: The Story of 1st Battalion Royal Warwickshire Regiment, 1914–18* (Solihull: Helion, 2000)

Aussaresses, Paul, *The Battle of the Casbah* (New York: Enigma Books, 2002)

Bergot, Erwan, *The French Foreign Legion* (London: Allan Wingate, 1975)

Bocca, Geoffrey, *La Légion! The French Foreign Legion and the Men Who Made it Glorious* (New York: Thomas Y. Crowell, 1964)

Bodard, Lucien, *The Quicksand War: Prelude to Vietnam* (London: Faber, 1967)

Boyd, Douglas, *The French Foreign Legion* (Stroud: Sutton, 2006)

Bringolf, Hans, *I Have No Regrets: The Strange Life of a Diplomat-Vagrant* (London: Jarrolds, 1931)

Bruckberger, R. L., *One Sky to Share: The French and American Journals of Raymond Leopold Bruckberger* (New York: P. J. Kennedy & Sons, 1952)

Carins, Gareth, *Diary of a Legionnaire: My Life in the French Foreign Legion* (Guildford: Grosvenor House, 2007)

Castellane-Novejan, Louis Comte de, *Souvenirs of Military Life in Algeria* (London: Remington, 1886)

Cendrars, Blaise, *Lice* (London: Peter Owen, 1973)

Chapman, Victor, *Victor Chapman's Letters from France* (New York: Macmillan, 1917)

Cooper, A. R., *The Man who Liked Hell: Twelve Years in the French Foreign Legion* (London: Jarrolds, 1933)

Cooper, A. R., *Born to Fight* (Edinburgh: Blackwood & Co., 1969)

Czapka, Jo, *Red Sky at Night* (London: Panther, 1959)

Debay, Yves, *The French Foreign Legion in Action* (London: Windrow & Greene, 1992)

Delmayne, Anthony, *Sahara Desert Escape* (London: Jarrolds, 1958)

Doty, Bennett J., *The Legion of the Damned* (New York: Century, 1928)

Ehle, John, *The Survivor: The Story of Eddy Hukov* (London: World Distributors, 1960)

Fall, Bernard, *Street Without Joy: The French Debacle in Indochina* (London: Pall Mall Press, 1964)

Fall, Bernard, *Hell in a Very Small Place: The Siege of Dien Bien Phu* (London: Pall Mall Press, 1967)

Genet, Edmund (ed. Grace Ellery Channing), *War Letters of Edmund Genet* (New York: Scribners, 1918)

Geraghty, Tony, *March or Die: France and the Foreign Legion* (London: HarperCollins, 2001)

Grauwin, Paul, *Doctor at Dien Bien Phu* (London: Hutchinson, 1955)

Habe, Hans, *All My Sins* (London: Harrap, 1957)

Hall, Bert, *In the Air: Three Years On and Above Three Fronts* (London: Hunt and Blackett, n.d.[1918])

Harris, Ted, *Escape from the Legion* (London: John Murray, 1945)

Hart, Adrian Liddell, *Strange Company* (London: Weidenfeld, 1953)

Harvey, John, *With the Foreign Legion in Syria* (London: Hutchinson, 1928)

Holmes, Richard, *Firing Line* (London: Jonathan Cape, 1985)

Horne, Alistair, *A Savage War of Peace* (London: Papermac, 1977)

Houseman, Lawrence (ed.), *War Letters of Fallen Englishmen* (London: Gollanz, 1930)

Jameson, Simon, *The French Foreign Legion: A Guide to Joining* (Yelverton: Salvo Books, 1997)

Jennings, Christian, *Mouthful of Rocks: Through Africa and Corsica in the French Foreign Legion* (London: Bloomsbury, 1989)

Joffé, Constantin, *We Were Free* (New York: Smith & Durrell, 1943)

John, Colin, *Nothing to Lose* (London: Cassell, 1955)

Jordan, David, *The History of the French Foreign Legion* (Staplehurst: Spellmount, 2005)

Jünger, Ernst, *African Diversions* (London: John Lehmann, 1954)

Kanitz, Walter, *The White Kepi: A Casual History of the French Foreign Legion* (Chicago: Henry Regnery, 1956)

King, David W., *L.M. 8046: An Intimate Story of the Foreign Legion* (London: Arrowsmith, 1929)

Klose, Fritz, *The Legion Marches: The Woes and Wrongs of the Foreign Legion* (London: John Murray, 1932)

Knight, E. F., *Madagascar in War Time* (London: Longmans, 1896)

Koestler, Arthur, *Scum of the Earth* (London: Jonathan Cape, 1941)

Laffin, John, *The French Foreign Legion* (London: Dent, 1974)

Lamping, Clemens, *The French in Algiers I: The Soldiers of the Foreign Legion* (London: John Murray, 1845)

Lapie, Pierre O., *With the Foreign Legion at Narvik* (London: John Murray, 1941)

Lartéguy, Jean, *The Centurions* (London: Hutchinson, 1961)

Le Page, Jean-Denis, *The French Foreign Legion: An Illustrated History* (Jefferson: McFarland & Co., 2008)

Le Poer, John Patrick, *A Modern Legionary* (London: Methuen, 1904)

Leulliette, Pierre, *St Michael and the Dragon: A Paratrooper in the Algerian War* (London: Heinemann, 1964)

Lodwick, John, *Bid the Soldiers Shoot* (London: Heinemann, 1958)

Löhndorff, Ernst, *Hell in the Foreign Legion* (London: George Allen & Unwin, 1931)

Low, Simon, *The Boys from Baghdad* (Edinburgh: Mainstream, 2007)

McCormick, Donald, *One Man's War: The Story of Charles Sweeny: Soldier of Fortune* (London: Arthur Barker, 1972)

Macdonald, Peter, *The Making of a Legionnaire* (London: Sidgwick & Jackson, 1991)

McGorman, Ewan, *Life in the French Foreign Legion* (Central Point: Hellgate Press, 2000)

McLeave, Hugh, *The Damned Die Hard* (Farnborough: Saxon House, 1974)

Magnus, M., *Memoirs of the Foreign Legion* (London: Martin Secker, 1924)

Manington, G. A., *A Soldier of the Legion or an Englishman's Adventures Under the French Flag in Algeria and Tonkin* (London: John Murray, 1907)

Martyn, Frederic, *Life in the Legion: From a Soldier's Point of View* (London: Everett, 1911)

Mercer, Charles, *The Foreign Legion: The Vivid History of a Unique Military Tradition* (London: Four Square, 1966)

Moore, Frederick, *The Passing of Morocco* (London: Smith, Elder, 1908)

Morlae, Edward, *A Soldier of the Legion* (Boston: Houghton Mifflin, 1916)

Morse, Edwin W., *The Vanguard of American Volunteers in the Fighting Lines and in the Humanitarian Service, August 1914–April 1917* (New York: Scribners, 1918)

Murray, Simon, *Legionnaire: An Englishman in the French Foreign Legion* (London: Sidgwick & Jackson, 1978)

O'Ballance, Edgar, *The Story of the French Foreign Legion* (London: Faber, 1961)

O'Keeffe, Pádraig, with Riegel, Ralph, *Hidden Soldier: An Irish Legionnaire's Wars from Bosnia to Iraq* (Dublin: The O'Brien Press, 2007)

O'Neill, James, *Garrison Tales from Tonquin* (Boston: Copeland and Day, 1895)

Parker, John, *Inside the Foreign Legion: The Sensational Story of the World's Toughest Army* (London: Piatkus/BCA, 1988)

Pechkoff, Zinovi, *The Bugle Sounds: Life in the Foreign Legion* (New York: Appleton, 1926)

Perrott-White, Alfred, *French Legionnaire* (London: John Murray, 1953)

Porch, Douglas, *The Conquest of Morocco* (London: Jonathan Cape, 1986)

Porch, Douglas, *The French Foreign Legion: A Complete History* (London: Macmillan, 1991)

Pyle, Ernie, *Here is Your War: The Story of GI Joe* (Cleveland: World Publishing Co., 1945)

Rankin, Reginald, *In Morocco with General D'Amade* (London: Longmans, 1908)

Rockwell, Paul Ayres, *American Fighters in the Foreign Legion 1914–1918* (Boston: Houghton Mifflin, 1930)

Rosen, Erwin, *In the Foreign Legion* (London: Duckworth, 1910)

Salazar, Jaime, *Legion of the Lost: The True Experience of an American in the French Foreign Legion* (New York: Berkley Caliber, 2005)

Seeger, Alan, *Letters and Diary of Alan Seeger* (New York: Scribners, 1917)

Simpson, Howard R., *The Paratroopers of the French Foreign Legion: From Vietnam to Bosnia* (Washington, DC: Brassey's, 1997)

Simpson, Howard R., *Dien Bien Phu: The Epic Battle America Forgot* (Washington, DC: Potomac Books, 2005)

Sloane, Tony, *The Naked Soldier: A True Story of the French Foreign Legion* (London: Vision, 2004)

Stamer, William, *Recollections of a Life of Adventure* (London: Hurst and Blackett, 1866)

Stuart, Brian, *Adventures in Algeria* (London: Herbert Jenkins, 1936)

Szajkowski, Zosa, *Jews and the French Foreign Legion* (New York: Ktav, 1975)

Tiira, Ensio, *Raft of Despair* (London: Hutchinson, 1954)

Todorov, Kosta, *Balkan Firebrand: The Autobiography of a Rebel, Soldier and Statesman* (Chicago: Ziff-Davis, 1943)

Travers, Susan, *Tomorrow be Brave* (London: Bantam, 2000)

Turnbull, Patrick, *The Foreign Legion* (London: Mayflower-Dell, 1966)

Ward Price, G., *In Morocco with the Legion* (London: Jarrolds, 1934)

Wellard, James, *The French Foreign Legion* (London: André Deutsch, 1974)

Weygand, Jacques, *Légionnaire: Life with the Foreign Legion Cavalry* (London: Harrap, 1952)

Windrow, Martin, *French Foreign Legion Paratroops* (London: Osprey, 1985)

Windrow, Martin, *The French Foreign Legion Since 1945* (London: Osprey, 1996)

Windrow, Martin, *French Foreign Legion, 1914–1945* (Oxford: Osprey, 1999)

Windrow, Martin, *The Last Valley: Dien Bien Phu and the French Defeat in Vietnam* (London: Weidenfeld and Nicolson, 2004)

Worden, James, *Wayward Legionnaire* (London: Robert Hale, 1988)

Wright, Louise E., *Maurice Magnus: A Biography* (Newcastle: Cambridge Scholars Publishing, 2007)

Young, John Robert, *The French Foreign Legion: The Inside Story of the World-Famous Fighting Force* (London: Thames and Hudson, 1984)

ARTICLES, CHAPTERS

Brooks, William, 'The French Foreign Legion Today, Part 1', *Soldier of Fortune*, Vol. 3, No. 4 (July 1978)

Brooks, William, 'The French Foreign Legion Today, Part 2', *Soldier of Fortune*, Vol. 3, No. 5 (September 1978)

Brooks, William, 'The French Foreign Legion Today, Part 3', *Soldier of Fortune*, Vol. 3, No. 6 (November 1978)

Debay, Yves, 'Foreign Legion Tests New Small Arms', *Soldier of Fortune*, Vol. 17, No. 3 (March 1992)

Fanshaw, Paul, 'Target Kolwezi', *Soldier of Fortune* (Special), (December 1983)

James, Erwin, 'Legion of Honour', *Guardian*, 13 January 2006

Lucas, Richard, 'Viva La Compagnie', *Soldier of Fortune*, Vol. 21, No. 12 (December 1996)

Lucas, Richard, 'French Foreign Legion in Afghanistan', *Soldier of Fortune*, Vol. 30, No. 9 (September 2005)

Lucas, Richard, 'Fight Like You Train', *Soldier of Fortune*, Vol. 32, No. 4 (April 2007)

Michels, Ekard, 'From One Crisis to Another: the Morale of the French Foreign Legion during the Algerian War', in Martin S. Alexander, Martin Evans, J. F. V. Keiger (eds), *The Algerian War and the French Army, 1954–62* (Basingstoke: Palgrave, 2002)

Milstein, Mark H., 'Foreign Legion Vendetta', *Soldier of Fortune*, Vol. 19, No. 5 (May 1994)

Moore, Molly, 'The French Foreign Legion: Legendary Force Updates its Image', *Washington Post*, 13 May 2007

Moynahan, Brian, 'Faithful Unto Death', *Soldier of Fortune*, Vol. 6, No. 12 (December 1981)

Simpson, Howard, 'Making the Most of R&R', *Soldier of Fortune*, Vol. 11, No. 9 (September 1986)

'Whatever Happened to the French Foreign Legion', *Military Review*, Vol. LI, No. 4 (April 1971)

IMPERIAL WAR MUSEUM

DOCUMENT ARCHIVE

Christie, J. F. (88/47/1); Haines, O. C. M. (95/16/1); Liskutin, M. A. (88/45/1); Spurgeon, S. H. K. (90/23/1); Trill, J. (85/34/1).

SOUND ARCHIVE (IWMSA)

Colman, John (17730); Demen, Erwin (9412); Foreman, Arthur (19923); Foster, Kevin (15438); Hasson, Eddy (14192): Harris, Jonathan (15102); Hill, Henry (9314); Mas Homs, Jaime (10627); Kendall, Maxwell (14949); Morris, Mark (14578); Parsons, Dennis (13759); Spier, Adolf (16583); Worden, Jim (14288).

INDEX